Pragmatism
Considers
Phenomenology

Current Continental Research
is co-published by
The Center for Advanced Research
in Phenomenology
and
University Press of America, Inc.

CURRENT CONTINENTAL RESEARCH 008

PRAGMATISM CONSIDERS PHENOMENOLOGY

Edited by
Robert S. Corrington,
Carl Hausman,
and
Thomas M. Seebohm

1987

Center for Advanced Research in Phenomenology
& University Press of America, Washington, D.C.

British Cataloging in Publication Information Available

Library of Congress Cataloging-in-Publication Data

Pragmatism considers phenomenology.

(Current continental research ; 008)
Includes indexes.
1. Pragmatism.   2. Phenomenology.   I. Corrington,
Robert S., 1950-   . II. Hausman, Carl, 1953-
III. Seebohm. Thomas M.   IV. Series.
B832.P757 1987   142'.7   87-22995
ISBN 0-8191-6581-6 (alk. paper)
ISBN 0-8191-6582-4 (pbk. : alk. paper)

TOP ROW: James Campbell, ?, Victorino Tejera, Doug Anderson, Hwa Jol Jung, Lester Embree, Bruce Wilshire, Henry Johnstone Jr., Armen Marsoobian, ?, ?, Albert Pacheco; SECOND ROW: Joseph Kockelmans, Kathleen Wallace, ?, Richard Mester, Robert Dostal, Aaron Druckman; THIRD ROW: Robert S. Corrington, Ed Petry, Carl G. Vought, Thomas Seebohm, Patrick Barker, John Anderson; BOTTOM ROW: Carl R. Hausman, Charles Hartshorne, John E. Smith, Sandra Rosenthal, Charles M. Sherover, Max Fisch, Charlene Haddock Seigfried, Beth J. Singer, Roberta Kevelson.

C O N T E N T S

PREFACE

Unless otherwise noted, the essays presented in this volume are based on papers read at a conference on Pragmatism and Phenomenology held at The Pennsylvania State University in the summer of 1984. The conference was co-sponsored by the Center for Advanced Research in Phenomenology, Inc. and the Department of Philosophy of The Pennsylvania State University.

The editors expecially wish to thank Felicia Kruse and Edward Petry for their valuable help with the conference and this volume. They also wish to thank Dr. Gail P. Corrington for taking time our of her busy schedule to help with the compilation of the indices.

INTRODUCTION AND REFLECTION

Robert S. Corrington (The Pennsylvania State University)

A. *Introduction to the Texts*

For some time there has been a growing suspicion that pragmatism and phenomenology converge on common insights into the nature and dynamics of lived experience and its relation to the horizonal structures of the world. Yet certain misconceptions on both sides have kept these two vital movements from developing the proper conceptual realignment which would reveal the striking contour of this common ground. Phenomenologists generally regard pragmatism as vitiated by a naive biological account of a 'merely' problem solving organism in search of periodic stabilities. The ideological constraints of a supposed scientism further limit the descriptive power of a pragmatic account of experience. Hence biological reductionism and a narrow scientistic epistemology are held to blunt the reach and depth of pragmatic frameworks. On the other side, pragmatists generally regard the Husserlian program as falling prey to the Cartesian idealism which the early pragmatists rejected in their drive to undermine traditional dualisms. Further, Husserl's architechtonic understanding of scientific insight runs counter to the general theory of inquiry as it emerged from the perspectives of Peirce and Dewey. The priority of the subject and its constituting acts stand in opposition to a pragmatic perspective which would place such a 'subject' within the larger horizon of communal and natural transactions. On the surface it would appear that intended syntheses of these two movements are faced with categorial divides of great scope and recalcitrance.

On further inspection, however, this seemingly unbridgeable chasm between two of the most vital trajectories of the modern period reveals a rich terrain which stands beneath each perspective and lives as the nourishing soil for both. This terrain is currently under exploration by a number of thinkers attuned to the need for the delineation of landscape which has just begun to show its complex contour. The essays in this volume can be seen to represent the results of this initial survey of a

Robert S. Corrington, Carl Hausman, & Thomas M. Seebohm, eds., *Pragmatism Considers Phenomenology,* Washington, D. C.: Center for Advanced Research in Phenomenology & University Press of America, 1987.

land long sensed but, until now, dimly perceived. For the most part, the forays were initiated from the side of pragmatism. Yet an assessment of the spoils returned indicates the immense subtlety and richness of the starting point. It is of especial interest that the writers presented in this volume have all developed both a reconstructed account of the pragmatic tradition and of the phenomenological movement. Perhaps it is no accident that the thinkers friendly to pragmatism tend to feel more at home in the writings of Schutz, Merleau-Ponty and Heidegger than in the writings of the early and middle Husserl. Yet the appropriation of these thinkers is one which forces their own perspectives back toward a renewed account of the origins and dimensions of the lived experience which nourishes all probings into common traits. From out of this appropriation both movements can only benefit.

The first essay by Sandra Rosenthal, "Classical American Pragmatism: Key Themes and Phenomenological Dimensions," recasts traditional understandings of scientific method in such a way as to avoid some of the more common charges leveled against a pragmatism which utilizes such a methodology. The scientific method is not one which counsels a reductionistic metaphysics of mechanistic causality but one which stresses a "noetic creativity" which evidences the role of thought in going beyond that which is observed in common experience. The noetic power of scientific method enables it to honor and preserve the "qualitative fullness of lived experience." Hence, the assumed divergence between a pragmatism aligned with scientific method and a phenomenology concerned with tracing out the fields of signification and meaning is seen to be illusory.

Rosenthal exhibits four traits of scientific method which all attest to its fundamental creativity. The first trait of this method is that it arises out of ordinary experience and refers back to it. However, this secondary reflection on ordinary experience can never return to its origin in a naive non-mediated manner. Experience articulated is experience changed. Yet any rendering intelligible of ordinary experience derives its validation from traits manifest within ordinary experience. The second trait of scientific method is that it always exhibits the intentional unity between knower and known. Dewey's classic reconstruction of the reflex arc (1896) stands as a foundational document of this rethinking of the unity between organism and environment. The known is to some degree the product of noetic acts which determine the relevant trait contour of any object. Further, the shape of the self is largely dependent upon the shape of the complexes known. The third trait of scientific method is its functional and teleological organization of qualities and qualitative fields. Our goal-directed activity establishes the mobile horizon within and through which objects are to become determinate and stable. Each intentional act serves the larger teleological drive toward partial wholeness and determinateness. So-called "qualities" can only be understood as consequent to methodic inquiry rather than as antecedent things-in-themselves. The fourth trait of scientific method is that it is prospective and self-corrective. Experience is constituted by a series of feed-back loops which serve to keep noetic creativity attuned to convergent structures within the phenomenal fields.

Rosenthal affirms that these four dimensions of noetic creativity emerge out of a phenomenological account of scientific method as it actually unfolds from within lived experience. Hence, pragmatism itself offers a phenomenological account of the noetic activity of science. Yet this account takes seriously the "hardness" and "bruteness" of a nature which sustains and ofttimes frustrates our noetic creativity. Disruptions and diremptions are as much a part of experience as are the habits which emerge out of multiform biological transactions. The habits of mental life are themselves continuous with antecedent biological and natural structures which belong to other organisms within nature. The presence of both habit and disruption attest to the naturalistic foundation for any just account of experience. Rosenthal insists that pragmatic naturalism is not incompatible with a phenomenological account of the field of irreducible meanings. Rather, pragmatism provides the metaphysical horizon which locates some of the more narrow phenomenological descriptions of signification.

Pragmatic naturalism functions within a general processive understanding of the world. This metaphysical account of process is actually the foundation for any analysis of temporality or inner time sense within the subject. "Felt temporality" derives its proper categorical location form a pragmatic analysis of the general processes of an evolving universe. The metaphysical boldness of pragmatic naturalism does not rest upon spurious transcendental arguments which drive beyond experience to 'produce' necessary and universal enabling conditions. This boldness derives from the dialectical traits of lived experience itself. Rosenthal insists that the exploration of lived experience shows such metaphysical categories as "qualitative richness, diversity, spontaneity, and possibility." The genius of pragmatism lies in its realization that our noetic creativity reveals fundamental traits not only of human subjectivity but of a processive universe. We must push through experience to the ontological features of the natural universe.

The second essay, by Charles Hartshorne, "An Anglo-American Phenomenology: Method and Some Results," criticizes Husserl's methodological notion that phenomenology must prescind from all presuppositions if it is to give a just account of so-called 'pure experience.' Presuppositions are both unavoidable and necessary if a non-trivial account is to be given of how experience occurs. The function of a non-Husserlian phenomenology is to account for the most relevant presuppositions which govern all understanding of reality. Any given observation, i.e., one not concerned with experience in its alleged universality and purity, must and will emerge from some definite theory or practical intent. Hence, Husserl's general problematic is vague and too indeterminate at the outset.

Hartshorne insists that several principles of formal logic provide us access to reality and experience in a way that is both necessary and universal. These modal analyses provide the framework within which more specific inquiries can occur. The first principle is that of "Dependence" (Peircean secondness) which asserts that successive experiences are dependent on antecedent experiences. The present is dependent upon the past and we must not assert an absolute distinction between logical and ontological dependence. This distinction is functional and reflects limitations in our finite human understanding. The second principle is that of "Contrast" which is related to Pierce's category of firstness. This principle states that relations can be independent of some of their terms and that genuine independence is real (thus complementing the first principle of dependence). One of the implications of this second principle is that something like Royce's notion of strict internal relation is rejected. This has obvious implications for a general metaphysical understanding of relational structures.

The third principle, "Asymmetry or Directional Order," shows in a striking manner the correlation between logical and ontological dimensions in a modal analysis. Symmetrical relations are merely special cases of the more pervasive nonsymmetrical relations. A nonsymmetrical dependence relation involves a directional movement which cannot be reversed or reduced to the antecedent. In logical terms we can assert that p is deducible from q while we may not be able to assert that q is deducible from p. The direction is not reversible. In ontological terms we may say that one event is derivable from another while the derivability cannot be reversed. Temporality 'intervenes' to change the relata and the meaning of their relation. The fourth principle of "Probabilistic Dependence" argues that future events have only a partial dependence on the past. Hartshorne asserts that this is what Peirce should have meant by his category of thirdness. Any ontological, i.e., temporal, deduction from p to q must introduce probability. Any 'necessary' deduction is non-temporal and thus cannot carry ontological weight.

The fifth principle, "Objective Modality," deepens and rein-forces the fourth principle by establishing that time involves a directional order. Metaphysical determinism remains tied to the limited account of symmetrical relations. The more generic asym-metrical structures of relation preserve genuine freedom. The sixth principle of "Logical Strength" asserts that the logically stronger cannot be deduced from the logically weaker. This holds for ontological deductions as well. That state of affairs which is the weaker is the one which, in essence, conveys less information. Thus, for example, the statement that x is material is logically weaker than the statement that x is a table. The being of the table cannot be deduced from the being of matter. This priority of the logically and ontologically stronger gives scope for the intervention of freedom or decision between antecedent and con-sequent states. Since the consequent state is not deducible from its weaker antecedent condition, it follows that something novel has intervened.

The seventh principle of "Practical Reason" goes beyond Kant by stressing the absolute priority of practical reason in our concrete knowledge of experience and the world. Practical know-ledge utilizes the past in order to determine at least part of the evolving contour of the future. The eighth and final principle, the "Zero Principle," asserts that the experience of positive traits is more decisive for our understanding of the world than our experience of absent traits. While both experiences are neces-sary, the experience of positive traits enables us to make more general statements about the structure of the world as a whole. Yet this ascription of positive traits, while more secure than so-called negative knowledge, rests within a larger understanding of metaphysical fallibilism. This fallibilism serves to limit any overly aggressive ascription of a given trait to the whole of reality.

Hartshorne's modal analysis functions to provide the cate-gorical foundation for the subsequent phenomenological obser-vations which make the modal account more concrete. Specifically, he argues that any just account of experience must pay heed to Whitehead's fundamental insight that experience is a "feeling of feeling." From this it follows that experience is social and that a subject does have access to another subject's feelings. Husserl's solipsism (akin to that of Leibniz) is firmly rejected. In my feeling awareness I can directly intuit what another may be feeling. A purely 'private' experience would be no experience at all.

Our access to the main traits of experience is improved when we take aesthetic experience as primary (a point missed by Husserl). Further, ethical and religious dimensions of experience are evocative of basic structures and point to the feeling dimension in all awareness. Experience is thus permeated by feeling and is open to the feelings of others. Hartshorne concludes his analysis by arguing for a basic realism which insists that experience is of real objects and not just of other experiences. Even dream experiences are, at the very least, of one's own body states at the time. Objects are present to feeling and cannot be bracketed out of a proper phenomenological account. The past itself is an intentional object of experience, not only through memory, but, more importantly, as present. The past and its objects are given in the present, this understanding of the richness of the present, and its relation to the other modes of time, takes us beyond the myth of the pure present.

The third essay, by John E. Smith, "The Reconception of Experience in Peirce, James and Dewey," shows how three major pragmatists developed a radicalized account of experience by criticizing and broadening classical British empiricism. This entailed the rejection of the epistemological starting point for an emphasis on experience as it actually shows itself to an active experiencer. James, as noted by Smith, was most aligned with the classical position and saw his own enterprise as one which developed several neglected dimensions in Hume's account of the "stuff" of experience.

Classical empiricism can be seen to affirm the following traits: the priority of the sensory element (and its separation from reason) within experience, that experience is of ideas rather than of objects, that experience is passive, and that experience is atomic, episodic, and has simples as its objects. Pragmatism, as understood by Smith, rejects these views in turn for an emphasis on relational and active dimensions of complex experience. The anti-Cartesianism of Peirce's early essays marks a divergence from naive intuitionism which has supported these classical conceptions of the knowledge relation. Further, the pragmatic emphasis on habit reinforces the natural and biological foundations of all forceful accounts of experience.

Turning to Peirce, Smith makes central the notion that experience is what is "forced" upon us by a world not of our own making. Compulsion is fundamental to the flow of experience and forces it to recognize certain general and repeated traits. Predication is tied to the forced element in experience and rests secure in the connections which emerge from real objects and classes. Peirce, echoing Hegel's critique of Kant, asserts that experience is of things-in-themselves rather than of mere representations. Of course, Peirce's fallibilism prevents him from asserting that we have some form of Absolute Knowing in which the full and complete reality of things is attained in the present. This experience is permeated with a lively sense of the secondness or resistance of those objects which force themselves upon our apprehension.

Peirce rejects the notion that experience is nothing more than perception by his insistance that contrast and resistance are part of experience while not possibly being objects of perception. To deny these elements within experience as lived is to narrow by fiat the list of traits found within the evolution of finite experience.

One of Peirce's greatest insights was into the role and structure of so-called familiar experience. This pervasive and general horizon for more specialized scientific experience is rarely grasped as it unfolds within the subject. In Peirce's example, our own heartbeat is not an object of experience so long as it functions properly to sustain life. Yet it remains as a part of the general horizon within which any experience will occur. Peirce's repeated affirmation of critical common sense must be understood against the background of this dimension of experience. It is much harder for philosophy to articulate this dimension of experience than for the epistemologist to render intelligible the traits of refined experimental experiences. Hence, the resistance of experience to our categorical probings.

Turning to James, Smith places emphasis on the more classical dimensions of the *Principles.* James ties knowledge to an analysis of sensation, albeit a much broadened account of the qualities within sensation. Like Peirce, James draws attention to the "fringe" or horizon of experience which lies outside of immediate apprehension. The distinction between focus and fringe functions precisely to direct our attention toward the fringe, or as put in the late writings, the subconscious dimension of experience. This forces a categorical shift of great import for a more properly generic *and* nuanced account of human awareness.

James stresses the reality of connection, relation, transaction and tendency within the flow of experience. This shifts the emphasis toward the event quality that came to be called "pure experience." The function of an analysis of pure experience is to prescind away from precipitate distinctions between the experiencing subject and its intentional objects. As Smith shows, the drive toward the realm of pure experience is fraught with difficulties which James was never fully able to overcome. At some level of analysis, the distinction between subject and object is essential. What is especially problematic is the role of the subject (of mineness) in the late writings of James. That experience is always mine is a fundamental affirmation of the *Principles*. This realization is blunted in the radical empiricism and the drive toward pure experience.

In reflecting on Dewey, Smith insists with ample evidence that Dewey is the most radical of the classical pragmatists in terms of a properly 'phenomenological' account of experience. The biological and social traits of experience become normative for understanding how any given experience fulfills its dynamic drive toward completion and, in aesthetic experience, fulfillment and consummation. Dewey rejects the classical notion of antecedent facts in order to affirm a transactional view which sees the "fact" as being the result of inquiry in the present and future. The full temporality of experience and its objects emerges within the instrumentalist analysis of knowledge.

Experience is both communal and shareable through forms a of communication not tied to simple assertive utterances. This communal dimension moves experience toward hoped for social convergence and has obvious political implications. It should be clear that Dewey's account of experience is tied irrevocably to a radical conception of democratic transaction in the forms of validation for experience. Experience thus discloses both nature and human community. The emphasis on the communal dimension of experience does, however, make many suspicious that Dewey does not have an adequate theory of the individual self. It is unlikely that this problem will receive a satisfactory solution through an analysis of Dewey's text's themselves.

Finally, Smith evidences the basic role of aesthetic experience for Dewey's account. Aesthetic experience, or the having of *an* experience, stands as the *telos* toward which all experience is moving. An experience is characterized as one which is fulfilled, consummated, completed, and filled with a qualitative integrity. In this fundamental kind of experience, the self and world interpenetrate in ways which go beyond the forms of experience tied to inquiry. Smith is surely correct when he points out that the analysis of aesthetic experience in the late Dewey saves him from collapsing human awareness into mere instrumental problem solving. In having an experience we redeem the claims of the present and allow a qualitative integrity to stand forth as an abidingness pure and simple. When Dewey's understanding of experience is read backward, as it were, from his account of

aesthetic experience, it promises to advance American phenomenology into a far richer territory than was possible previously.

The fourth essay, by Beth J. Singer, "Signs, Interpretation,
and the Social World," utilizes basic concepts from the writings
of Justus Buchler and Alfred Schutz in order to develop a general
theory of signs which she claims is more generic in scope than
that developed by Peirce. The basic concept of the social world is
held to cover both human communities and the common sense world of
every day life. Singer is concerned with overcoming certain biases
in more traditional semiotics which distort the internal and
external reality of the social world. These misconceptions stem
from both an inadequate theory of judgement and from a misunderstanding of the relation between judgement and interpretation.
Buchler's general metaphysics of natural complexes is held to
provide fundamental directives for overcoming these confusions.

Most writers in semiotics tie sign function directly to the
reference function. Yet, as Singer points out, certain signs,
e.g., connectives such as "and" and imperatives such as "Stop!",
do not refer to given complexes but stand alone, as it were,
without pointing to something other. A more properly generic
semiotics must allow for sign meanings which are non-referential.
The emphasis thus shifts from reference to the sign's relation
with other signs and interpretants.

Yet before semiotics can reach this more generic ground,
certain basic distinctions and reconceptions have to be made.
Singer utilizes Buchler's notion of the "natural complex" to
provide a universal categorical identification which situates
signs in a larger context. As Buchler affirms, anything discriminated in any way is a natural complex. A complex is an order of
related or relevant traits. These constitutive traits form the
"integrity" of the complex in a given order. At the same time, any
given complex will be located in other complexes, that is, will be
a constitutive trait (subaltern complex) in the other order or
orders. A complex thus locates traits 'within' itself and is
located by other complexes. Any complex can become a sign if it
becomes available for human judgement. In so far as a complex is
judged, it has meaning or meanings.

Buchler's general theory of judgement requires that we go
beyond assertive judgement to envision two other modes of judging.
Assertive judgments concern themselves with statements which pur-
port to be either true or false. The second form of judgment is
active judgment which involves human action or manipulation of
complexes or traits. Active judgments need not take the form of
propositions or function through any use of language. The third
form of judgment is exhibitive judgment, which involves the

manipulation of traits as ends-in-themselves. Art most frequently utilizes exhibitive judgement to display carefully discriminated traits in order to show a rich contour of qualities. It is important to note that each form of judgment has its own forms of validation. Any judgement, whether assertive, active, or exhibitive, must struggle toward some form of validation. It is clear that something like Dewey's notion of inquiry and instrumental validation remains tied to assertive judgments even though Dewey struggled to move his theory of validation into something akin to the other two modes.

A sign is, as noted above, any complex which has meaning. Yet a sign is not to be understood as a static repository of determined meanings. Rather, a sign directs further judgment so that interpretants will emerge to govern and direct the interpretation process. Hence an interpretation is concerned with interpretants rather than with signs per se. As Singer puts it, "An interpretation is a judgment that determines an interpretant." More specifically, an interpretant emerges from a judgment about a sign. This interpretant becomes available for further judgment and interpretation. The complex relationship between an interpretant and its sign is articulated or presented by an interpretation. While judgments are concerned with complexes, interpretations are concerned with the relation between any complex with meaning and its interpretant. It is perhaps helpful to see interpretation as a specific kind of judgment, a subclass.

Of fundamental importance for Singer is Schutz's use of Husserl's notion of "appresentation," which refers to the analogical or constructive process by which hidden dimensions of an object become available to intuition. Appresentation is not a process involving inference but one which produces a unity of intuition. To use Buchler's term, the "contour" of a complex, that is, its unity across numerous ordinal locations, is arrived at by a special form of intuition which 'fills in' the hidden or recessed dimensions. The use of appresentation is especially helpful when dealing with such realities as dreams or fantasies. A fuller sense of the contour of these complexes becomes possible through this special method of phenomenological seeing.

Moving beyond her analysis for Buchler and Schutz, Singer probes into the nature of interpretation and sign function. She introduces the notion of an "interpretive Scheme" to show that any interpretation must occur within an order of judgments which govern an order of interpretants. This scheme is the horizon within which any meaningful interpretation must take place. The order of signs delimited by the interpretive scheme is the "province of meaning." We can say that the province of meaning

represents the concrete signs which are the 'body' of the interpretative scheme. For Schutz, such a province is incommensurate
with other provinces. It remains cut off from active interaction
with other signs which might occupy a different domain. For
Singer, any given province will interact with other provinces. It
remains cut off from active interaction with other signs which
might occupy a different domain. For Singer, any given province
will interact with other provinces. The province may be a constituent in another province or it may share some of its signs with
several provinces. In either case, some form of interaction is
possible.

Returning to the problem of communication, Singer insists
that the individual communicates with him or herself and with
other members of the community. Further, in my reflexive communication I may, in fact will, belong to a large number of communities. The individual is thus the place where more than one community will prevail in its sign domain. All the modes of judgment
are utilized by the individual in an attempt to stabilize these
various sign communities into some meaningful contour. All signs
are amenable to communication in some form and this essential com-
municability stands as the horizon for our ability to enter into
alien provinces of meaning.

The fifth essay, by Richard J. Bernstein, "Heidegger and
Humanism," locates Heidegger's 1947 essay *Letter on Humanism*
against the backdrop of Greek and modern reflections on the nature
and meaning of *praxis.* Heidegger's own efforts to overcome the
history of metaphysics and its attendant humanism are seen to
represent and extreme danger for practical human moral and political community. The American pragmatists are evoked as thinkers who
made *praxis* central to philosophical speculation and who were thus
in a stronger position than Heidegger to reveal the fundamental
traits of authentic community.

Heidegger represents one extreme of a mood (*Stimmung*) which
has become pervasive in the 20th century. Unlike the 19th century,
with its belief in positive overcoming and qualitative birth or
rebirth, our century is characterized by a spirit of negation and
a sense of cultural entropy. Many thinkers evoke the end of metaphysics or the end of philosophy and its attendant culture while
bemoaning the fate of technical selfhood. Both self and history
are under an eclipse which shows no signs of ending. Rather a
deepening of the midnight consciousness emerges as the horizon of
our time. Heidegger's "rage against Humanism" must be seen as a
particularly acute expression of this general malaise.

Ironically, Bernstein points out that the Heidegger of *Sein
und Zeit* would feel at home with the classical American pragma-

tists on such issues as human finitude, the critique of subjectivity, the non-centrality of epistemology, and the emphasis on the necessity for prejudgments. Heidegger's rejection of the so-called technocratic essence of pragmatism deepens the irony. Heidegger's drive to overcome metaphysics, an extremely dubious notion, renders him unable to share with the pragmatists their deep commitment to social and moral *praxis*. In his writings on Aristotle, long appreciated by Gadamer, Heidegger blurs important differences between *praxis, poiesis, techne,* and *phronesis.* The failure to make appropriate distinctions blunts an insightful apprehension of the positive traits of *praxis.*

Heidegger lumps these Aristotelian distinctions under the one term of action (*Handeln*). Action is concerned with bringing about an effect, whether physical or moral. The essence of all action is found in a humanism which itself is but one expression of the essence of technology. The enframing (*Gestell*) of technology gathers human identity under its movement and reduces the human in persons to the merely controllable, The positive Greek understanding of *praxis*, and its relation to *ethos* and the *polis,* is ignored in favor of a view which disparages all so-called will-to-will. This rejection of the autonomy and the priority of *praxis* made Heidegger vulnerable to political currents which unleashed powers of evil on a scale which is still impossible to comprehend.

Bernstein takes pains to point out that serious efforts have been made by such thinkers as Dallmayr and Caputo to rescue a form of "higher" humanism from the Heideggerian texts. Yet this "higher" humanism, even with its positive emphasis on retrieval (*Wiederholung*), fails to give adequate weight to the reality of *Mitdasein* and the community which supports it. Neither *praxis* nor community play a role in the reconstructed Heidegger of these thinkers. It is clear that the negative appropriation of Heidegger by such a thinker as Derrida is fraught with difficulties. The deconstructive 'rage against metaphysics' is itself guilty of a profound anti-humanism which leaves us with little more than an extreme, and highly exaggerated form of relativism. It should be clear that the Heidegger of Dalmayr and Caputo is of greater value to us than the Heidegger of the deconstructionists.

Bernstein concludes by stating the points of convergence and divergence between the pragmatists and Heidegger. As noted above, the points of comparison are basic and pervasive. Both agree on the dangers of the metaphysics of subjectivity with its attendant emphasis on epistemology and its forms of validation. Both positions relentlessly strive to overcome those categorical dualisms which have vitiated the tradition of Western metaphysics. Both perspectives insist that human beings exist *in medias res* and thus have neither absolute origin or predetermined *telos.*

Yet this partial list of common traits should not blind us to several profound differences between pragmatism and the writings of Heidegger. Chief among these are the pragmatic emphasis on the centrality of *praxis* and the pervasive commitment to the growth of critical community. Thinkers as diverse as Peirce, Royce, Mead, Dewey, and Buchler have all made human community central to philo- sophic reflection. By developing what can be called a metaphysics of community, the pragmatists and their heirs have provided ample room for a *true* humanism which vindicates the fundamental aspirations of finite selves in search of authenticity and moral regeneration.

The sixth essay, by Charles M. Sherover, "Royce's Pragmatic Idealism and Existential Phenomenology," shows a number of key parallels between Royce's Absolute Pragmatism and the basic categories of Heidegger's *Sein und Zeit.* Royce is discussed in the context of his diary notations and in terms of the metaphysical categories of his 1901 *World and the Individual.* Specifically, the notions of intentionality, sociality, and temporality are examined to show how Royce anticipated insights of the early Heidegger. Sherover maintains that Royce developed a more profound understanding of the role of sociality in determining individual reality than was possible for Heidegger with his emphasis on the priority of *Dasein* and its relation to nature and equipmental totalities.

Both Royce and Heidegger can be seen to work with a basically Kantian understanding of the role of categories in constituting human being and social structures. This Kantian legacy converges on the basic problems of intentional consciousness and its role in sustaining integral and coherent unities of experience. Further, both thinkers assume the priority of ontology in any reflection on the world or nature. While Royce does not raise the *Seinsfrage* as such, he does strive to locate anthropology and cosmology within the context of basic conceptions of Being.

Intentionality is understood to function within a teleological process in which an "internal meaning" of an idea seeks fulfillment in an "external meaning." Royce understands the internal meaning of an idea to be its purposive intent toward some form of external embodiment or confirmation. The finite self imposes its will by projecting these internal meanings onto a field of hoped for consummation. The emphasis on this internal dimension supports Royce's basic Idealism. The external meaning of an idea is its descriptive meaning. Traditional correspondence theories of truth grasp this side of the intentional relation. The teleological aspect of intentionality drives each internal meaning toward fulfillment in its proper external meaning. Royce states that the Absolute lives in the realm of fulfilled internal meanings (pertaining to its world of appreciation) while finite selves must move toward external expression. The intentionality of finite consciousness manifests itself in the movement from internal to external meanings. The will functions as the motor force for this movement.

Sherover points out that, contrary to common misconceptions, Royce did not posit a monistic Absolute but insisted, instead, on what Sherover calls a "pragmatic contextualism." This contextual view of reality rules out any 'block universe' which would stultify the teleological drive of the self. All intentional acts prevail within specific contexts which add to the life of the Absolute. Individuality is not eclipsed in Royce's general categorical scheme.

Royce advances four conceptions of Being in *The World and the Individual* in order to affirm the final position as the one leading toward truth. He rejects the perspectives of mysticism, realism, and so-called neo-Kantianism in order to prove the truth of the fourth conception. This fourth conception, perhaps best named as that of "Absolute Pragmatism," insists on the social and temporal dimensions of both the human self and of nature as a whole. Sociality is fundamental to the life of the Absolute, and this is itself normative for the life of the finite and time-bound self. Human self-consciousness is emergent out of the primordial sociality which exhibits systems of contrast that enable the self emerge in distinction from the not-self. We cannot start our reflection from the priority of self-consciousness but must derive any such 'starting point' from sociality itself.

Our awareness of human community, of the contrast between our self and those of others, is prior to our awareness of nature. This reverses Heidegger's understanding, which starts from *Dasein's* relation to the present and ready-to-hand inorder to move toward the social world of *Mitdasein*. Sherover insists that Royce has more clearly grasped the true starting point for our knowledge of reality. For Royce, echoing Peirce, nature is what is or will be known by the community of finite minds. The priority of community is established for both self-knowledge and the knowledge of science and metaphysics. Sociality is the most basic category in Royce's metaphysics as it serves to govern and locate categories of lesser scope.

Royce's phenomenological framework is most clearly manifest in his presentation of the traits of temporality. Like Heidegger, he sees temporality as the horizon within which the self can stand into and before a world which becomes disclosed through time. Royce drives beyond James' "specious present" to an understanding of the conceptual priority of the three modes of time over the perceptual present. The conception of past and future govern and locate any experience of the present. Royce, like the pragmatists in general, places priority on the future as that mode of time which governs our intentional acts. Truth is not an antecedent state but must await validation in the future convergence of the community and the Absolute. Unlike some medieval thinkers, Royce envisions the Absolute as itself part of an all-inclusive temporality rather than as something which stands outside of time in a self-contained eternal present. Hence temporality and the time-order characterize the life of the Absolute and of finite human selves.

In Royce's later writings, especially his 1913 *The Problem of Christianity*, the role of temporality and sociality is developed along the lines of Peirce's triadic epistemology. Perception and conception are united in the interpretation which manipulates signs for both interpreters and interpretees. One can say that the later Royce becomes even more phenomenological in his portrayal of intentionality, sociality, and temporality as they function within the community of interpretation. The metaphysical structures of community guide the phenomenological descriptions of the interpretive process. Sherover concludes that these metaphysical structures provide a grounding for concrete phenomenological investigations. Royce's systematic structure gives his perspective a scope and power which remained out of Heidegger's reach. If nothing else, Royce showed that a phenomenology bereft of metaphysics was a phenomenology without depth and without a horizon.

The seventh essay, by John J. McDermott, "Experience Grows by its Edges: A Phenomenology of Relations in an American Philosophical Vein," makes an impassioned plea for personal and moral transformation through the extension and liberation of the relational networks which potentially surround us. Phenomenologists and pragmatists can be understood to advance a method rather than a conception of the universe. The methodic nature of these movements makes them especially fruitful in the enterprise of establishing relations between selves and between a given self and its personal universe. Human consciousness is unique in nature in its ability to allow the world to interpenetrate into its evolving life. This complex interpenetration is fraught with both novelty and the deadening routine of mechanical habit. The function of a proper phenomenology of relations is to help us emerge from the confines of habitual structures which freeze the number of relational potentialities.

One forceful way to enter into an analysis of relations is through medical case studies of those extreme conditions which can befall the human organism on its way toward death. McDermott cites several such studies in order to reawaken us to the hidden richness of everyday being-in-the-world. The case of Lillian T. involves a woman who was revived after years of suffering from the devastating "sleeping sickness" which ravaged Europe from 1916 to 1927. Her every movement required complex prior planning if a successful outcome was to be expected. In the case of a brain-damaged soldier, Mr. Zasetsky, even the simplest feat of concentration was beyond reach. His detailed efforts to remember something as simple as a handshake evoke admiration and wonder at the effortless movements common to the majority of mankind. In extreme case histories such as these we are forced to recognize the utter complexity of those thoughts and movements which we so casually take for granted.

Philosophically, we can advance our understanding by taking note of the writings of James and Dewey. James both described and preached a Promethean self which has the task of building its own personal world of relations and meanings. Dewey, more skeptical of such hubristic optimism, insisted on the social and natural limitations of any human transaction with a world not of human construction. Yet Dewey affirmed fundamental dimensions of the Jamesian conception of the person, specifically, the power of the problem-solving self to reconstruct a lived world along the lines of its own felt desires. Going beyond James and Dewey, we must further locate the self in a larger social cosmology which attests to the utter plenitude and scope of the physical universe. No grasp of the self is complete which fails to account for the new physical cosmology.

Yet the growth of the Promethean self is not without its difficulties. Chaos and frustration await any self who tries to remake the universe out of whole cloth. Circumspection and wisdom must intervene to preserve the contour of the relational self. For McDermott, the greater danger lies in the deadening of relation which emerges from the imperial power of language and its substantive ascriptions of objective realities. James' radical empiricism shows us that objects are themselves secondary products of human attention and conceptualization and that these objects emerge out of a continuum which is ontologically prior. The continuum can be described as a relational network which has neither center nor circumference. Social and linguistic pressures keep this continuum from being a proper 'object' of personal and philosophic attention.

Of course, finite selves cannot hope or desire to have an unlimited number of relations. Some narrowing of pure possibility is necessary for biological and social survival. What is important, however, is that this narrowing serve genuine needs for preservation rather than the illusory drives of self-protection. McDermott analyses five negative forms of relationality which go beyond a genuine and healthy drive for proper limitation.

The first, relation-starvation, comes from a profound fear of the novel. The imperial power of repetition stands duty guarding the self against any relation which would bestir its illusory tranquility. This flight from new relations gives birth to the "incarnation of the *a priori*" which gives categorical sanction against that which would be new or novel. Other selves are seen as a threat to our assumed plenitude, and we project imperial biographies which reduce their novelty or greatness to accustomed models cut to our own measure.

The second, relation-amputation, radically cuts off newness. The twin compulsions of fright and habit conspire to keep the self within grooved patterns of response and identity. This entails a fundamental shrinking of the contours of the person.

The third, relation-saturation, goes to the other extreme in its drive toward stimulation and massive repetition of experiences which are neither deep nor long lasting. This "frenetic activity of multiple involvement" blunts the proper sociality of the self by reinforcing a deep solipsism. Quantity of experience becomes the measure of human existence.

The fourth, relation-seduction, is perhaps the most dangerous of the five. A "second fringe" beyond the ordinary becomes the lure and beacon for a self driven to leave the world of everydayness far behind. Religious or political messianism lift the self beyond common aspiration and blind it with a vision which is neither real nor valuable. When mind-altering drugs enter the mixture, the self may be forever beyond recall to the tasks of the real social order. These seductions do not forebode liberation but serve to deepen the addictive nature of relations beyond the pale.

The fifth, relation-repression, is attested to in psychoanalytic literature, which warns of the dangers of repressed contents. Nothing repressed can remain forever outside of manifestations through the 'cracks' in consciousness. As has been well documented, these repressed contents take on a life of their own and function as autonomous centers of power and affect. Whether through creative sublimation or through proper translation, these relations must find expression if the self is to avoid reversal and the humiliation of the irrational.

McDermott concludes with an affirmation, in spite of these dangers, of the need for an expanded world of relation. The self is presented with the existential task of building its own personal universe in the face of a larger universe of indifference and neutrality. Armed with insight into the dangers of the wrong type of relationality, the self can emerge into a world which vastly outshines the world of our own compressed isolation.

The eighth essay, by Charlene Haddock Seigfried, "Hodgson's Influence on James' Organization of Experience," traces James' interest in so-called "pure experience" back to the writings of British philosopher-psychologist Shadworth H. Hodgson. She cites a letter written by James in 1910 where he affirms that Pierce and Hodgson were the two major influences on his notion of pragmatism. James was especially attracted to Hodgson's emphasis on common sense and the conversion of the question of being to the question of what being is "known as." Hodgson is seen as a thinker who struggled to free philosophy from the Kantian legacy which would insist on the existence of a transcendental ego or transcendental unity of apperception as the basis of unity in the life of experience.

For James, the unity of the self could not be founded on something posited outside of experience as undergone. The philosopher could not appeal to a substantive self outside of phenomenal appearance, nor could the Kantian formal structures be introduced through a transcendental argument moving from what is the case to what must be the case in order to account for experience. James located the principle of unity in "passing thought" which tied together the modes of time as well as the the various thoughts isolated from the flow of experience. The ego, whether transcendental or empirical, emerges out of the passing thought as its own moment of present unity.

Both James and Hodgson rejected the Kantian notion that experience is chaotic until it receives unity from the formal structures of a constituting consciousness. Hodgson prefers to speak of a quasi-chaos *within* experience which must receive further orderliness through human intention. To talk of a chaotic manifold prior to experience is to engage in the type of speculation from which pragmatism sought to free itself. James affirmed that experience is already unified and organized in perception. Unity occurs within experience or not at all.

Seigfried maintains, against James, that the unity of experience must come from something besides "passing thought." James did not, of course, have a unitary account of the self in the *Principles*, but wavered between several possibilities. But he was correct in seeking that unity from within experience.

Hodgson, like contemporary phenomenologists, believed that we could examine experience without introducing presuppositions which come from a realm outside of experience. Further he insisted that we 'bracket out' the question of the agency behind experience. Such concerns must await a careful and thorough account of experience itself.

For James, this bracketing extended to the realm of metaphysical categories in general. The real is what which we find important and interesting. The unreal is that which fails to draw our attention. Yet James gives a broader definition of the real as that which is not contradicted by anything else which we think. From this weak definition we must assume that there are some things which are more real than others. Anything which does not generate contradictions is real while the more real is that which remains at the focus of our interest or attention. Beyond the problem of existence predication, James strove to return all metaphysical categories to their original appearance within common experience. No generic notion can emancipate itself from the stream of consciousness which gave it birth. Hence James envisioned pragmatism as a method for bringing speculative metaphysics back to its home base in finite experience.

James had another motive for attempting to return metaphysics back to the stream of consciousness. He insisted throughout that philosophic categories remain tied to real and vital moral issues. From this commitment he moved towards a conception of metaphysics which insisted on its practical import for giving meaning and direction to the self. Any given metaphysical category derives its validation not from formal argumentation but from its efficacy in turning a drifting and empty life into a meaning filled and future directed existence. His famous notion of the will or right to believe is part and parcel of this sense of the pragmatic value of general categories. The phenomenological dimension fo James can be most clearly seen in his effort, inspired by Hodgson, to show the origin of all metaphysics in the stream of consciousness, which is the spawning ground for all categorial systems.

The ninth, and final essay, by Thomas Olshewsky, "Toward a Hermeneutical Realism," argues that hermeneutic theory must overcome linguistic relativism if it is to advance more fully toward a proper understanding of the reality which confronts persons in their actions towards the world. Peirce's semiotics is held to provide a generic framework on interpretation which moves beyond the linguistic framework of both Gadamer and Habermas. In addition, the utilization of Peirce's three categories saves the act of interpretation from the nominalism an conventionalism which have vitiated all attempts to understand both texts and the world.

Philosophy, unlike theology, is engaged in a hermeneutics of hermeneutics whereby the main traits of the interpretative process itself are laid bare for our inspection. The classical view of hermeneutics is tied to a realism which drives towards a direct confrontation with the texts themselves. For someone like Martin Luther, Scripture interprets itself to the proper hermeneute along the lines dictated by the Spirit. By the time we arrive at the Romantic hermeneutics of Schleiermacher, the texts become problematic as interpretation shifts its interest to the inner spiritual evolution of the author. The intentions of the author become the genetic norm by and through which the text becomes open to our gaze. Schleiermacher locates the evolution of an author's thought within the evolution of a particular language. The Romantic movement stressed a hermeneutics which sought to divine the author, often with reference to 'unconscious' thoughts, better than the author understood himself. It was assumed that this process was capable of textual and psychological validation.

Dilthey's empiricist-historical hermeneutics, to a large degree based on Schleiermacher, struggled to find a form of validation appropriate for the *Geisteswissenschaften*. An intuitive emphasis on *Verstehen* attempted to find direct access to the mind of the author as that mind emerged out of concrete life. In many respect, Dilthey remained bound to the model of science from which he tried to free himself. He can be read as having tried to legitimate the domain of the human studies by a translation of methodology from the sciences of nature.

Gadamer moved Hermeneutics in the right direction by shifting from epistemology to ontology, that is, by moving towards an analysis of the structures of being-in-the-world as these structures show themselves in language. For Olschewsky, this shift advanced the study of interpretation beyond the previous stages. Yet Gadamer, like Schleiermacher and Dilthey before him, rejected a general semiotics in order to insist that all meaning takes place in language. No complex can show itself, can become unhidden, outside of the evocative Saying of language. Hermeneutics thus has language alone as its 'object.'

Peirce, utilizing a more forceful categorical framework, insisted that anything thought can function as a sign. Of course Peirce often hints that reality itself is nothing more than innumerable signs. In either case, signs can certainly exist outside of the natural human languages. Any complex can function as a sign provided that it convey something to someone in some respect. Peirce's semiotics is thus held to provide a more just account of the 'object' of hermeneutics than the linguistic accounts of the

Continental thinkers. The task becomes that of grafting semiotics to a non-linguistic conception of hermeneutics.

Any sign will exhibit all three of Peirce's categories. Of course, any given category may appear in degenerate form. Thus for example, a merely thought of possibility for action may contain secondness (resistance) in only a degenerate form while it may contain thirdness (generality) in a non-degenerate form. Regardless of the 'strength' of an instantiated category, it will be present in some respect.

Gadamer and Peirce do share several perspectives on the interpretive process. Both reject any form of Cartesianism which would insist on pure intuition into something like essences. Both reject the notion that interpretation has a presuppositionless starting point in a first sign or interpretation. And both, albeit it in different ways, make aesthetics primary for understanding interpretation.

Olshewsky's "hermeneutical realism" rejects the relativism and nominalism to be found continental thinkers. Gadamer, it is held, remains free from some of the more extreme implications of the "linguisticality thesis." That is, he places hermeneutics on a more secure, and potentially realistic, footing than do others. Yet his linguisticality keeps him from recognizing the existence of signs outside of language. Specifically, Peirce's three categories provide parameters within which any given interpretation must move. Nature functions as a system of seconds which limit the reach of any interpretive act. The world embodies firsts and thirds independently of our attempts to understand them. Any sign must exhibit all three categories and must exert its own forms of constraint on the hermeneutic process. Once this is recognized, we can leave behind the relativistic and idealistic hermeneutics of the past and advance toward a richer awareness of how our interpretations relate to a nature not of our own making.

B. *Through Temporality to Ordinality*

In the introduction to his 1913 work *Ideas*, Husserl takes pains to show how phenomenology stands opposed to the so-called "natural attitude." The attitude common to most philosophy and to the domain of the everyday assumes that the intentional objects of consciousness occupy different orders of being and that some complexes are more or less real than others. This ontological bias makes it difficult to move from the realm of facts to the realm of pure essentiality. Transcendental phenomenology utilizes an eidetic reduction in order to drive beyond the mere matter-of-fact and arrive at essential universality. Yet the success of this eidetic reduction rests on a prior *epochē* which puts all ontological positing out of action so that the pure phenomenality of the phenomenon can appear. This bracketing (*Einklammerung*) shatters the power of the natural attitude, which insists on degrees of being:

> Indeed, what makes so extraordinarily hard the acquisition of the proper essence of phenomenology, the understanding of the peculiar sense of its problems, and of its relationship to all other sciences (in particular to psychology), is that, for all this, a new style of attitude is needed which is entirely altered in contrast to the natural attitude in experiencing and the natural attitude in thinking.[1]

The entrance into phenomenology proper is the *epochē*, which frees the quest for essence from any commitment to a peculiar understanding of complexes which would bypass one domain or order for another.

Husserl demands a "perfect freedom" for phenomenology which would universalize doubt about the existential status of any complex under investigation. What remains intact after the *epochē* is pure consciousness. The traits of any consciousness whatsoever become available to the specific kind of sight peculiar to phenomenology. From the self-evident foundation of the pure subject emerges all intuition into essences of whatever kind.

Methodologically it is clear that Husserl's return to the "things themselves" is facilitated by this rejection of the natural attitude and its ontological hierarchies. While he does posit hierarchies of essences, he refuses to intrude pre-thematic metaphysical hierarchies.[2] Every complex discriminated must receive full and detailed treatment if it is to show its proper trait contour. Physical objects do not assume priority over phantasy objects or ideational structures. The motive behind the *epochē* is the desire to be ontologically fair to any phenomenon regardless of its regional or ordinal location in some pre-reflective scale of nature.

Yet for all of Husserl's sensitivity to different ordinal or regional structures, there remains the perplexing problem of the "phenomenological residuum," the realm of pure subjectivity. Methodological fairness does not always foreclose metaphysical bias. The intention of the *epochē* is clear enough, yet its curious alignment with Cartesian subjectivity betrays its fundamental purpose. The priority of subjectivity distorts an otherwise judicious sensitivity to difference and ordinal placement. What is required is a thematic sense of metaphysical fairness to support and encompass the methodological openess.

Husserl's intent to save the 'reality' of all phenomena no matter what their existential status is best fulfilled in a more properly metaphysical understanding of the equality of all complexes. This understanding emerges with greatest clarity in the categorial scheme of Justus Buchler when he contrasts ontological priority with ontological parity. Unlike the methodological tactic of bracketing, the metaphysical commitment to parity remains free from any bias toward the subject who might engage in such bracketing. There is no sought-for 'residuum' which would stand secure against the assaults of a puritanical drive against positing. No privileged location or complex emerges which would govern or locate the 'bracketed' intentional objects.

Philosophers traditionally assume that some complexes are more real than others, often confusing type of being with degrees of being. Pervasive throughout human history are versions of a commitment to ontological priority. This perspective makes probing into traits difficult because of a recurrent methodological bias toward those 'realities' which are permanent, inevitable, or spatio-temporal. For Buchler, this confusion is one which blunts the generic spread of any systematic articulation of the world:

> Philosophers, less concerned than men of affairs with making their world manageable and more with making it intelligible, develop types of trust and distrust comparable to those of common life. Some aspects of the world provide them with clues to other aspects. Some provide them with the impetus to build their guiding concepts. Those which they are compelled repeatedly to acknowledge, those to which they feel they are led back irresistibly in their interpretations, get accredited as "real" or "most real." Degree of explanatory usefulness gets transformed into degree of "being."[3]

Foundationalisms assume that translation into certain categorial primitives moves us from the less real to the more real. Method becomes the servant of metaphysical shortsightedness. Both reductive methodology and metaphysical hierarchy conspire to narrow the reach of cumulative human probing. A privileged perspective makes it difficult to render account of novel or vagrant complexes.

In strict contrast to ontological priority is the sense of ontological parity. For Buchler, the *poet* comes closest to this difficult but fundamental sense of ontological parity:

Some complexes may have more or less importance, more or less pervasiveness, more or less moral significance, more or less interest, for the poet; but none has more or less being than any other. The poet's working attitude is an acceptance of ontological parity. "Acceptable" is the term rather than "assumption." Ontological parity does not function for the poet as a theoretical commitment or assertive presupposition. It functions as an unwillingness to deny the integrity of any complex discriminated.[4]

Poetic query insists that any trait discriminated is as real as every other. Of course, one trait may be real in a very different way than another. Yet this difference is not one which pertains to degrees of being.

The import of this realization should be obvious. Phenomenology, like the poetic attitude, represents a commitment to ontological parity. No phenomenon, no matter how tenuous or 'unsubstantial,' should be precluded from sustained analysis and articulation. Any intentional object has 'being' in so far as it is available to noetic consciousness. To deny the reality of any phenomenon is to let ontological priorities foreclose query.

Unfortunately Husserl's *epoché* only carries us part way toward the proper sense of parity. The refusal to allow any "positing" of being curiously reinforces the primacy of pure subjectivity and its assumed transcendence of the world. Husserl fails to apply the insight into parity to the 'residuum' which remains intact after the *epoché*. His critique of the natural attitude violates a more profound naturalism which would insist on the locatedness of the self in complexes of unlimited complexity and scope. To bracket the world in order to preserve the integrity of phenomena is to subvert a proper sense of methodological fairness for a hidden, and highly destructive, metaphysical privileging.

What is desired is a categorial clearing of unlimited scope and power which would give us access to any trait or complex no matter what its ontological location. The sense of parity is absolutely basic to any judicious articulation of the world and nature. Husserl's' Cartesianism occupies a redoubt from which only shortsighted expeditions may embark. A less confined categorial location must be sought which would allow for unlimited movement in all directions. Before this clearing can be articulated, several further steps must be taken.

We will take our initial clues from another perspective, that of Heidegger. Shortly after the publication of *Sein und Zeit*, Heidegger gave a series of lectures later published as

Grundprobleme der Phänomenologie. Initially given in 1927, these lectures represent an advance beyond the concepts of "World" and "Worldhood" as previously articulated in *Sein und Zeit*. The analysis of these notions required an understanding of temporality and its relation to Dasein's openness to anything whatsoever. Our concern in what follows will be to show how Heidegger's articulation of the concepts of World itself violates the sense of ontological parity. Temporality will be shown to be an inadequate horizon for understanding our being-in-the-world. The phenomenon of ordinality will emerge as the ultimate categorial clearing which locates both Temporality and the phenomenon of the "Worldhood of the World."

In *Sein und Zeit* Heidegger grounds his understanding of care (*Sorge*) in the three ecstatical modes of Temporality (*Zeitlichkeit*). In the movement from inauthentic to authentic being the modes of time become transformed. In inauthentic existence time is experienced as awaiting (future), presentation (present), and oblivion (past). The richness of temporality becomes reduced to a truncated and flattened understanding of beings and Being. In authentic existence time is experienced as anticipation (future), the moment of vision (present), and repetition (past). Heidegger took St. Paul's eschatological account of fulfilled time quite seriously in the late 1920's and strove to develop a phenomenological account of the primitive Christian understanding of expectation. Like Paul Tillich, who showed the political implications of eschatological time in his brilliant work *The Socialist Decision,* Heidegger recognized that a transformed relation to time would alter human nature on its most fundamental level.

Authentic Temporality, with special attention to the anticipatory resoluteness which would gather us fatefully toward death, became the horizon by and through which human nature could be recaptured from the tyranny of the everyday. In utilizing such notions as *kairos* and *Augenblick* Heidegger advanced beyond the chronological notion of time inaugurated by Aristotle. Temporality became the thematic clearing for any human understanding of beings or Being.

The world in its Worldhood was rendered intelligible through an analysis of the equipmental totalities (*Zeug*) which radiate outward from our various pre-thematic involvements. By articulating the traits of the ready-to-hand, the present-at-hand, and the being with others (*Mitdasein*) Heidegger built up a conception of the World as a phenomenon in its own right. *Dasein's* access to this world was itself made possible by the fundamental clearing

provided by Temporality. The ecstases of Temporality were seen as
the basic moments of 'holding-open' which allowed for the un-
veiledness of any beings whatsoever.

By 1927 Heidegger had come to focus more specifically on the
nature of the Worldhood of the World. In *Die Grundprobleme* he
attempts to reveal the inadequacies of traditional accounts of
that phenomenon which is neither *a* being nor Being itself.

> A glance at the history of philosophy shows that many
> domains of   beings were discovered very early - nature,
> space, the soul - but   that, nevertheless, they could not
> yet be comprehended in their   specific being. As early as
> antiquity a common or average concept of   being comes to
> light, which was employed for the interpretation of   all the
> beings of the various domains of being and their modes of
> being, although their specific being itself, taken expressly
> in its   structure, was not made into a problem and could not
> be defined.[5]

Orders, and their attendant traits and subaltern configurations,
emerged from ancient speculation in an array which has changed but
little. Yet the problem of the being of that which 'governs' these
domains has remained in eclipse. The issue is not only that of the
ontological difference between Being and beings but that of the
full phenomenality of the World and its ordinality.[6] Temporality
still remains as *the* horizon for our understanding of the World
yet the phenomenon of Worldhood has become more thematic.

In *Vom Wesen des Grundes* (1929), Heidegger gives a condensed
account of the categorical reflections of *Die Grundprobleme*.[7]
Specifically, he radicalizes the concept of the World in such a
way as to go beyond any understanding which would see the World as
the mere totality of what is. He compresses his analysis into four
aspects:

> 1. World means a *How of the being* of Being rather than
> being itself.   2. This How defines being *in its totality*. It
> is ultimately the   possibility of every How as limit and
> measure (*Mass*). 3. The How in   its totality is in a certain
> way *primary.* 4. This primary How in its   totality is itself
> *relative* to human *Dasein.* Thus the world belongs   strictly
> to human *Dasein*, although it encompasses (*umgreift*) all
> being, *Dasein* included, in its totality.[8]

The How (*Wie*) becomes the encompassing clearing through which the complexes *of* the world become available to *Dasein*.[9] Let us analyze these four points in turn.

The World as a phenomenon is neither a being nor Being itself. As such it stands between both extremes of the ontological difference. Since the world is not a complex it cannot be understood in terms applicable to beings or complexes. World is the How through which any complex or order becomes intelligible. The How of the world *locates* beings.

Secondly, the World governs beings (complexes) in their totality. This is not to reduce the World to the totality of all complexes but to show it as the measure for complexes. When we say that the world is the limit (*Grenze*) for beings we mean to affirm that it is the non-located location for any complex whatsoever. Any given being will, of course, be regionally located. Heidegger's understanding of the history of philosophy gives priority to the orders (space, matter, etc.) which have emerged as primary for human reflection. Each order is governed by a regional ontology with its own regional a priori structures. Yet 'beneath' these orders is the World which locates both beings and their attendant orders.

Thirdly, the How of the World is primary. That is, it is foundational for any understanding of beings and their orders. Categorial reflection drives inward from both sides of the ontological difference to make Worldhood primary for holding-forth the between which sustains the poles of the difference.

Finally, this How of the World is relative to the human *Dasein*. This is not to assert that the World is dependent upon *Dasein* for its being or its How but that it becomes unhidden as a phenomenon only for *Dasein*. Yet the World also stands as the encompassing for all beings including *Dasein*. It both encompasses and measures all complexes.

Returning to *Die Grundprobleme*, we can see how the concept of the World is tied to an understanding of *Dasein* and Temporality:

> Since the world is a structural moment of being–in–the–world and being–in–the–world is the ontological constitution of the *Dasein*, the analysis of the world brings us at the same time to an under standing of being–in–the–world and of its possibility by way of time. Interpretation of the possibility of being--in-the–world on the basis of temporality is already intrinsically interpretation of the possi blty of an understanding of being in which, with equal originality, we understand the being of the *Dasein*, the being of fellow–*Daseins* or of the

others, and the being of the extant and handy entities always encountered in a disclosed world.[10]

Temporality grounds our understanding of *Dasein* while the World is seen to be only part of the larger 'phenomenon' of being-in-the-world. Temporality thus remains as the horizon for any understanding of beings, Being, and World. The ready-to-hand (handy) and fellow *Daseins* become available to us only through temporality.

Dasein is the only known being who exists within the three ecstases of Temporality. *Dasein* is thus ontologically prior to any other complex within the World. Its own trait structure becomes normative for any understanding of beings of whatever constitution. Heidegger does not, of course, project anthropocentric categories onto pre-human complexes. Yet his emphasis on the absolute priority of the *Dasein* and its unique Temporality does preserve an ironic chapter in the history of Cartesian metaphysics. The concept of the Worldhood of the World remains tied to an anthropocentric and privileged complex. In order to exhibit this bias more forcefully we must examine another understanding of the phenomenon of World which does not give ontological priority to the human and its unique traits.

In his watershed article, "On the Concept of 'The World,'" (1978), Buchler criticizes several traditional notions pertaining to the nature of the World. Chief among these are: the World is a totality, the World is the overarching unity, the World is the overarching continuity, the World is an organism, and the World is a machine. Each of these views betrays metaphysical problems of great recalcitrance. Yet each view in turn struggles to preserve some sense of the encompassing nature of the World as opposed to that which is encompassed by the World. Positively put:

> The World provides conceptually what is greater in scope, incom parably greater, than anything "in" it or "of" it. But this contrast imposes itself even where the emphasis, plurally, is on worlds. A distinguishable or circumscribed world is yet indefinitely greater in scope than any discriminandum of that world.[11]

Both 'the' World and a world are encompassing of any order or trait isolated by human probing. This sense of encompassment is fundamental to an initial grasp of the Worldhood of the World. Buchler, like Heidegger, insists that the phenomenon of the World is unique. No analogies from specific orders or traits are applicable to the notion of Worldhood itself.

Traditionally, spatial analogies function to reinforce some notion of the World as an aggregate or as a container. The astronomical orientation has served to produce serious problems for a metaphysical understanding of the phenomenon of Worldhood. A just and generic account must move beyond spatial analogies. Can we say, for example, that possibilities are "in" the World in the same way that spatio-temporal particulars are? And what sense would it make to say that the World is itself "in" something more inclusive? Some complexes are spatial and some are not. The World in its Worldhood is neither spatial nor temporal. Process metaphysics imposes a similar confusion when it elevates the notion of epochal time to a fundamental trait of Worldhood. Whatever the World is, it is not 'the space of spaces' or 'the time of times.'

It should be clear that the World cannot be located by something more inclusive. While a world is located in other worlds, and locates subaltern worlds within itself, 'the' World has no primary or extrinsic location. Buchler states:

> The World cannot be located, for it would have to be located in an order which would be more inclusive. The World cannot be included, for it would then be not the World but one more order, one more sub- complex. The World cannot be environed, as every order can and must be, for that which environs would be a complex distinctly additional to the World - an absurdity.[12]

In striking parallel to Heidegger, Buchler denies that the Worldhood of the World can be understood in terms applicable to a being or a complex. World stands between complexes and the Being (prevalence) which 'sustains' them. Its unique phenomenal status requires alternative categorial articulation.

To advance a more positive definition, the World can be seen as "innumerable natural complexes" with no correlative integrity or 'shape.' The World cannot have a collective unity or contour but stands as the clearing 'within' which any complex can become known. We cannot isolate any one order, say the order of the *Dasein*, and make that order primary in all respects. Buchler states, "Since the Innumerable Complexes do not constitute an Order, and since in consequence no order has an 'ultimate' location, it follows that no order has absolute priority over any other."[13] The phenomenon of the Worldhood of the World can be exhibited without any reference to persons or their internal forms of Temporality or time consciousness. Any complex, when rendered metaphysically intelligible, provides us access to that which is not a complex. While it is clear that persons have a unique openness to the World it does not follow that the categorical articulation of this phenomenon requires an analysis of the traits of persons.

Heidegger's insistence on the absolute priority of *Dasein*, as a constituent in the complex of being-in-the-world, returns to a muted subjectivism which darkens the generic drive toward a fuller understanding of Worldhood. Buchler's methodic and metaphysical utilization of ontological parity prohibits the notion of a privileged order or complex.[14] It is significant the Buchler advances his concept of the World *without* reference to human existence. Worldhood can be articulated without benefit of those categories which are applicable to persons, or, in Buchler's language, to "proceivers."

The Worldhood of the World, as a primary phenomenon, emerges into its own true measure when the traits of *Dasein* are bypassed for categories of greater generic encompassment. Temporality may be *part* of the access-structure of human dwelling but it is not constitutive of Worldhood itself. The most generic categorial clearing for gaining access to Worldhood is that of *ordinality.*

Buchler takes pains to distinguish between the Innumerable Orders constitutive of the World from the fundamental ordinality which stands as the ultimate dimension of Nature. In his 1978 essay, "Probing the Idea of Nature," he makes this distinction:

> The conceptions of nature as providingness and as ordinality are continuous with one another and with the conception of nature as "orders." This continuity can be conveyed by utilizing both members of the twin *natura naturans* and *natura naturata*. Nature as ordinality is *natura naturans*; it is the providing, the engendering condition. Nature as "orders" is *natura naturata*; it is the provided, the ordinal manifestation, the World's complexes.[15]

When we probe more fully into the phenomenon of the Worldhood of the World it becomes necessary to work through this distinction in such a way as to come closer to what Heidegger has called the *How* of the World.

World is neither an aggregate of enumerated complexes nor the Being which would somehow stand 'behind' complexes as a creative or ejective power. It stands between complexes and the ordinality which governs them. Nature and World can be differentiated from each other through the reappropriation of Spinoza's distinction between nature naturing and nature natured. Heidegger has understood both sides of the distinction but in a manner which does not achieve the level of clarity desired.

Nature is the ordinality which provides the innumerable complexes of the World a 'place' within which to arise and function. The World is the engendered complexes themselves. The phenomenon of the Worldhood of the World encompasses both dimensions. The engendering condition *for* the World's complexes is prior to any engendered complex itself. Providingness is certainly 'more' than the 'sum' of all providings within Nature. It is best seen as "bringing forth" or as "sheer geniture" rather than as an agency behind the World. This providingness encompasses any provided or engendered traits yet it is not itself an order or complex.

Ordinality, as another name for the providing, for providingness, is the fundamental dimension of Nature. Further, it is prior to the Innumerable complexes of the World because 'it' abides as the seed bed for what does emerge as *a* world or as *a* complex. Ordinality embraces the World's complexes by freeing them for their proper manifestation as orders. Returning to Heidegger's *Die Grundprobleme* we can appropriate his re-fashioning of Aristotle's understanding of time for our understanding of ordinality:

> If we remain with the image of embrace, time is that which is *further outside*, as compared with movements and with all beings that move or are at rest. It embraces or *holds around* the moving and resting things. We may designate it by an expression whose beauty may be contested: time has the character of a *holdaround*, since it holds beings – moving and resting – around. In a suitable sense we can call time, as this holder-around, a container, provided we do not take "container" in the literal sense of a receptacle like a class or a box but retain simply the formal element of holding-around. [16]

Ordinality is "outside" of the orders which constitute the World. Yet its being-outside does not remove the World from it. It holds around all complexes and embraces them in their unfolding and withering. To call this *holdaround* "time" is to extend too much metaphorical charity towards a concept of only limited applicability. There are orders which are not held around by time, no matter how time or temporality come to be understood. Heidegger comes closer to a proper understanding of the holdaround when he rejects spatial or container analogies. What is unclear is the reason behind the insistence that temporal analogies or metaphors are sufficiently free from order--specific connotations.

The holdaround of temporality is but one element of the holdaround of ordinality. The later notion is the more generic and stands as the encompassing measure for the former. Ordinality stands even "further outside" than temporality. As such it is the Encompassing itself.

Ordinality and the Encompassing itself are actually the same phenomenon from two different perspectives. Our concluding remarks will concern themselves with showing how this is the case.

Ordinality stands as the *measure* for the World's complexes. This is not to say that ordinality "locates" complexes in the same way that orders locate and are located. Rather, ordinality measures and enables complexes. As the enabling 'ground,' ordinality makes all arising and dying possible. No complex can be non-ordinal. Each complex will have an "ordinal environment." This environmentality is fundamental:

> The foregoing conception of nature means that no complex can be   regarded as, so to speak, transcendentally free-floating, as non ordinal, as superseding all orders. It means, for example, that what   are labelled as fictions, illusions, and contradictions also have an   ordinal environment and an integrity or integrities, whether these be verbal or logical or emotional. It means that nothing is "contrary to   nature," nothing distinctively "in accordance with nature."[17]

On one side, no complex can extricate itself from its ordinal environment or its relation to ordinality. On the other side, ordinality remains bound to that which is ordered, to orders in their unlimited complexity. Ordinality encompasses the innumerable orders of a World which has no ultimate shape or contour. Any given complex (order) will stand under a dual encompassment. A complex is encompassed by other complexes; is located in an order of larger scope. But a complex is also encompassed by the ordinality which stands as the provision of traits and orders.

While it is easy to see how a complex stands under this dual encompassment, it is less clear how the World in its worldhood relates to the Encompassing. For if the World, as Innumerable complexes, has no shape or 'outer' contour, it makes no sense to speak of that which encompasses the World. 'Where' would the encompassment occur?

We have an initial clue guiding us to the heart of this problem. Earlier we spoke of ordinality, of Nature in its

naturing, as that which is the "holdaround" of the World's
complexes. Yet we also indicated that this holding around is not
to be identified with the notion of ordinal location. It is not
something which somehow lifts itself completely 'outside' of the
World's complexes. What is needed is an understanding of ordiality
which evokes a proper sense of the Encompassing.

Ordinality is the *measure* for the orders under its care. It
measures without at the same time being measured. This measuring
is not that of a spatial system which assigns a given three- or
four-dimensional place to that which is measured. It cannot be a
static or atemporal fore-structure for the "in" relation. Yet
ordinality cannot in turn be measured. It would make no sense at
all to speak of the contour of ordinality. Ordinality has even
'less' of a contour, if a descriptive license may be allowed, than
the World. Ordinality resists being measured or encompassed. The
Encompassing is that side of ordinality which cannot be measured.
Ordinality is that side of the Encompassing which lives as the
providingness of all complexes. The phenomenon itself may perhaps
be best described as the measureless measure which provides
traits. This measureless measure provides for the arising of
persons, temporality, spatiality, and all complexes outside of the
human.

The Encompassing is not arrived at through a transcendental
argument which would posit some hidden structure to account for
that which is manifest. The Encompassing is present to complexes
whenever they 'recognize' (if we may stretch this psychological
notion) that they do not stand as their own measure but receive
their measure, their being measured, from that which is without a
measure. Philosophy can be best understood as the movement toward
encompassment. Each addition to our categorial stock deepens the
sense of generic spread. Philosophers would better serve their
chosen craft if they would recognize the encompassing lure which
lives within the very act of philosophizing itself. As we move
through orders to the World, as we move through the World to
ordinality, and as we move toward the Encompassing which lives at
the heart of ordinality, we experience that measureless measure
which provides the very 'space' within which thought moves. The
lure of the Encompassing is the fundamental clearing-away which
gives us World. Would it not behoove philosophy to open *itself* to
this lure.

NOTES

1. Husserl, *Ideas Pertaining to a Pure Phenomenology and to a Phenomenological Philosophy*, trans. by F. Kersten (The Hague: Martinus Nijhoff Publishers, 1983), p. xix.

2. pp. 24-25.

3. Buchler, *The Main of Light*, (New York: Oxford University Press, 1974), p. 124.

4. p. 126.

5. Heidegger, *The Basic Problems of Phenomenology*, trans. by Albert Hofstadter, (Bloomington: Indiana University Press, 1982), p. 22.

6. For another discussion of this issue see my "Naturalism, Measure, and the Ontological Difference," *The Southern Journal of Philosophy*, XXIII, No. 1 (1985), 19-32.

7. The important internal relation between his *Die Grundprobleme* and *Vom Wesen des Grundes* was pointed out to me by Dr. Raymond Gogel, who has worked on problems parallel to those treated here. See his *Quest for Measure: The Phenomenological Problem of Truth*, Peter Lang Publishing, Inc., 1987.

8. Martin Heidegger, *The Essence of Reasons*, trans. by Terrence Malick (Evanston: Northwestern University Press, 1969), p. 51.

9. We have been using the words "being" (*Seiendes*) and "complex" interchangeably throughout. However, the notion of the natural complex, "complex" for short, is the more generic of the two. The concept "being" often has the conotation of spatio-temporal particularity which the concept "complex" avoids.

10. Heidegger, *The Basic Problems of Phenomenology*, p. 294.

11. Justus Buchler, "On the Concept of 'The World'," *The Review of Metaphysics*, XXXI, No. 4 (June, 1978), 556.

12. *Ibid.*, p. 573.

13. *Ibid.*, p. 576.

14. The methodic side of ontological parity is found in Buchler's utilization of his general concept of query. For an elaboration of query see his *The Concept of Method* (New York: Columbia University Press, 1961). This work has recently been reprinted by University Press of America.

15. Justus Buchler, "Probing the Idea of Nature," *Process Studies*, III, No. 3 (Fall, 1978), p. 165.

16. Heidegger, *The Basic Problems of Phenomenology*, p. 252.

17. Buchler, "Probing the Idea of Nature," p. 165.

CHAPTER I

CLASSICAL AMERICAN PRAGMATISM: KEY THEMES AND PHENOMENOLOGICAL DIMENSIONS

Sandra B. Rosenthal (Loyola University, New Orleans)

Three interrelated themes within classical American pragmatism[1] – the positions of Peirce, James Dewey, Lewis and Mead – are naturalism, the biological approach to the emergence of mental activity as a function of organism–environment adaptation, and the focus on scientific method as the method of gaining knowledge. The intertwining of these issues has been a key factor in the historical alienation of pragmatism and phenomenology, for phenomenology firmly rejects what it calls natural or empirical or scientific methodology in order to focus on an irreducible field of meanings by which man constitutes his world, and on the irreducibility of the qualitative fullness of lived experience.

The tendency to conflate the pragmatic focus on nature and scientific method with one or another of the various scientific reductionisms rejected by phenomenology is nurtured by the general fact that the method of gaining knowledge which was the backbone of the emergence of modern science was confounded with the results of the first "lasting" modern scientific view – the Newtonian mechanistic universe. An illicit reification of scientific content, resulting from an inadequate understanding of scientific method, led to a world view which gave rise to a quantitatively characterized natural universe and to various types of causal accounts of knowledge.

Pragmatism is indeed naturalism in that humans are within nature, but the nature into which man is placed within pragmatic naturalism contains the qualitative fullness revealed in ordinary experience, and man's grasp of nature within his world is permeated with the irreducible meaning structures by which he and his world are intentionally bound. Further, it is precisely in the

Robert S. Corrington, Carl Hausman, & Thomas M. Seebohm, eds., *Pragmatism Considers Phenomenology*, Washington, D.C.: Center for Advanced Research in Phenomenology & University Press of America, 1987.

context of the pragmatic focus on scientific method *as method*, as the lived experimental activity of the scientist, rather than on the illicit reification of scientific contents, that these features of pragmatism can best we explored. Perhaps this is to be expected, for an understanding of the method to which a particular philosophical position is linked is often the key to understanding any philosophical position. Thus, while a misunderstanding of the linkage of pragmatism with the method of scientific endeavor has been a crucial factor in the historical philosophical alientation of the movements of pragmatism and phenomenology, the clarification of this linkage can provide a key pathway to the exploration of their affinities.

What, then, does the pragmatist find when examining scientific method, or lived experimental activity, as the model for understanding the nature of knowledge? The beginning phase of scientific method, not as a formalized deductive model, not as a metaphysical enterprise illicitly reifying supposed ultimate truths, but as lived experimental activity, exemplifies human creativity. The creation of scientific meanings requires a noetic creativity that goes beyond what is directly observed. Without such meaning structures there is no scientific world and there are no scientific objects. A focus on such creativity will reveal several essential features of scientific method.

First, such scientific creativity arises out of the matrix of ordinary experience and in turn refers back to this everyday primary experience. The objects of systematic scientific creativity gain their fullness of meaning from, and in turn fuse their own meaning into, the matrix of ordinary experience. Though the contents of an abstract scientific theory may be far removed from the qualitative aspects of primary experience, such contents are not the found structures of some "ultimate reality" but are rather abstractions, the very possibility of which require and are founded upon the lived qualitative experience of the scientist. As Mead observes, "Controlled sensuous experience is the essential basis of all our science.[2] Further, "the ultimate touchstone of reality is a piece of experience found in an unanalyzed world. . . . We can never retreat behind immediate experience to analyze elements that constitute the ultimate reality of all immediate experience, for whatever breadth of reality these elements possess has been breathed into them by some unanalyzed experience."[3] In Dewey's terms, the refined products of scientific inquiry "inherit their full content of meaning within the context of actual experience."[4] However, the return to the context of primary experience is never a brute returning, for, as Dewey continues, "We cannot achieve recovery of primary naivete. But there is attainable a cultivated naivete of eye, ear, and thought, one that can be acquired only through severe discipline."[5] Such a return to everyday primary experience is approached through the systematic categories of scientific thought by which the richness of experience is fused with new meaning. Thus, the technical knowing of second level reflective experience and the "having" of perceptual experience each gain in meaning through the other. With this model, then, of the relation between the objects of reflective experience and the objects of primary perceptual experience, it can be understood why the model of scientific method, as itself an object of philosophic reflection, can serve to illuminate the dynamics of primary experience.

This illumination can begin to emerge when we turn to the second implication of creativity as the starting point of scientific reflection, the resulting intentional unity between knower and known. Dewey well encapsulates this in discussing the significance of Heisenberg's principle of indeterminacy: "What is known is seen to be a product in which the act of observation plays a necessary role. Knowing is seen to be a participant in what is finally known."[6] Further, either the position or the velocity of the electron may be fixed,[7] depending upon the context of meaning structures in terms of which the interactions of what exists are grasped. Thus, both perception and the meaningful backdrop within which it occurs are shot through with the intentional unity between knower and known. Using this characteristic of the model of scientific methodology in understanding primary experience, Dewey can observe, "What, then, is awareness found to be? The following answer. . . represents a *general trend of scientific inquiry*. . . of maximum doubt and precariousness of subject-matter, means things entering, via the particular thing known as organism, into a peculiar condition of differential -- or additive - change."[8] As Peirce emphasizes the same point, the creative abductions of scientific endeavors "shade into perceptual judgments without any sharp line of demarcation between them."[9]

In brief, for the objects of everyday perceptual experience, as for the objects of science, the role of the knower enters into the object known; there is, on both levels, an intentional unity between knower and known. And, true to the reciprocal relation established above between the objects of secondary and primary experience, the dynamics of primary or everyday perceptual experience disclosed with the help of the model of scientific method in turn help make more meaningful the model itself. Thus, Lewis clarifies the noetic creativity ingredient in scientific objects by turning to common sense objects to understand the nature of "thinghood" common to both levels,[10] while Dewey, in his discussion of the dynamics of everyday perceptual awareness, asserts, in clarifying the model, that the scientific object "marks an extension of the same type of operation."[11] Such dynamics of perceptual awareness, however, lead to a further characteristic of the model of scientific method.

Turning to a third feature of scientific method, it can be seen that such a creative noetic structuring of experience brings objects into an organizational focus from the backdrop of an indeterminate situation, and, as constitutive of dispositional modes of response, yields directed, teleological, or goal-oriented activity.[12] The system of meanings both sets the context for activity and limits the direction any activity takes, for such meaning structures are constituted by possibilities of acting toward a world. Thus, James remarks that a conception is "a teleological instrument,"[13] while in Peirce's words, the "general idea is the mark of the habit."[14]

The objects of everyday experience, like the objects of second level reflection, are the results of dispositionally generated meaning organizations used to turn a potentially problematic or indeterminate situation into a resolved or meaningfully experienced one. At the level of ordinary perceptual experience, as well as at the level of science, 'the object' is an abstraction or meaningful focus marked off within the larger context of the richness of concrete experience. At neither level can 'the object' be hypostatized as absolute independently of the meaning structures through which it emerges in experience. Further, just as the second level object gives added significance to the level of everyday experience, so the object of everyday experience gives added significance to the more concrete immediacies of experience.

Such a parallel between the levels of science and common sense thus clarifies the relation between perceived object and appearance within the context of primary or everyday experience. In terms of the above discussion it can be seen that habit or dispositional modes of response organize experience in terms of enduring objectivities, while enduring objectivities give significance to the immediacies of more concrete experience.[15] Thus, our dispositional modes of response fund with enriched meaning the felt immediacies or the pervading qualitative appearances of everyday experience; these latter emerge for conscious awareness within the context of a meaningful world of perceived objects. True to the model of the relation between the more concrete and the more abstract, qualitative immediacy conditions all the constituents of a given objective experience, but in turn the constituents of a given objective experience enrich the felt[16] qualitative immediacy with the meaningfulness of the transactional context within which it emerges. As Mead summarizes, "in the end what we see, hear, feel, taste, and smell depends upon what we are doing, and not the reverse."[17]

In brief, felt qualitative appearances or "sensations" are understood in functional terms. They emerge within the context of a problem to be solved, and are meaningful in terms of the meaningful world of objectivities within which they emerge, be it the "world" of science or the "world" of everyday experience; for, in Dewey's words, "if by sensations or sensa are meant something qualitative and capable of objective reference, then sensations are but one class of meanings. . . . They are primary only in logical status; they are primary as tests and confirmations of inferences concerning matters of fact, not as historic originals."[18] In this case, felt quality is the most fundamental level for verification in experience in the sense that it is the level most devoid of interpretive elements, and, as indicating the way a thing "feels" as opposed to the way a thing is, is itself devoid of the future reference of perceptual claims. Thus James holds that sensation and perception are "names for different cognitive functions, not for different sorts of mental fact." The former represents "the word that says the least," and contains the minimum of subject–object distinction.[19] As Lewis expresses this point, such a level is known not by introspection or by extrospection, but simply by "spection."[20]

This level says the least, is most devoid of interpretive elements, precisely in the sense that reference to future experience contained in assertions of objectivity is withheld. In a certain sense, however, interpretation is very much in evidence, since to focus on the felt quality is to focus on that which emerges via abstractive attention or a change of focus because of a problem which does or may present itself in the coordination of activity. Such a qualitative feel is not a building block but a verification level. It belongs to "the class of irreducible meanings which are employed in verifying and correcting other meanings."[21] Here, then, can be seen the way in which the view of experience as experimental contains within itself the need for a focus upon immediate "felt" quality, though this felt level itself arises for conscious awareness from within experience of the world that is there, and its very feeling quality is funded with precisely that meaningful backdrop which the change of focus is attempting to withhold.

A discussion of verification, however, leads to a fourth and final characteristic of scientific method. It can be seen that the adequacy of meaning structures in grasping "what is there," or in allowing "what is there" to reveal itself in a significant way, must be tested by consequences in experience. Only if the experiences anticipated by the possibilities contained within the meaning structures are progressively fulfilled – though of course never completely and finally fulfilled – can truth be claimed for the assertion made. Such experimentalism is again reflected in prereflective modes of experience, for such prereflective experience, notes Dewey, "as far as it has meaning is neither mere doing nor mere undergoing, but is an acknowledgement of the connection between something done and something undergone in consequence of the doing,"[22] and hence must be verified by future experience. Or as he translates the same point from the language of experimental activity into the language of intentionality:

> An experience is a knowledge, if in its quale there is an experienced distinction and connection of two elements of the following sort: one means or intends the presence of the other in the same fashion in which itself is already present, while the other is that which, while not present in the same fashion, must become so present if the meaning or intention of its companion or yolk-fellow is to be fulfilled through the operation it sets up.[23]

Thus, wherever there are rudimentary, lived habits of expectation, there is knowledge; there is "common sense knowledge."[24] And, as Pierce so well notes, "There is no span of time so short as not to contain. . . something for the confirmation of which we are waiting."[25] Thus, Mead concludes that experimental method is embedded in the simplest process of perception of an object,[26] while Pierce asserts that scientific method, as representing a self-corrective rather than a building-block model of knowledge, is the only "correct method of fixing belief."[27]

At this point one may object that after all, scientific knowledge is theoretical knowledge and thus can surely not provide the model for understanding everyday perceptual experience. Is not the pragmatist, in dealing with knowledge in this way, once again, though in a different manner, confusing the world of science with the world of ordinary perceptual experience? The answer here is a decisive "no." The use of the model is in no way an attempt to assert that perceptual awareness is really a highly intellectual affair. Rather, the opposite is more the case. Scientific objects are highly sophisticated and intellectualized tools for dealing with experience at a "second level," but they are not the product of any isolated intellect. Rather, the total biological organism in its behavioral response to the world through feeling, brute activity, and ingrained habits of response is involved in the very ordering of any level of awareness, for, as Dewey observes, all "knowing is, for philosophical theory, a case of specially directed activity instead of something isolated from practice."[28] Indeed, the pursuit of scientific knowledge is an endeavor throughout which are "writ large" the essential characters of any knowing, and it partakes of the character of even the most rudimentary ways in which organism-environment interaction involves habits of anticipations of a "next experience to come."

Pragmatism, in focusing on scientific methodology, is thus providing a phenomenological description of the lived-through activity of scientists which yields the emergence of their objects. In so doing, it is focusing on the explicit, "enlarged" version of the conditions by which any object of awareness can emerge within experience, from the most rudimentary contents of awareness within primary perceptual experience to the most sophisticated objects of scientific knowledge. In providing a phenomenological description of the lived experience of doing science, pragmatism is uncovering the essential aspects of the emergence of any objects of awareness. Thus, it is at the same time revealing the essential dimensions of the everyday level of experience as foundational for science.

It has been seen that a proper understanding of the lessons of scientific method reveals that the nature into which humans are placed contains the qualitative fullness revealed in lived experience, and their grasp of nature within their world is permeated with the meaning structures by which they and their world are intentionally bound, both at the level of common sense experience and at the level of scientific reflection. Only through such meanings does that which is brutely there, and within which humans have arisen, reveal itself to them. And it is only within this context that the biological approach to the emergence of meanings as a function of organism-environment adaptation can be understood. The being of humans is within nature. Neither human activity in general nor human knowledge can be separated from the fact that humans are a natural organisms dependent upon a natural universe. However, the externally real does not, at any level of human activity, cause a reaction as does a stimulus. Rather, it has a significance, and is a being which is acted upon even as it acts upon us, The structures which come to awareness in experience are an interactional unity of such activities.

The human organism constitutes its world in the sense that the world is the encompassing frame of reference or field of interest of organism environment interaction; the "outermost" horizon of meaningful rapport by which the human organism is intentionally linked with the natural universe or the independently real. The human organism both creates and responds to its environment. An environment is what it is in relation to the purposive activities of a biological organism, while the purposes of the organism have developed in the course of its need to deal successfully with the environment. As Mead concisely sets forth the two directions of this reciprocal unity, the dependence of the organism upon its environment is generally stated in causal terms, while the dependence of the environment on the organism must be stated in terms of the meanings which appear.[29]

The dependence of the organism on the environment from which it and its habits have emerged is causal or ontological, but this has nothing whatsoever to do with a causal or reductionistic theory of perception, with causality as expressed in scientific categories, or with a related reductionistic ontology. Rather, it concerns the fact that there is an independent "hardness" or "bruteness" to that which is there which will either frustrate or allow to progress the purposive activities of the organism. In this sense one may speak of the adequacy of meanings in terms of the objective categories of the ongoing conduct of the biological organism immersed in a natural world. However, the dependence of the perceived environment on the organism is also noetic, and it involves neither the above excluded features nor objective categories but rather is an intentional mind-object relationship which can be phenomenologically studied from within. In this second sense one speaks of the adequacy of meanings in terms of the appearance of what is meant.

The significance of dispositions or habits not as objective categories but as phenomenological categories is that such dispositions, habits, or tendencies are immediately experienced within the passing present and pervade the very tone and structure of immediately grasped content. Such "felt" dispositions provide that fixity and concreteness to objective meanings which outrun any indefinite number of experiences to which they give rise precisely because felt dispositions and tendencies are felt continuities which outrun any indefinite series to which they give rise. Concerning a certain "unboundedness" inherent in dispositional modes of response as a readiness to respond to more possibilities of experience than can ever be specified, Peirce observes that because they are, as felt continuities, "immediately present but still embracing innumerable parts. . . a vague possibility of more than is present is directly felt."[30] Such dispositionally generated meanings grasp the independently real in a direct but not-spectatorial knowing of reality.

Thus, the irreducibly meaningful behavior of the organism in interaction with its environment is the very foundation of the intentional unity by which man is bound to his world. As Peirce states, in indicating this vital intentionality at the level of sensibility, "Desire creates classes."[31] Human behavior is meaningful behavior, and it is in behavior that meaning is rooted. As Lewis observes, "The earliest cognitions of a mind like ours are continuous with those modes of animal behavior which foreshadow explicit knowledge."[32] Further, the "mode of behavior" which man brings to experience, "and which represents its meaning, dictates the explicit concept and implicitly possess it already."[33] In James' terms, the essence of a thing is relative to the "interests of the conceiver."[34] The inseparable relationship between human biological organisms, bound to their natural environment, and humans as knowers who constitute their world, is concisely delineated in Mead's assertion:

> Objects about us are unitary objects, not simple sums of the parts into which analysis would resolve them. And they are what they are in relation to organisms whose environment they constitute. When we reduce a thing to parts we have destroyed the thing that was there. We refer to these differences as the meanings these things have in their relationship to the organism.[35]

Thus, there emerge from organism-environment interaction, irreducible meanings within the structure of experience. The pragmatic focus on scientific method leads to a biological approach to humans which is not in opposition to a view of human awareness in terms of a field of irreducible meanings by which they constitute their world, but rather, when properly understood, it is purposive activity out of which consciousness of meanings emerge. There is vital intentional unity at a primordial behavioral level which is the context from which an intentional unity at the conscious level emerges. From the context of organic activity and behavioral environment there emerge irreducible meanings which allow objects to come to conscious awareness. Such meanings are irreducible to physical causal conditions or to psychological acts and processes; yet they emerge from the biological, when the biological is properly understood, for the content of human perception is inseparable from the structure of human behavior within its natural setting. It is this foundational understanding of experience explicated within pragmatic naturalism which phenomenology is

attempting to extricate from the philosophically destructive confusions of the modern scientisms.[36]

The focus on a foundational view of nature and a primordial
level of experience can be further clarified, and again this can
best be done from the backdrop of science. It has been claimed
that the dynamics of everyday experience reflect throughout the
dynamics of scientific method, and that since "the object" of
science is an abstraction from a richer or more concrete transactional experience and hence cannot be hypostatized as absolute,
the perceptual object is likewise an abstraction from a richer,
more concrete experience and hence cannot be hypostatized as
absolute. Thus, Mead states of the universe at the "boundary" of
experience or at the "outer edge" of noetic activity, "At the
future edge of experience things pass, their characters change and
they go to pieces,"[37] while Lewis holds that the "absolutely
given" is a "Bergsonian duration": "The absolutely given is a
specious present, fading into the past and growing into the future
with no genuine boundaries. The breaking of this up. . . marks
already the activity of an interested mind."[38] As Dewey observes,
"Structure is constancy of means, of things used for consequences," discriminated out of a more uninformed experience.[39] The
pragmatic characterization of the concrete matrix of activity
which makes possible the dynamics by which the everyday perceived
world emerges through the experiential activity of organism-environment interaction is a philosophical claim which helps fund
with meaning the philosophical understanding of the dynamics of
experience as experimental, as revealed through phenomenological
description.

The concreteness of the continuum of primordial organism-
environment activity is "there"; it is that which we always experience, but which we always experience through the web of
meanings we have woven into it through the dynamics of experience
as experimental as manifested in the vital intentionality of
meanings as dispositional. It is that primordial processive
activity within which we project a world as the meaningful
background for the delineation of objects, and which is foundational both for the human mode of being in the world and for the
human mode of knowing the world, both at the levels of everyday
lived experience and of scientific theorizing. It is primordial
processive activity which can be philosophically reflected upon
through interpretive description, which can be used philosophically to fund with enriched meaning the dynamics of everyday
experience, and which can in turn be verified by everyday experience. The content of such an undertaking is at once more
abstract and more concrete than everyday experience. It is more

abstract in that it emerges from a second level philosophic *reflection on* ordinary experience. But that which is clarified by such philosophic reflection is the *more concrete basis* of everyday experience, that primordial processive continuity of organism-environment interaction as expressed in a primordial vital intentionality which is partially constitutive of our lived world.

Thus, Dewey's characterization of the concrete matrix of undifferentiated activity and James' world of pure experience, as well as his radical empiricism, are interpretive descriptions which direct the manner in which one actively gazes at everyday experience, which both emerge from and bring enriched meaningful understanding to everyday experience, and which are in turn verified by the structures of everyday experience.[40] These features of the relation between the reflections of philosophy and its meaningful grasp of everyday experience are precisely the features previously revealed through the examination of scientific method. But these also are the essential features of general phenomenological exploration of the existential characteristics of experience at a foundational level.[41] This is to be expected, for if scientific method is indicative of the dynamics of all levels of cognitive activity, then it is indicative of the dynamics of philosophic activity, for philosophy is a cognitive enterprise. Thus James can observe the similarity of method between science and philosophy as second level reflective endeavors, while yet allowing for a diversity of content.[42]

However, the focus on scientific method reveals that a more speculative level can be reached within the structure of pragmatism. If, as the pragmatic naturalist holds, experience is that rich ongoing transactional unity between humans and their environment, and only within the context of meanings which reflect such an interactional unity does that which is given emerge for conscious awareness, then the nature of experience reflects both the responses they bring and the pervasive textures of that independent reality which enters into experience. There is for pragmatic naturalism a "two-directional openness" within experience.[43] What appears opens in one direction toward the structures of the independently real or the surrounding natural universe and in the other direction toward the structures of the human modes of grasping that independently real, for what is experienced is in fact a unity formed by each in interaction with the other.

There is an independent ontological dimension of what appears which reveals itself in experience and which forms a limit on the possible meanings through which it can be revealed, or, in other terms, on the meanings which will work. The pervasive textures of experience which are exemplified in every experience are at the

same time indications of the pervasive textures of that independent universe which, in every experience, gives itself for our
responses and provides the touchstone for the adequacy of our
meanings. All knowing involves an intentionally founded unity
between man's noetic activity and the independently real, both
poles of which enter into the character of his experienced world
of objects, from the most concrete level of primordial experience
to the most abstract reflections of science. Thus, phenomenological description of the general structures, dynamics, or
features of experience, as integral to pragmatic naturalism, provides the basis within pragmatic naturalism not only for the
philosophic exploration of the structure of the knowing activity
and its objects in all of its aspects and at all of its levels,
but also for the speculative extrapolation from experience of the
pervasive textures, tones, or characteristics of the independently
real which enters into all experience, but whose reality is
"there" independent of such experience. Furthermore, it should be
noted here that there is a vast difference between the illicit
reification by past philosophies of common sense or scientific
meanings, reifications to which phenomenology so rightly objects,
and the speculative extrapolation from within experience of the
pervasive tones and textures of the ontologically real universe
which enters into all experience.

   This speculative endeavor, which is rooted in the previously
analyzed levels of experience, gets beneath both common sense and
primordial experience to that independent element which enters
into all experience. The categories of such a speculative metaphysics of nature emerge as philosophically reflective structures
or tools for delineating the interwoven pervasive textures of the
concrete, independent reality which provides the concrete basis
for all experience. As second level explanatory tools, they are a
step more abstract than the second level philosophic interpretive
descriptions of primordial experience. But, that to which they are
applied and within which they delineate is one step more concrete
than primordial experience in the sense that it is the *basis for*
both primordial and common sense experience. It is that independent, natural "thereness" within which man has emerged and upon
which or within which intentionality operates in the projection of
a world.

   Metaphysics of nature as system, then, is, for the pragmatist, a systematic speculative endeavor rooted in and verified by
lived experience. It offers an "explanation" of lived experience
by providing a "speculative description" of the features of the
independently real universe which presents itself in the immediacy
of organism-environment interaction, which is "open to" certain

meanings, and which is known only through such meanings. Pragmatists, as speculative metaphysicians, are led ultimately to an explanatory hypothesis which accounts for the textures of that which is independently there and which enters into all experience. They are led to a speculative analysis, via extrapolation from lived experience, of what that independent reality must be like in its character as independent to give rise to the primordial level of experience and to "answer to" the meanings by which it becomes known to us.

Such an emerging characterization of nature in its deepest sense, as inclusive of all that is and all the ways of being, does not yield the illicit reification of the derived objects of scientific and metaphysical reflection to which phenomenology rightly objects. Rather, such a characterization is a speculative philosophic reflection which must be grounded in everyday experience and be constantly fed by such experience. It is tentative, not certain. It is reflective content rooted in lived experience, not direct grasp of "being in itself." And, though rooted in the lived level, it is never completely adequate to the lived level. It is open to change and development, just as all second level interpretations are open to change and development. Although this speculative route is not taken by phenomenology, such an endeavor is a viable extension of the phenomenological path.

What, then, are the basic textures of the independently real which emerge from such philosophical extrapolation of the textures of everyday experience? Or, in other terms, what are the categories of speculative metaphysics of nature which emerge from philosophic reflection on the independently real concrete basis for all experience, the textures of which are embedded deep within the structure of everyday experience?

The very formation of metaphysical categories as a reflective system of meanings reveals process as fundamental, for as has been seen, the very structure of meaning grounds in lived experience a primordial grasp of time as process. What occurs within the present awareness is not the apprehension of a discrete datum in a moment of time, but rather the time extended, dispositionally based, experiential "feel" within the passing present of a readiness to respond to more than can ever be specified. Further, it has been seen that for the pragmatists, the structures of objectivities grasped by the knowing mind do not reach a reality more ultimate than do the processive interactions of primordial experience, but rather the lived-through primordial grasp of felt temporality opening onto a processive universe is the very foundation for the emergence within experience of meaningful structure. James indicates this in a way which both clears the path for a metaphysics of process and reflects the interactional unity, at the primordial felt level, of knower and known, self and world, consciousness and object, observing;

> In the pulse of inner life immediately present now in each of us is a little past, a little future, a little aware-ness of our own body, of each other's persons, of these sublimities we are trying to talk about of earth's geography, and the direction of history. . . Feeling, however dimly and subconscious all these things, your pulse of inner life is continuous with them, belongs to them and they to it. You can't identify it with either one of them rather than with the others.[44]

In the immediate flow of experience, in the immediate "feel" of temporality, knower and known cannot be distinguished because the flow belongs to both. The flow of primordial experience re-flects the temporality of the knowing subject and the temporality of a processive universe.

Such a processive universe which reveals itself in the per-vasive textures of my experience is the home of the whole of the sensory, with its richness and spontaneity,[45] the home of the brute otherness of the independently real with which I interact and to which I respond; the home of the continuities and regulari-ties which pervade my commerce with it and allow me to anticipate the type of presence to be contained within the approaching moment. Thus, all the pragmatists, through their respective ter-minologies, converge toward a process metaphysics of nature which can be characterized in terms of the categories of qualitative richness, diversity, spontaneity, possibility; interaction over-againstness, shock, presentness; dispositional tendencies, poten-tialities, lawful modes of behavior.

Such an emerging metaphysics envisions a universe in which humans are at home and with which their activities are continuous; a universe in which their lived qualitative experience can grasp real emergent qualitative features of reality and in which their creative meanings, embodying dispositionally generated noetic potentialities, can grasp the real dynamic tendencies of reality to produce operations of a certain type with a certain regularity. A universe, in short, which is both grasped by, and reflected within, the structure of meaning.

The pragmatic vision developed above, which emerges directly through its focus on scientific method as lived experimental activity, and on the natural biological approach to the emergence of meanings as a function of organism-environment interaction, reveals both the irreducibility of meaningful experience to the causal categories of scientific explanation and the access to the real through the richness of primary, pre-scientific experience, the very features which phenomenology is attempting to illuminate in its radical rejection of all philosophical remnants of the inadequate Modern World View understandings of the nature of science and the status of its objects. As long as pragmatic naturalism is interpreted in terms of even the slightest vestiges of the very philosophical inadequacies to which it, like pheno-menology, is reacting in its own rejection of Modern World View empiricism's understandings of nature, knowledge, science and experience, then the phenomenological endeavor must remain exter-nal to, and ultimately incompatible with, pragmatic thought. How-ever, when properly understood, the pragmatic vision stands neither in opposition to, nor as a limitation of, phenomenological description. Rather, such a vision reveals both a broadly based philosophic need for, and a natural ontological foundation for the validity of, the method of phenomenological description, as it uses such description both to understand experience in its various aspects and to forge a philosophic path leading through experience outward toward the ontologically rich features of that natural universe which is foundational for the worlds of both common sense and science.

NOTES

1. By "pragmatism" this essay intends the positions of the classical American pragmatists: Charles S. Peirce, William James, John Dewey, George Herbert Mead, and C. I.Lewis. While this essay will not attempt to argue the case for pragmatism as a systematic unity containing minor "family differences" within its central structure, the presupposition underlying the entire discussion will be that there is indeed such a unity.

2. George Herbert Mead, "The Definition of the Psychical," in *Mead, Selected Writings*, ed. A. J. Reck (New York: Bobbs-Merrill Co., 1964), p. 34.

3. George Herbert Mead, *The Philosophy of the Act* (Chicago: University of Chicago Press, 1938), p. 32.

4. John Dewey, *Experience and Nature* (New York: Dover Publications, 1958), p. 31.

5. *Ibid.*, pp. 37-38.

6. John Dewey, *The Quest for Certainty* (New York: G. P. Putnam's Sons, 1960), p. 204.

7. *Ibid.*, pp. 206-207.

8. John Dewey, "The Practical Character of Reality," in *The Philosophy of John Dewey*, Vol. I, ed. John McDermott (New York: Putnam's Sons, 1973), p. 219. (Italics added.)

9. Charles S. Peirce, *The Collected Papers of Charles Sanders Peirce*, Vols. I-VI ed. Charles Hartshorne and Paul Weiss (Cambridge: Harvard University Press, 1931-1935); Vols. VII-VIII ed. Arthur W. Burkes (Cambridge: Harvard University Press, 1958) (hereafter cited using only the standard form of volume number followed by a period and paragraph number), 5.181. Scientific abductions and perceptual judgments differ, however, in that the latter are beyond criticism.

10. C. I. Lewis, *Mind and World Order* (New York: Dover Publications, 1929), Appendix A especially, pp. 395-399.

11. Dewey, *The Quest for Certainty*, p. 238.

12. That objects of knowledge perform this function, not only at the level of secondary objects but also at the level of every-day experience, can be seen from Dewey's insightful discussion of "the table":

> Nothing is more familiar than the standardized objects of reference designated by common nouns. . . "*the* table" is both more familiar and seemingly more substantial than *this* table, the individual. This undergoes change all the time. . . This is an indefinitely multiple and varied series of thises.
> But save in extreme cases, these changes are indif-ferent, negligible, from the standpoint of means for con-sequences. *The* table is precisely the constancy among the serial "thises" of whatever serves as an instrument for a single end. . . . In the degree in which reactions are in-choate and unformed, "this" tends to be the buzzing, blooming confusion of which James wrote. As habits form action is stereotyped into a fairly constant series of acts having a common end in view: *the* table serves a single use, in spite of individual variations. . . . The object is an abstraction, but unless it is hypostatized it is not a vicious abstrac-tion. It designates selected relations of things which, with respect to their mode of operation, are constant within the limits practically important. (*The Quest for Certainty*, pp. 237-238).

13. William James, *Principles of Psychology*, 2 Vols; (New York: Dover Publications, 1950), II, 335-336.

14. Peirce, *Collected Papers*, 7.498.

15. As Dewey so clearly indicates as he continues with his example of the chair:

> The abstracted object has a consequence *in* the indivi-dualized experiences, one that is immediate and not merely instrumental to them. It marks an ordering and organizing of responses in a single focused way in virtue of which the original blur is definitized and rendered significant. Without habits dealing with recurrent and constant uses of things for abiding purposes, immediate esthetic perception would have neither rich nor clear meaning immanent within it. (*The Quest for Certainty*, p. 238).

16. As will be seen in the following pages, the term "feeling" or "felt" indicates a noetic level, not a psychological category.

17. Mead, "The Definition of the Psychical," p. 37.

18. Dewey, *Experience and Nature*, pp. 326–327.

19. James, *Principles of Psychology*, II, 1; I, 222.

20. Lewis, *An Analysis of Knowledge and Valuation* (LaSalle, Illinois: Open Court, 1962), p. 444.

21. Dewey, *Experience and Nature*, p. 327.

22. Dewey, *The Quest for Certainty*, pp. 177–178.

23. John Dewey, "The Experimental Theory of Knowledge," in *The Philosophy of John Dewey*, I, 182.

24. Dewey, *The Quest for Certainty*, p. 87.

25. Peirce, *Collected Papers*, 7.675.

26. George Herbert Mead, *Philosophy of the Act* (Chicago: University of Chicago Press, 1938), p. 25.

27. Peirce, *Collected Papers*, 5.316.

28. Dewey, *The Quest for Certainty*, p. 204.

29. Mead, *Philosophy of the Act*, pp. 115-116.

30. Peirce, *Collected Papers*, 6.138.

31. Peirce, *Collected Papers*, 1.205.

32. Lewis, *An Analysis of Knowledge and Valuation*, p. 260.

33. Lewis, *Mind and the World Order*, p. 88.

34. James, *Principles of Psychology*, II, 335–336.

35. George Herbert Mead, *Philosophy of the Present*, (Chicago: University of Chicago Press, 1934), pp. 116–117.

36. Heidegger finds problems with philosophy's concept of nature for the same reason he finds problems with its concept of reality and with epistemology. He takes 'nature' and 'reality' as derived levels and holds that epistemology fails to get below these derived modes of being. Thus, he is addressing the same problems which pragmatism addresses when it establishes nature and reality as foundational for derived levels and brings epistemic considerations to this foudational level.

Merleau-Ponty takes nature in a derived sense when he states, "By nature we understand here a multiplicity of events external to each other and bound together by relations of causality" [*The Structure of Behavior*, trans. Alden Fisher (Boston: Beacon Press, 1963], p. 3). However, he at times touches on a view of nature as foundational and speaks of "a truth of naturalism" (*ibid.*, pp. 201-224).

37. Mead, *Philosophy of the Act*, p. 345.

38. Lewis, *Mind and the World Order*, p. 58.

39. Dewey, *Experience and Nature*, p. 72; *The Quest for Certainty*, pp. 237-238.

40. The brute meaningless feel of interactive immediacy is a philosophic abstraction or limiting concept analogous to that of a moment within process or a point on a line. It represents the idealized moment of organism-environment interaction, and the pure concrete having, within such a moment, of the indefinitely rich universe within or upon which the dynamics of experience as experimental operate to create a world of perceived objects. Brute having or brute qualitative feel, devoid of the meanings implicit in dispositional modes of response, would be brute interaction at an instant. But, the concept of interaction at an instant is an abstraction from the reality of process, and brute activity is an abstraction from the continuity of a dispositional mode of response. Such an abstraction represents the limiting point of the boundary of consciousness; the postulated 'moment' of the brute 'feel' of the surrounding universe, of the contact with the brute stuff of immediate experience in that idealized instant before past and future enter into the very grasping of that which is "felt". As James says of such an idealized moment, "It reduces to

the notion of what is just entering into experience. . . the merely ideal limit of our minds," (*The Works of William James: Pragmatism*, ed. by F. H. Burkhardt [Cambridge: Harvard University Press, 1975], p. 119.), for "there is literally no such object as the present moment." (*The Works of William James: A Pluralistic Universe*, ed. by F. H. Burkhardt [Cambridge: Harvard University Press, 1977], p. 128.)

41. At this point it should not be surprising, in retrospect, that both pragmatism and phenomenology are led to similar understandings of the nature of experience and of the relationships among various experiential levels. For if, as phenomenology holds. there is really a pervasive structure to all noetic activity, and any one instance of knowing can become the initial focal point for the interpretative description and imaginative variation which yield its pervasive features, then pragmatism can well begin with scientific knowing as an instance to be analyzed for its pervasive features and, with it as a model, proceed to understand all levels of noetic activity, including its own as philosophical. Conversely, if pragmatism is correct in its understanding of the method of science as yielding the pervasive features of all knowing, then such primordial knowing as depicted by the descriptive interpretations of phenomenology should include these features derived from the characteristics of scientific knowing, and phenomenological method should, as itself a noetic activity, reflect these features.

42. James, *Principles of Psychology*, II, 671. (Although philosophic investigation, like scientific investigation, is a second level reflective activity, yet their respective objects are quite different. For the object of philosophical inquiry here is the concrete basis for all experience and all objects of awareness, be they the objects of common sense or the more abstract objects of science.)

43. The existential phenomenology of Merleau-Ponty and Heidegger are reaching this point of two-directional openness of interactional unity or, in Merleau-Ponty's language, "reciprocal implication," but do not follow through, to the extent of pragmatism, the recognition of the character of the independent pole.

44. James, *A Pluralistic Universe*, pp. 286-287.

45. Such a universe displays not less qualitative richness and diversity than found in experience, but more, for the organizational possibilities for experiencing contained within meaning as dispositional are ingredient in the experience of sameness and repetition.

CHAPTER I I

AN ANGLO-AMERICAN PHENOMENOLOGY:
METHOD AND SOME RESULTS

Charles Hartshorne (University of Texas)

A. *Why Phenomenology?*

With most modern philosophers, I take Descartes to have demonstrated that, whatever else we know, we know that experiences occur. According to Husserl, before we try to reach anything beyond experience we should make a thorough study of what is in experience. We should inhibit all presuppositions, such as that we are in a world along with a host of other experiencing creatures and with some things seemingly without experience. We should bracket these beliefs and simply say what our experience for itself is and what, with absolute evidence, it discloses. When I first heard Husserl saying all this, I thought him naive.

Intellectual history strongly suggests that we are bound to have presuppositions, that they are not made harmless by blanket declarations of their dismissal or bracketing and that it is better to make the most relevant ones explicit from the start. We also have good reason to think that observation, to be effective, needs to be motivated by the desire to answer definite questions or test definite theories. The question, "What are the data of direct experience?" is much too vague.

B. *Phenomenology and Some Principles of Logic*

The principles of formal logic have a degree of generality that should make them relevant to our theory of reality, or of experience, in general. They are not dependent on the accidental features of our actual world but express features of correct thinking about no matter what. Moreover, if we are to *understand* and not merely intuit reality or experience, we should consider from the outset what logic can teach us about understanding.

Robert S. Corrington, Carl Hausman, & Thomas M. Seebohm, eds., *Pragmatism Considers Phenomenology*, Washington, D.C.: Center for Advanced Research in Phenomenology & University Press of America, 1987.

1. Logical Principle: Dependence or Peircean Secondness

Relations of dependence alone make deductive inference, or indeed any inference, possible. Without this possibility, what understanding have we? Hence we should ask of any experience as sample of reality, "Upon what does it depend?" And when we confront an ontology like Hume's (repeated more recently by Russell and many others), which tells us that successive experiences have no intrinsic dependence upon their predecessors and might conceivably have had entirely different predecessors (in short, that there are no strictly necessary conditions for experiences), we should not be impressed. If in the present we can experience or infer the past, the present must depend on the past. Hume's view could not be right.

If it is said that one must distinguish logical from ontological necessity, modality *de dictu* and modality *de re*, I agree, but comment that the extent of the difference is a measure of the limitations of human knowledge. The better we see realities or experiences as they are the less gap there will be between the two modalities. That none of us could have existed without our ancestors is not a consequence of how we talk about ourselves or our ancestors, but of the way things, as (indistinctly and partially) disclosed in experience, are. Equally, as we shall see presently, the truth that, granted those ancestors, we might have developed otherwise than we have, or might never have been born, is not a consequence of how we talk but once more of how things as experienced are. It is also how, with enough insight, we will talk.

2. The Principle of Contrast

If there must be dependence, there must also be independence, or what Peirce called Firstness. The point of 'X depends on Y' is that it is true of some but not of all values of X and Y. Similarly, if 'p entails q' (or depends for its truth on that of q) were valid for every pair of propositions, then logicians – but there could be no logicians: for they would have no subject matter. Any inference we could formulate would be valid. Yet how many writers (including Royce, Bradley, and Blanshard) have told us that each thing or event depends on every other, or that no relation can be external to any of its terms! This opposite extreme to Hume is equally unacceptable on logical grounds. Reality must admit real dependence and equally real independence.

3. Asymmetry or Directional Order

The basic relation among propositions is entailment: p strictly implies q. If q also implies p, this symmetry is the special case of equivalence. A logic with only equivalence in some cases and mutual independence in all others would be useless. We would either be going from the same to the same or (arbitrarily) from the different to the different. The ontological moral is: Look for nonsymmetrical dependence relations, with symmetrical ones their special case – cases in which the distinction implied by "asymmetrical" reduces to zero. It is symmetry that is the partly negative idea, the absence of difference. The positive notion is *directional order*, symbolized by a single arrow.

The first three principles together tell us not only that both dependence and independence are necessary but also that they normally occur together, though without inconsistency, just as the deducibility of p from q is entirely compatible with the nondeducibility of q from p. We shall find this a reliable guide to phenomenology and hence ontology.

4. Partial, Non-Strict, or Probabilistic Dependence

If p entails q and q is true [(p——>q) & q], although it does not follow that p is true, still we can conclude something about p, which is that it belongs to the class of propositions, Cq, such that each member entails q and some member (or members) must be (or become) true. I have argued elsewhere that real or causal probabilities for the future are explained by this logical truth plus certain ontological assumptions about the meaning of 'concrete and singular actuality or experience.'[1] If q is an ideally complete description of some experient event or occasion, and if events are necessary conditions for all later events, also, if no event can be the last, then there *will be* future events dependent upon, their full description entailing the description of, the given event. I have also argued that this constitutes what Peirce ought to have meant, and partly did mean, by Thirdness, the probabilistic mean between strict dependence and sheer independence, the real possibility relating events to their successors in time. Today's events do not depend strictly upon those of tomorrow, but they do depend upon there being real possibilities and probabilities for the future. Prospective probability is the third category, as retrospective dependence or necessity is the second, and complete independence of any event from its particular successors is the first. Over and above dependence and independence there is the third relation of *partial* dependence. Events must have successors, but not necessarily the very ones that subsequently occur. But events not only must have predecessors, they require the ones that actually took place. Each of us required the very childhood that he or she actually enjoyed or suffered in order to be what we now are. Yet the child that one once was might never have grown up or might have grown up differently. We face the future intuitively as partly open, the past as closed. Life, and indeed becoming itself, is *given* as the constant closing of the openness in question, as Bergson was, with Peirce, among the first to hold.

To say, "p entails q," is to say, "given p, q necessarily follows." The 'following' is here nontemporal, and the semantic ambiguity has not been harmless. Strict deductive derivability is not only not from cause to effect, it is in an important sense opposite to this temporal relation. Given the present, it is the actual past, not the actual future (there is no actual future), that in the logical sense follows. Given an adult, there has been a corresponding child; but given a child, a corresponding adult is only possible or probable.

5. Objective Modality

If asymmetrical dependence is ontological as well as logical, then so is modality. For "Y depends asymmetrically on X" has strict meaning only if 'X *and* Y,' 'X but not Y,' are both possible; whereas 'Y but not X' is impossible. Or: possible X alone, possible X and Y, not possible Y alone. This models the essential logic of time. Peirce put it in a nutshell: "Time is objective modality."

6. Logical Strength, or Degrees of Abstractness

'X is an animal' says less about X than does 'X is a fox.' Since the more cannot be contained in the less, nonequivalent inferribility can go only from the stronger to the weaker or thinner statement. Here again is our logical asymmetry. Notice, too, that temporal asymmetry is also involved. Animality had instances long before foxness, and this was no accident. Foxes could only be produced out of simpler animal predecessors, and the later might not have evolved into what we now know as foxes. We may pretend to imagine foxes coming first and the primordial protoplasm afterward; but this is juggling with words or superficial images and contributes nothing to understanding.

That the logically stronger cannot be deduced from the logically weaker is the key to Firstness in Peirce's sense of independence, both logical and ontological, just as the deducibility of a logically weaker from a logically stronger, but not otherwise differing, statement is the key to causal dependence or (conditional) necessity. The present is the past *and more*; for the past, as Peirce said, is "the sum of accomplished facts," while the present is the sum as being integrated into a new emergent synthesis embracing additional facts.

The foregoing view, like so many other true ones, is a mean between two extremes. These are: that all facts are timeless (like omniscience in classical theism), and – at the opposite extreme – that the only facts or actualities are those now taking place. Since all our concrete knowledge is of the past, to reserve the word "actual" for the bare present is to imply that all our concrete knowledge is of next to nothing. For if it is not of actuality what can it be of? Surely not mere possibilities. Realized possibilities are what we should *mean* by 'actuality,' and any realization is past by the time we know it. (It is satisfying to find Peirce saying flatly, "The past is what is actual.")

To regard facts, truths about occurrences, as timeless is to imply that the sum of truths is fixed at all times. Yet we intuit ourselves as in the process of *deciding* some of the events that make certain truths true. If we decide some events, do we not decide truths about those events? Three great logicians are in agreement here: Aristotle, Peirce, and Whitehead.

7. The Primacy of Practical Reason

We seek to know what has been happening and what *could* happen in the future, not simply in order to know these things, but also in order wisely to decide, so far as is within our power, what ought to, and can, be made by us to happen. Concrete knowledge is, in principle, of the past, and its value is partly that we may enjoy the interest and beauty of the past and the presumptive future, and above all that we may rightfully and wisely do our part in making the future. We do not live exclusively to know, but partly to decide what, until it is decided, is not there to know. Thus practical reason is even more "primary" than Kant, with his deterministic view of becoming, could fully realize. Our total response to the past (which is alone knowable in its concreteness) is at the same time our creative contribution to the future.

If practical reason is primary, then Peirce's "conceivably practical bearings" are a valid test of meaning in science and philosophy.

8. The Zero Principle, or the Hazards of Negative Judgments

Presences are easier to establish by experience than are absences. If we consciously experience a positive property, something with that property must be there; but if we do not consciously experience a property, this failure knowingly to experience it may not suffice to establish its absence either from the experience or from the experienced world. We do not ordinarily and knowingly experience the properties of atoms, molecules, or cells; but, in all that we directly experience, these things must be there. The Greek materialists thought brilliantly about this matter.

My conclusion from these and other considerations is that positive deliverances of direct experience are in principle decisive, but negative ones are not. Thus perceived change is real somewhere, and not only in our perceiving; but failure to perceive change is compatible with (slow, slight, or microscopic but real) change being present in the perceived. Similarly, the apparent lack of definite details in much of our past as remembered proves neither that the past lacked details nor that we are not genuinely aware of that past; it shows only that our present awareness is indistinct. Leibniz said (and Peirce and Whitehead followed him in this) that all our intuitions are indistinct to a greater or lesser degree. Leibniz often used the word 'confused' for this lack of definiteness.

C. Some Phenomenological Results

1. The Actual Past is Given in the Present

Against this, certain arguments have been proposed. We often claim to "remember that" p, although p is false. Here, however, we have not merely memory but a verbalized description of the remembered. The verbalization is a present creation; it is not the past events merely as remembered. Verbalizing our never entirely distinct experiences is of course a fallible procedure and always involves elements of theory. I have yet to encounter an argument for a radical distrust of memory that adequately allows for these theoretical elements. This becomes clear when we note that the usual examples are taken from long-range memories where thousands, even hundreds of thousands, of intermediate experiences, each with its own memories, present a treacherous maze of subtleties. We have, each moment, some memories going back less than a second; what mistakes in *these* have been shown? When a note (other than the first one) of a melody new to us is heard, we experience it as *following* the previous note or notes. This is a relatively simple and not noticeable fallible functioning of memory. (Giving the exact pitches of the notes is, for most of us, much more than mere memory.)

Another argument against the givenness of the past is that only present realities are real. If this proves anything, it proves infinitely too much; for causes, as science and much common sense conceives them, are past events. Do unrealities produce realities?

A third argument is that all claims to have absolutely given data of knowledge have been shown unsound. Wilfrid Sellers speaks of "the myth of the given." But here 'given' is taken as equivalent to "consciously detected or detectable." No such equivalence need be assumed. The other animals, also infants, experience but do not have any, or much, conscious knowledge *that* they do so. They may have the right feelings or impulses in responding to the data but not necessarily much *thought*, or in this sense consciousness, about them. The general theory of givenness is one thing, a theory of thoughtful knowledge is something else. We are trying to know or understand not just knowledge or understanding but experiencing, which can be both more and less than knowledge. The non-givenness of the past cannot be shown.

2. The Social Structure of Experience

Language, as the British analysts insist, is essentially social. But this sociality is a high-level special case of a vastly more pervasive feature of experiencing. Whitehead's account of experiencing as "feeling of feeling," meaning that one subject directly feels the feelings of other subjects, expresses what I already believed when I knew nothing of Whitehead. In contrast, Husserl followed Leibniz (and many others) in supposing that no subject directly intuits the feelings of any other subject. This is giving perceptual solipsism the benefit of far too much doubt. It is acting on a very bad hunch.

If we are directly aware of anything other than our own experiencing, it should be of our own bodily constituents. These are organized, living individuals, cells. No evidence from science seems to falsify the supposition that cells have their own feelings and that in our bodily awareness we participate in these feelings. Our physical pains and pleasures are then simply described and partly explained as *participatory*, as spanning two evolutionary levels, that of the metazoa and the protozoa. No simpler or more direct way of understanding the relation of our minds to our bodies is thinkable. To me its truth is intuitive. It

gives the social structure apparent in language and science
another dimension and suggests a way to overcome dualism. How many
other ways are there?

3.   The Aesthetic Principle (Croce, Whitehead, Heidegger)

If experiences are to be studied, the question arises, "What
persons, by their occupations and talents, are most interested in
experiences as such? Is it scientists?" They care about their
experiencing so far as it registers the states of measuring apparatus, or the movements of animals. "Philosophers?" They deal
with ideas, as captured in words or other conventional symbols.
Also, because they try to understand the methods and results of
science, they are likely to share the emphasis of scientists on
quite abstract, accurately measurable aspects of experienced
reality.

There is one group of persons interested in experiences in
something like their concreteness. I refer to artists and students
of the arts, including poetry and music. Benedetto Croce is among
those aware of this point. Also Schopenhauer.

Of all metaphysicians, Whitehead stands out as having drawn
the reasonable conclusion from the foregoing considerations.[2] This
is that, in trying to reach reality through experiences, we should
pay special attention to poets (Wordsworth, for example) and
others who seek to create and communicate experiences. Husserl did
not, so far as I know, do this. He came to experience from logic
and mathematics, and shared some of the abstractions from the
concrete of logicians and scientists. I felt this vividly, since I
had come to philosophy from prolonged attempts to write poetry and
from intensive reading in the romantic poets. In this respect
Heidegger, and still more, when I came to study him, Whitehead,
seemed closer to actual experience. Whitehead was also more aware
of religious and, I think, ethical aspects of experience than
either Husserl or Heidegger. Yet Whitehead was, to say the least,
as concerned about and familiar with mathematics, logic, and
science as Husserl. I cannot see Husserl as a genius comparable to
Whitehead or Peirce.

As for Heidegger, although more aware of what experience is
than Husserl, he was remote from logic and science, had little
appreciation of Anglo-American thought, had a tendency to retreat
either into the remote past of intellectual history or into a
brand of mysticism notably devoid of ethical content, and was too
much given to being evasive and oracular. He was right in holding
that *Dasein*, or Human Being in the World, is the given vestibule
to an ontology, also in saying that God is better conceived as

"infinite temporality" than as timeless immutability. But he erred in making too sharp a distinction between Being and Deity. He was also wrong and pretentious in implying that only he had discovered the distinction between Being and beings, or ontic and ontological. Moreover, 'Being' seems to imply a contrast with becoming that is incompatible with his own analysis of *Dasein.*

4. Retrospective Realism

It is time to inquire, "How are experiences themselves known? Do we experience, and *simultaneously* experience that very experience? If so, do we also experience that very experience? If so, do we also experience that very experience of that very experience. . . ?" This seems to be a vicious regress. What then is introspection?

That an experience is always *of* something, not just the experience or any mere aspect of it, is the natural realistic notion, and to give it up is to open the door to radical skepticism. Bergson in his essay on dreams has shown (and my observation of dreams confirms it) that even in dreaming we are always (though more or less vaguely) aware both of our own past and of our bodily states. There is no way to prove, though it is often assumed, that in dream experiences nothing of the experienced is there but only the experience itself. On the contrary, we dream of being cold and find, on awakening, that we are so; of being sexually excited, and so we are; of hearing a sound and it is actually sounding; of needing to go to the toilet and we do; of suffering from an itch and finding an insect bite; of floating on a cushion of air when we are indeed on a cushion, though not of air only, but of similarly soft mattress material containing air. The list can go on and on. Always there are actual sounds, at least of one's own or a sleeping companion's breathing, also tactual and kinaesthetic stimuli; often, too, some more or less faint light, and always some sense, however vague, of 'ourselves' as having a past. What it comes down to is, as Bergson says, that dreams have a genuine likeness (in spite of Norman Malcolm's denial of this) to waking experiences in that in both states memory and the sensory apparatus are *always* functioning. What is different is that in sleep the sensory apparatus functions in a low key: the eyes, for instance, are usually closed so that there are no sharp visual images under the relatively direct control of light coming from shapes and colors in our surroundings. There are also differences in the way data are evaluated or interpreted. But in all cases some features of the actual bodily conditions and the past are given.

In waking perception, what we are aware of or feel is never simply our very awareness itself, but something else, at least our bodily condition. How then are we aware of our awareness? Ryle and Whitehead, for once agreeing, hold that it is by memory that we experience -- not indeed that very experience - but previous experiences, most directly those in the preceding second or less. This seems to have been Peirce's view. We feel how we have just been feeling, or experience how we have just been experiencing. The regress is into the past; also, but less definitely, into the future, in the opposite sense that we feel our experiences as about to be remembered in following moments. The structure of experience is temporal and is most clearly illustrated in memory.

5. Perception as Retrospective

Whereas memory is manifestly a relation of the present to the past and of experience to other experiences, sense perception is easily and commonly taken to be a relation of present experience to equally present realities very different from experiences – mere insentient material processes. Thus we find philosophers either treating memory and perception as doubly opposite to one another (one can see this in Husserl's book *Ideen*) or trying to escape this extreme dualism by forcing memory into the assumed pattern of perception. In the latter case, memory is supposed to be awareness of an image that comes to be in the present and somehow refers not to past experience but to past physical objects. "I remember, I remember / The house where I was born." Actually the poet (Hood) remembered his past *experiencing* of that house, not simply the house. The double-opposition theory of memory and perception lacks clear phenomenological warrant. Memory in extremely short-run cases (less than a second or two) is easily confused with simultaneous experience of that very experience, suggesting a similar confusion (e.g., by Husserl) in the supposed simultaneity of subject and its data in perception. This simultaneity is contradicted, for all extra-bodily processes as data, by scientists and some Buddhists, and for bodily processes, even those in the nervous system, by Whitehead.

The fact that nonsimultaneity, temporal asymmetry, of experience and experienced is less manifest in perception than in memory is easily explained. We remember our past remembering and so we intuit the temporal relation between experience and experienced, but we do not equally distinctly *perceive* either perceiving or remembering – except, and then a little indirectly, when we see or hear ourselves or other animals. So of course it is memory, more obviously than perception, that manifests relations to the past. But the relations may be equally there in both cases. Neither memory nor perception can be proved to relate experience directly to simultaneous rather than past processes.

Since it is intuitive that later events cannot influence earlier ones, realism favors the view that the given is always past. Objects simultaneous with their subjects should either interact with them (and then how could we know what in the experience characterizes the subjects and what the objects?) or they should (like distant events in relativity physics) be mutually independent, and then how can the subjects have any immediate information about the objects? Although Whitehead is a metaphysical idealist, he is also, and quite consistently, a radically realistic epistemologist. The given is immune to present production or alteration, because it is past process.

Husserl, taking perception to be only of the present, further misses the realistic truth in another way. Whereas he terms experiences *Erlebnisse*, implying processes or events, he talks not about physical *events* but about physical "things" or "objects," and, like Kant, defines an object as an enduring pattern, more or less reliably projected into the future, in our kind of experiencing. But then we can doubt if the projection into the future is warranted. And so, since no objects are securely given, no realities other than human experiences are securely given. What is overlooked is that the given is always a *past process*, and this can be given only because it has really occurred.

In memory the past process is one's own previous experiencing; in perception the past process is not another experiencing by the same individual, but seemingly a vastly different kind of process. Still, consider the state of the nervous system that we feel as pain, or as cold. That state was real and our now feeling it proves as much. (There are indeed pains that originate in states of mind, but the psychosomatic origin does not mean that there is no physical state corresponding to the pain. I had, at one time in my life, a nervous tension about my eyes which made me think my eyes or glasses were defective; but by the time I could feel pain about the eyes, the emotional source had produced a physical alteration that became apparent when the tender spot was touched with a finger. The trouble began as psychic but ended as bodily, and only then was it felt as pain. I see no evidence that physical pain is ever merely imaginary, though imaginings may be among its indirect causes.)

6. The Emotional Quality of all Experience

Colors most of all, sounds a bit less so, physical pains and pleasures least convincingly, appear to some as essentially *neutral* emotionally, although, it is supposed, elements of feeling may be added by associations from past experience, varying widely from individual to individual. This theory, found in Husserl, is often asserted, but no hard evidence establishes it. My first book argued against it, and although not all of the book's arguments now seem to me cogent, most of them still do. Nor have they been refuted, unless being ignored is a refutation.

Consider the case of pains and physical pleasures. Some adults may masochistically "like" pain, but no infant does. What further proof is needed that the equation pain = suffering is *not* established by mere association? There is no better evidence that the relation between certain sexual sensations and enjoyment is merely a result of association. There are sweet sounds, smells, tastes, all like bits of enjoyment. Moreover, the pleasingness of the tastes of many fruits is (or was, under the conditions of early human life) adaptive, since the fruits are wholesome and the unpleasant bitterness or sourness of some fruits is also adaptive, since they are, in quantity at least, dangerous. Thus nature had produced (doubtless by long testing under natural selection) emotionally appropriate sensory qualities for those animals that we are. The "association" involved is not individual; it is built into the sense organs and took hundreds of thousands or millions of years to effect -- bringing together emotionally appropriate sense qualities with the real uses or dangers of the environing processes. Feeling motivates behavior; merely neutral sensations, even if possible, would not be comparably adaptive.

When Whitehead speaks of the subject-object relation as "feeling of feeling," he expresses an aspect of experience that Peirce also hinted at, but that most philosophers, including Husserl, James, and Dewey, have overlooked or denied. The socio-emotional structure of experience has been my most basic philosophical conviction since 1918, when I knew no one else who believed it. Later I argued with Husserl about this. He said, "Perhaps you have something." By that time I knew there were others who agreed with my position, not with Husserl's, on this point.[3]

NOTES

1. See my essay, "Creativity and the Deductive Logic of Causality," *The Review of Metaphysics*, XXVII, no. 1 (September, 1973) 62–74.

2. I thank Douglas Anderson, the commentator on this paper when it was read at The Pennsylvania State University (August, 1984) for reminding me that Peirce also acknowledged the aesthetic principle, as one can see in many passages in his writings, e.g., in *The Collected Papers of Charles Sanders Peirce*, ed. by Charles Hartshorne and Paul Weiss, V (Cambridge, MA: Harvard University Press), 5.42. I agree with Anderson also that Peirce did connect thirdness with futurity. My complaint is that he did not use this connection in *defining* thirdness as dependence on two other things, in contrast with firstness as dependence on no, and secondness as dependence on one, other thing. Nor did he make explicit the connection of thirdness with futurity and probability or partial dependence in characterizing thirdness as "representation," in contrast to "feeling" and "reaction." Peirce was close to the truth but partly missed it by his emphasis upon the number of other phenomena on which there was dependence, rather than upon the *kind* of dependence or independence involved.

3. It may have occurred to the reader that the "zero fallacy" listed in section B is not a principle of formal logic. However, we know that one must not divide by zero, which, although called a number, is a very special one indeed; also that failure to find a proof for a mathematical theorem does not amount to a disproof. All other ways of knowing are fallible. Husserl wrote in the margin of the *Ideen* where the idea of absolute *Evidenz* is set forth, "perhaps this is only an ideal." Subsequently he crossed out this comment. He was right the second, not the first or third time, on this point. Moreover, zero is an absolutely definitely quantity, to justify which may require absolute precision in our means of detecting or measuring. Absolute simultaneity, zero temporal difference, between perception and perceived, or absolute affective neutrality of sensory qualities such as redness, may exceed our ability to detect.

CHAPTER III

THE RECONCEPTION OF EXPERIENCE

IN PEIRCE, JAMES AND DEWEY

John E. Smith (Yale University)

The attempts to interpret Pragmatism as set forth in the writings of Peirce, James and Dewey as a continuation of British empiricism with a dose of action and American practicality thrown in, are not only misguided in their basic intent, but they have served as well to obscure the important fact that these philosophers, in different but related ways, were engaged in a full-scale critique of that empiricism because they regarded the conception of experience associated with Locke and Hume, especially, as inadequate, or, in Dewey's word, non-empirical. If a short formula is needed, no better can be found than to say that the American philosophers all appealed to experience but that they were not "empiricists" because they were developing a new and broader conception of experience based not on what experience "must" be if it is to serve the purpose of founding knowledge, but on what actual experiencing shows itself to be in the course of human life. This truth will be missed if one seeks to understand these thinkers by looking to their supposed answers to all the standard epistemological questions – the status of sense data, the conditions of verifiability, the relativity of perception, the problem of how to reach the "external world" and the like – which have been the stock in trade of British philosophy from Hume to Russell and beyond. On the contrary, not only did Dewey especially express serious doubts about the validity of the "epistemology industry," as he called it, but all three aimed at reconceiving experience in terms sufficiently broad and rich to provide a matrix for philosophy, science and ordinary human pursuits. Philosophy for them did not begin and end with the theory of knowledge.

The task at hand, then, is to provide some understanding of the new and reconstructed conception of experience to be found in writings of Peirce, James and Dewey. In view of the great volume

Robert S. Corrington, Carl Hausman, & Thomas M. Seebohm, eds., *Pragmatism Considers Phenomenology*, Washington, D.C.: Center for Advanced Research in Phenomenology & University Press of America, 1987.

of material involved, however, it will be necessary to confine the present discussion within manageable limits; this can be done by starting with some general characteristics of the new conception and some brief comparisons with the classical view, followed by a more detailed account of the analyses set forth by the three thinkers in question. It is important to avoid at the outset the supposition that the Pragmatists were in complete agreement or had one single view of the nature of experience, for James, it is clear, accepted more of classical empiricism than either Peirce or Dewey, and the position of the latter is the most radical of the three in the sense that it leaves little of the classical theory standing. On the other hand, as the sequel will show, there was a consensus, in the current idiom a "family resemblance," concerning what was deficient in the older empiricism and what new features must be taken into consideration in arriving at a more satisfactory account of what is involved when we speak of experiencing ourselves and the world, of having experience and of being experienced.

For the philosophers representing modern empiricism, experience was construed as the domain of *sense* and the qualities of things in the world apprehended through the standard sensory organs. As such, experience was set in contrast to the understanding or reason so that the two were made to appear as occupying separate domains. Even Kant, who aimed to show that experience could not be correctly conceived as anything less than a synthesis of sensory material and conceptual form, still referred in many passages to "experience" as if it coincided with the sensory element alone. Because of the emphasis placed on the immediate perception or the first impressions of sense, the classical empiricists came to regard experience as a tissue of subjectivity or even as a veil somehow standing between the one who experiences and the so-called "external world." Accordingly, it was but a short step to the conclusion that what we really experience is only our own ideas -- the experience of "experience." And indeed the long discussion that followed concerning how we are to reach the external world was initiated by the belief that, since we are supposed to know from the outset that the material of experience is internal to our consciousness, some way must be found to surmount or transcend this inner world and thus come into contact with the outer world of objects. In addition to thinking of experience in terms of sense and subjectivity, the classical empiricists saw it as a product of passivity on the part of the one who experiences, the result of adopting the stance of a spectator whose role is to record, if not exactly to copy, what experience writes on the mind regarded as a sheet of blank paper.

Closely connected with the spectator view was the belief that experience is itself knowledge and must be analyzed in terms of what it would have to be in order to serve as a foundation for an ediface built upon it. The latter requirement placed a great strain on the interpretation of experience because attention was diverted away from the complexities of actual experiencing and directed instead to the analysis of the supposedly simple and atomic datum which is to supply the meaning for all conceptual thought. As a result, experience was construed as itself atomic and episodic; its ultimate constituents were taken to be sensible simples, hence the emphasis on the *term* as the basic unit of meaning, and episodic in the sense that it was not possible to think of a course, a growth, an internal development of experience, but only of a series of moments each clear and distinct both in themselves and in their relations to other moments.

By contrast, the Pragmatists expressed serious doubts about the validity of this entire picture and set out to develop a new conception of experience more in accord with the facts of the matter as they saw them. With the possible exception of James, whose thought is at certain points ambiguous, they rejected the identification of experience with sense taken as a clearly defined realm standing over against reason. The clearest indication of this rejection is found in the arguments advanced by Peirce and Dewey in support of the claim that experience has within it an "inferential stretch" which is inconsistent with the view that it is sealed off from reason and rational activity. They were, moreover, opposed to the belief that experience is a screen of subjectivity standing between us and the so-called external world since they regarded it as a public and reliable disclosure of that very world. Consequently, they could not subscribe to the thesis that what we experience is experience and not the world. Peirce laid the ground for this conclusion in his early anti-Cartesian papers, where he showed that there is no intuitive certainty that what is immediately apprehended is wholly internal to the consciousness of the one who apprehends it. Thus if we do not start on the "inside," so to speak, the perennial empiricist problem of the external world is set aside. In addition, the Pragmatists did not accept either the spectator view of experience or the passivity of the one who experiences. For them the stance of the spectator or theoretical observer, while of great importance, is not *the* stance of experience itself but one approach, attitude, or, in their language, a context, among others. As regards the matter of passivity, we find here what is the most basic point of contrast between the two views, namely, the emphasis laid by the Pragmatists on the activity and engagement of the subject in experience and especially on the close connection between experience and the formation of habits or patterns of behavior in response to the challenge of the situation. Finally, there is the refusal to accept the atomization of experience into singular moments or episodes and the insistence instead on the continuity and cumulative character of experience making up a course of life and the biography of an individual. As will become clear, it is the latter feature of experience together with the elements of habit and response which led the Pragmatists to think of an "experienced" person as one who has become familiar with the tendencies of people and of things to behave in certain ways and thus is prepared or "knows how" to respond appropriately according to the circumstances. The introduction of "know how" into the picture marks the appearance of a new dimension in the conception of experience, one which has no counterpart in the classical view.

Having indicated, albeit in general terms, the main drift of the two conceptions, I should like to consider in more detail some typical pronouncements by Peirce, James and Dewey on the nature of experience with the aim of clarifying further the positive features of their new position. For it is these features which, in addition to constituting a break with the older empiricism, provide significant points of contact with the phenomenological approach. In carrying out this part of my task, I must, as before, impose some limitations, and hence I used the phrase "some typical pronouncements" as a way of dealing, within the confines of a relatively brief discussion, with the extensive literature at hand.

We are all familiar, in the case of Peirce, with the complaint that his views on any topic are spread over an enormous range of writings of various kinds and in different contexts so that it is a matter of some difficulty to determine what his views really were. I am not unaware of this difficulty, but I am convinced that, thanks to the efforts of many scholars and with help from Peirce's own insistence that we approach things experientially, a persistent reading of the relevant writings on a given topic results in the emergence of a consistent view. In the end it is the repetitions and recurrences which count and I am assuming that when Peirce says essentially the same thing five times that is a reliable indication of the position he is taking. Fortunately, throughout his numerous analyses and discussions of experience there are such recurrences and I intend to focus on them. I do not claim to have established an order of importance among the features to be singled out, but I do believe that Peirce's repeated insistence on the idea that experience is what is "forced" upon us has a claim to head the list, and therefore I shall begin with that.

In the many passages where Peirce identified experience in terms of compulsion or constraint standing over against willfulness and prejudice on the part of the individual, he was careful to note that he was talking about a pervasive experience persisting over time for which he generally used the phrase "the course of life." It is not with a singular or isolated occasion that we are dealing but with something cumulative and lasting. "Experience," he wrote, "is that determination of belief and cognition generally which the course of life has forced upon a man,"[1] and in an account of the meaning of assertion, Peirce pointed out that the compulsion involved in experience is of a permanent sort in contrast to the temporary force exerted by individual "thises" encountered on singular occasions. The attachment of predicates to subjects in an assertion, Peirce claimed, continues in force on every relevant occasion so that experience assumes the character of law (3.435, 2.138-39, 7.437, 1.426, 7.391). In stressing the element of compulsion or force, Peirce was not supposing that the relation between the experiencer and what is encountered is that of the pure dyad, if such there be, but rather that in experience there is a direct awareness of something reacting against us which, though we may set our minds against it, cannot in the end be resisted. Hence he could speak of the "overwhelming rationalizing power of experience" (7.78) with the clear understanding that this power is shot through with thought and the interpretative activity of the one who experiences. Consequently, even when Peirce claims that experience is "brutally produced" (6.454), he hastens to add that the effect is conscious and contributes to a habit as something that is self-controlled. The point is reinforced in one of Peirce's analyses of consciousness (7.437) where experience is construed as a "sum of *ideas*" (italics mine) distinguished by the fact that they "have been irresistibly borne in upon us . . . by the tenor of our life." In summary at this point, we may say, first, that for Peirce experience is essentially an invasion of the inner world of ideas by independent reals which modify our ways of thinking in accordance with what is really there. And, we must add, these reals are not confined to things or objects since Peirce included propositions and truth among the items which resist our efforts to ignore them. Secondly, he attached great importance to the pervasive, continuing and cumulative character of experience as something general and poles apart from the primitive simples of a sensory sort which were thought to constitute experience on the classical view (2.138-39).

Closely connected with the compulsory nature of experience was Peirce's repeated claim that experience is experience of the independent reals and not of representations; in short, he clearly rejected any form of the belief that what we experience is already some form of "experience." "Nothing can be more completely false," he wrote, "than that we experience only our own ideas. . . . That is indeed without exaggeration the very epitome of *all* falsity" (6.95). And to underline the point he went on to claim that "we have direct experience of things in themselves" (ibid.), clearly echoing Hegel's rejoinder to Kant, except that in Peirce's view such experience is relative and conditioned by the limited capacities of fallible beings. In this connection, moreover, we must not lose sight of the many points at which Peirce insisted that the reals to be experienced are not themselves opinions, but what opinions are *about*. Peirce's well known theory of reality and truth in terms of the community and the convergence of opinion has often been misunderstood because of failure to take seriously his insistence that such opinion must be under the constraint of both a proper method of inquiry and the independent reals. In this sense Peirce did not identify truth and reality.

On the all-important question of the relation of experience to sense, I think it is fair to say that, taking a large number of discussions into account, Peirce not only refused to confine experience within the bounds of sense, but he regarded it as wider than perception as well (1.335 ff.). In an important analysis of experience, Peirce declared that he would not go so far as to say that all experience consists in sense perception, but only that every element of experience is "in the first instance" applied to an external object. That this qualification is important appears in the sequel, where he claimed that when a person wakes up in a bad humor the tendency is immediately to project this state on the objects and persons with whom one comes in contact, but that, whereas the persons and objects are perceived, the bad humor is not perceived although it is *experienced*. This important distinction is given further confirmation in what we may call the "locomotive" example (1.336). There Peirce explicitly states that experience is "more particularly applied" to *events* and that these, as such, are not perceived. When a locomotive passes by with whistle sounding, says Peirce, the person perceives the whistle, but as the train passes the person the note is changed – for reasons not relevant to the point – and while, on Peirce's view, the change is experienced, it is not perceived. Experience is of changes and contrasts in perception, from which it follows that experience is broader than perception and includes much that is not perceived. As he put the point in another section (1.358),

secondness, limitation, conflict, restraint "make up the teaching
of experience," and no one of these features can be put down to
perception alone. Obviously, much more would need to be said on
this point, especially in connection with what Peirce has to say
about the perceptual judgment, but I am focusing here exclusively
on the point that experience goes beyond both sense and perception. Consider another instance, one taken from the Neglected
Argument, in which experience is again construed as extending far
beyond the boundaries set by traditional empiricism. In this
discussion Peirce refers to the three "Universes of Experience"
and describes them as (1) mere ideas whose being consists in their
capability of being thought; (2) the brute actuality of things and
facts manifesting the action and reaction of Secondness; (3) signs
or the active power to establish connections not only between
items in the same Universe but between those in different Universes as well. The fact that Thirdness is included within the
scope of experience is sufficient to show that, for Peirce, experience cannot be exhausted by sense content. There is yet another example, one which I regard as very important in this connection especially because Peirce repeated it several times. I
refer to his distinction between experiencing a *proof* and experiencing the *object* of a proof. Peirce, that is to say, was
insisting on the difference between encountering a proof – actually tracing out the steps, particularly in the case of what he
called Argumentations – and encountering its object in another
context (3.35). It would, then, seem clear that the bounds of
sense are too narrow to contain Peirce's conception of experience.

No account of Peirce's view can fail to include at least some
indication of the way he conceived of general or universal experience as both distinct from and related to what he called
special experience. Sometimes he expressed the distinction as that
between familiar experience and recondite, the former being open
and generally accessible while the latter, chiefly the minute
observations of the sciences, obviously is not (6.560 ff). To
begin with, he regarded what is familiar, the most pervasive
experiences, as very difficult to apprehend because, as he says,
they surround us so completely with their constant presence that
there is no background against which to contrast them. As long as
our heart beats we do not know even that we have a heart, nor do
we have any clear grasp of how our own voices sound. Consequently,
familiar experience is likely to make little impression on us and
comes to be neglected without being understood. On the other hand,
recondite experience concerning particulars and details – Peirce
is clearly thinking of experiment and controlled observation –
will not, in the nature of the case, escape our notice, but he was

concerned that the prominence and authority attached to special experience would lead to the subordination of general experience and the loss of its contribution. To paraphrase his vivid expression of this point, we find him saying that "Young America" (6.564) "will take familiar experience as if it were just so many squeezed lemons – whatever they had to teach has already been learned – whereas it will be dazzled by the recondite – gunpowder, the steam engine, the telephone – and will recall nothing else." Important as this observation is in the way of social commentary, its deeper significance is to be found in its serving as an introduction to Peirce's idea of the relation between science and philosophy. His thesis is that the great facts of nature, ultimately grasped and articulated through the medium of science, are all initially embodied in familiar experience also described as commonplace or universal. Such experiences, he claimed, cannot "have their juices sucked out of them and be cast aside" (6.565) because they are both inexhaustible and indispensable. The history of the principle of the conservation of energy – "all that man has ever learned about force" (6.566) – shows that the entire investigation "rested almost exclusively upon familiar experiences" in which they served for scientists "as almost their sole premises" (6.567). Science as essentially special reasoning and experimentation always sets out from the matrix of familiar experience and is always dependent upon it for certain truths – for example, that there is a reason in nature and an affinity with the human mind – which are at the root of science but which at the same time surpass the power of science to support them. Here Peirce is arguing for the role played by general experience in the formation of common sense transmitted from each generation to the next, and he even described general experience as a "far more valuable reservoir of truth than the aggregate of man's special experiences" (6.571). It should be obvious that Peirce was not engaged in disparaging science, but rather in securing a ground for philosophy which, as he says, must attend to normal and pervasive experience that otherwise goes unnoticed (1.241). By contrast with the special observational techniques of the sciences, philosophy has no experimental apparatus but must concern itself with the reflective elucidation of that universal experience from which the sciences abstract. Peirce's view is a bold one, and perhaps only a philosopher with his credentials in science could sustain it; a purified, disciplined and consistent philosophy based as it must be on pervasive experience has a force of evidence which continually outstrips the power of special experience. Such is the price of precision and the vindication of vagueness.

Turning now to James, we must bear in mind that, despite his concern to broaden the classical conception of experience, he found that conception more congenial than either Peirce or Dewey, and he was alone among them in allowing that there can be knowledge based on sense alone. On the other hand, it will not do to ignore, as have many who seem not to have made their way to the end of the second volume of the *Principles of Psychology*, the fact that in his discussion of the "house-born" ideas he came down on the side of the *a priori* and declared the failure of empiricism at this point. In what follows, I should like to concentrate on four focal points in an effort to elucidate James's conception of the nature of experience.

There is, first, his insistence on distinguishing within experience a central focus of attention from what he called the "fringe." Adopting a "field" theory, an approach which he described at the time as the most important advance to take place in psychology for decades, he claimed that there is always more in experience than is being attended to by what we may call the "spotlight" consciousness. Attention, as selective and hence abstractive, must in the nature of the case ignore the fringe but from that it does not follow that it does not exist. How seriously he took this conception can be seen in the *Varieties* where the "trans-marginal" consciousness plays a key role in the analysis of the phenomena of religion. There is far more in experience than is presented at any time since it has sub-conscious depths which may surface only on certain crucial occasions in the life of an individual. For James, the experience that figures in science and its accompanying theoretical stance is not experience *par excellence* but it rather the product of a special context, one among others. And the same holds true for everyday consciousness and experience which selects and retains only what is needed for practical purposes. One of James's main contentions in his analysis of experiences cited by mystics is that these do not occur unless the mundane consciousness has been surmounted and no longer commands the field.

Closely connected with this first point is James's insistence on analyzing actual *experiencing* - James was above all a thinker of participles - in order to grasp, as he liked to put it, the "particular go" of the thing. Consider the example of the clap of thunder. The experience of thunder is not exhausted as an instantaneous datum of sound, a sensible simple or impression, but is part of a temporal episode which James sought to represent by the use of hypens. What is experienced is a sudden, sharp booming which breaks in upon a preceding silence, making us vividly aware of the interruption and the contrast so that, if we may so say, we now "hear" the silence which was shattered since, as part of the familiar, prevailing situation, we had no occasion to notice it before. The experience has the character of an event and belongs to the ongoing biography of the one who has it; to abstract from the total episode the bare sense quality of sound and call that the delivery of "experience" is, in James's view, to confuse the concrete experiencing with an abstraction and one which has been dictated by the demand that experience be preeminently sensory in character.

James's conception of "radical empiricism" follows in the same vein since it involves both a criticism and an expansion of the classical view, particularly that of Hume. Describing his own position as akin to Hume's in the sense that both are, in James's words, "mosaic" philosophies (presumably because both emphasize a putting together of facts), James maintained that Hume had not gone far enough in his inventory of the contents of experience. He did not get beyond the delineation of discriminable items, sensory impressions to be expressed as *terms*, and consequently he failed to take note of the connections, continuities, relations, transitions and tendencies which, according to James, are no less present in experience than the items they connect. Stated in other terms the point is that Hume gave priority to the relation of "other than" in his belief that what is distinguishable is also separable and in so doing overlooked the relation of being "with" which, on James's view, is a genuine feature of experience. The cover of the book is other than the pages, but it is quite ob-viously with the pages and belongs to the unity of the object. We need not go into James's underlying concern here, which was to combat the view that, since relations and connectives are absent in experience as such, a supervening or transcendental subject is needed to supply what experience supposedly lacks. More important is his effort to expand the scope of experience by calling atten-tion to all that it contains. Since, however, James included within his conception of the connective tissue in experience a number of items, not all of which are the same, a word is in order concerning one that is of special importance, namely, the idea of tendency. The inclusion of relations in the doctrine of radical empiricism has been much discussed, but tendency as a factor has sometimes been overlooked. One of the reasons for the stress on the atomic in classical empiricism was the difficulty of not being able to find an acceptable "impression" answering to the direc-tionality we encounter in processes of both the physical and organic worlds, to say nothing of the experience of change and growth in ourselves. James was aware of the problem, as is evi-denced by his use of the figure of the "stream" in his description of thought and consciousness. If the field of awareness is basically a flow or succession in which states interpenetrate each other, and those which have passed leave traces on those yet to come so that at each point there are indications of what might or could come next, any analysis of these states into clear-cut and atomic units must result in the banishment of tendency from experience. The same point reappears in James's account of what he called the experience of effort or activity. In pushing a table from one place to another we are directly aware of the effort involved in the form of the weight, the friction between the table and the floor, and we experience the continuity of our action and the tendency of the movement. If, however, we analyze the movement into a set of states complete and distinct in themselves, the continuity and tendency disappear.

We may summarize the radical empiricist doctrine by repeating James's own description of it as involving a postulate, a statement of fact and a generalized conclusion. The postulate is that only what is capable of being experienced is legitimate subject matter for philosophy; the statement of fact is that the connections are as real in experience as the items connected; the generalized conclusion is that since experience contains its own connective tissue there is no need for a supervenient reason to supply it.

The fourth focal point to be noted in presenting James's position is his notion of "pure experience." There is, of course, far more in this conception and its implications than we need to consider for our purposes; the main aim is to see what further light it throws on our central topic. The return to what James called "pure experience" means an attempt to recover what we actually live through and without the encumbrances of such habitual constructions as "mind," "body," "subject," etc. Such constructions, although they later develop from pure experience, are to be suspended at the outset so that the content can shine forth in its own light. Taking pure experience for a start, we can, James says, describe it "as subjective and objective both at once,"[2] and this precludes our saying that it is exclusively one or the other. John Wild is, I believe, correct in calling attention to an ambiguity in James's account at this point.[3] On the one hand, James construed experience as having a generic structure which is neither exclusively subjective nor exclusively objective, but allows for both. On the other hand - and here I see the lingering influence of the classical conception in his thought - James described pure experience as composed of units which remain neutral to the subjective/objective distinction. Consider what James says:

By the adjective 'pure' prefixed to the word 'experience' I mean to denote a form of being which is as yet neutral or ambiguous, and prior to the object and subject distinction. I mean to show that the attribution either of mental or physical being to an experience is due to nothing in the immediate stuff of which the experience is composed - for the same stuff will serve for either attribution. . .[4]

The question now arises whether this account is consistent with the view of the generic structure of experience set forth in the *Principles.* There he maintained that all experience belongs to a personal self; there is no thought or experience "which is nobody's thought,"[5] and this would suggest that no experience is without the intentional structure ingredient in the personal stream to which it belongs. The question is whether James was not sacrificing the personal element upon which he had previously insisted by declaring the "neutrality" of pure experience in an effort to overcome the prevailing dualism. It is, moreover, curious that in *Essays in Radical Empiricism*, where James was concentrating his argument on the defense of pure experience, he should have introduced the dualistic note himself. Referring to experience, he wrote, "It supposes two elements, mind knowing and thing known, and treats them as irreducible. Neither gets out of itself or into the other, neither in the way *is* the other, neither *makes* the other."[6] Without proposing to resolve the ambiguity, I would merely suggest that James was not in the end denying the validity of a subject-object distinction, but rather maintaining instead that it is not primordial and develops consequently as the result of reflection. In short, I take James to be defending the view that in actual experiencing the experiencer and the experienced are together and that, while one can distinguish them from each other conceptually, that distinction itself is not a constant and proper part of the concrete experience as it is undergone.

While James was working out the details of his doctrine of radical empiricism, Dewey was engaged in an even more radical reconstruction of the nature of experience in accordance with the biological orientation of a position he was to call by the name of instrumentalism. The shift in focus is by no means unimportant for, while Peirce's thought was shaped by his logical and speculative interests and James's by his humanistic psychology and moral and religious concerns, Dewey's philosophy was largely determined by his social and biological approach to problems. In considering Dewey's position, we have, of course, the concise comparison he set forth between his own conception of experience

and that to be found in Aristotle and in Locke, whom he took as
the representative of British empiricism, to be found in his
essay, "An Empirical Survey of Empiricisms." Since I have discussed that article at some length in other places, I shall, while
not ignoring its contents, attempt a fresh approach not determined
exclusively by the contrasts Dewey pointed out.

In describing Dewey's conception of experience as "radical" I
meant first of all to point to a significant break with the tradition; many philosophers prior to Dewey had laid great stress on
the need of experience to *conform* to antecedent fact or what he
called antecedent being, whereas he made paramount the idea of
transformation and construed experience in terms of its role in
resolving problematic situations or in transforming the indeterminate, unsatisfactory situation into a determinate and non-pro-
blematic one. It is important to notice that, for Dewey, the
intelligent attack upon any problem does not end with the correct
theoretical explanation of the difficulty but only with the
development, thought experience, of the *means* whereby the difficulty is to be overcome. If I may avail myself of a nice ambiguity, Peirce was intent on "fixing" belief, while Dewey was
aiming in the end at "fixing" the broken radiator! The emphasis on
transformation itself transforms the discussion, because experience appears no longer as a registry of finished fact but as
the funded product of many interactions between the organism and
the environment in which the former aims at overcoming the
challenges presented by the latter. It was for this reason that
Dewey was critical of the idea of experience as a kind of subject
matter – the matter of sense – to be received by a spectator whose
task is to copy it as closely as possible. On the contrary, as
Santayana was among the first to see, experience has now become a
weapon or a means for introducing such change as is necessary for
transforming precarious human existence into something more
stable.

Accordingly, Dewey attacked the idea that experience is coincident with the domain of the senses or even that it can be
defined in any differential way whatever in terms of some subject
matter, since experience embraces all that is encountered by an
intelligent being in interaction with nature and the cultural
world. Like James, Dewey maintained that there are numerous ways
in which the things and events of experience can be taken or
interpreted, many contexts – scientific, moral, social, political,
esthetic, religious – representing different interests and purposes from which these same things and events are viewed. In
rejecting the coordination of experience with the deliverences of
sense, Dewey was also denying the validity of the opposition

between "experience" and reason or thought as envisaged by traditional empiricism. This opposition seemed to him mistaken on at
least two grounds; first, there is the development of modern
science made possible by the interpenetration of observation and
rational construction so that any view according to which the two
elements are totally distinct and opposed to each other would then
have to account for their continuity and togetherness in bringing
about the knowledge we actually possess. In the second place,
Dewey, like Peirce, would not accept the view that experience is
itself devoid of inference. Experience, he claimed, is shot
through with clues that, in Peirce's term, "suggest" connections
whereby thought is able to pass logically beyond the items presented to other items and to other features of the same item. Dewey
even offered a biological argument in this connection, insisting
that if experience were no more than the series of atomic sensations of the empiricist view, mankind would never have been able
to infer and retain such knowledge as was needed for survival.

It is not necessary to do more than mention Dewey's rejection
of the subjective bias inherent in the traditional conception of
experience, because the point is so well known. The main consideration is that, for Dewey, experience, in virtue of its being
the meaningful and funded result of many interactions between the
individual and the environment, attains a *public* character evi-
denced, among other things, by the fact that it can be communicated, shared and compared. On Dewey's view, it was the psycho-
logistic tendency and the belief that experience is what is exclusively connected with the "mind" that led to the idea of its
being a private content which is not only immediately available to
the one who has it, but, as was noted earlier on, is something of
a screen standing between the individual mind and the external
world. By contrast, Dewey held that experience is a genuine medium
of disclosure, reaching down into nature and not doubling back
upon itself. One might say that Dewey laid such stress on the
objective and public nature of experience that there are grounds
for questioning whether he did justice to its personal and indivi-
dualized aspects. As I shall point out, he did not indeed omit
this dimension of experience, but no reader of Dewey can entirely
suppress the impulse to ask from time to time the question, "Whose
experience?"

Another significant feature of Dewey's reconstruction of
experience concerns his refusal to equate experience and knowledge. This feature is more complex than any of the preceding and
demands a lengthier discussion than is possible here, but at least
the main point can be indicated along with the problem Dewey was
trying to resolve. It is clear that the classical empiricists saw

in the experience they acknowledged not only knowledge but a sure foundation capable of supporting a body of knowledge. Kant, who sought to broaden the empiricist conception, also took experience and knowledge as co-extensive, as can be seen from the many passages in which *Erfahrung* is said to be *empirische Erkenntnis*, an expression customarily translated as "empirical cognition." Dewey rejected the identification for a number of reasons, among which was his claim that knowledge is always mediated, the outcome or result of a critical process of inquiry, and hence is not something to be read off, as it were, from the direct course of experience. He sought to deal with the problem by distinguishing between "having" and "knowing," a distinction which at once expresses his refusal to identify "Being" and "Being known" and his claim that many experiences are simply "had" or undergone without the need for them to become matters of theoretical knowledge. If such knowledge is called for, then these experiences must become the material and set the conditions for the controlled inquiry which alone can issue in knowledge. It is clear that Dewey was trying to allow for the sort of thing which has been designated by others as "pre-thematic" experience, or the ongoing encounters and interactions between individuals and the world, including the world of other individuals, which make up the course of human life. According to Dewey, were experience *ipso facto* knowledge, the dimension of having, which he tended to identify with the esthetic, would be done away with, and experience would become one with science. This view, of course, as has been pointed out by a number of critics, is thoroughly dependent on Dewey's identification of knowledge with science so that it is fair to raise the question whether there is any noetic element in what he called having, or, to put the question in another form, whether knowledge is exclusively an affair of the sciences. I cannot join that issue here; suffice it to say that Dewey was on the right track in seeking to liberate experience from its traditional indentification with knowing and the spectator attitude which went along with that view. In this regard, Dewey has affinities with the attempts made by others to recover lived experience with all its vividness and import.

Perhaps I should have considered earlier in this discussion a feature of Dewey's view of experience which many have regarded not only as novel but as expressive of something distinctive on the American scene. I have in mind the connection between experience and intelligent activity and practical skill; in short, the role of experience in the development of "knowing how." This feature was little emphasized in the classical view because of its emphasis on the perceiving of sense qualities without regard to their dynamic meaning as manifest in the way in which things possessing those qualities would react in relation to other things. Like Peirce, Dewey asked what things "would do" if they possessed a certain character or belonged to a certain kind and then used these expectations as a basis for preparing the proper response to be made when we are in the presence of these things. The central point can be made by considering what we mean when we say that someone is "experienced" in dealing, for example, with horses.[7] To begin with, we do not mean primarily that such a person has "perceived" many horses since that will be taken for granted and, in any case, that fact alone would not qualify one as "experienced." What we mean is essentially that a person has come to understand the behavior of horses and to interpret signs of what they are likely to do under particular circumstances as a basis for "knowing how" to respond, knowing what to do in the presence, for example, of a frightened or unfriendly horse. It should be obvious that gaining experience in this sense cannot be a matter merely of singular occasions when one perceives the qualities of horses, but requires a continuous and cumulative interaction with the animals in the course of which one becomes familiar with how they behave and how we are to respond in dealing with them. It is in this sense that experience for all three of our thinkers is essentially related to the formation of habits and skills which serve to direct our actions and shape the course of our lives.

Finally, we would do injustice to Dewey if we failed to take into account his conception of the esthetic and its expression in works of art as having their roots in those experiences where the present alone is significant, experiences which transcend instrumentalities and place us beyond direct concern for past and future. Dewey's attack on the "museum" conception of art according to which it is too "fine" to have grown out of or to be associated with ordinary experiences, is well known. The key to overcoming this conception is a new understanding of the experiential roots of art in all its forms and, in turn, a new perception of the meaning bestowed upon experience when its esthetic dimension is taken fully into account. I know of no better passage in Dewey's writings for conveying his central contention about the relation between experience and art than the following from *Art as Experience*:

> It is mere ignorance that leads. . . to the supposition that connection of art and esthetic perception with experience signifies a lowering of their significance and dignity. Experience in the degree in which it *is* experience is heightened vitality. Instead of signi fying being shut up

within one's own private feelings and sensations, it signifies active and alert commerce with the world; at its height
it signifies complete interpenetration of self and the world
of objects and events.

   . . . Because experience is the fulfillment of an organism in its struggles and achievements in a world of
things, it is art in germ. Even in its rudimentary forms, it
contains the promise of that delightful perception which is
esthetic experience.[8]

In addition to its reenforcement of the idea that experience
cannot be confined to an internal world, this statement is noteworthy for its emphasis on experience as a matrix within which
self and world interpenetrate, an actual overcoming of the sub-
ject--object dichotomy. I regard this way of viewing experience as
a significant counterbalance to Dewey's tendency, especially evident in his discussions of the role of experience in science, to
equate experience with method and thus bring it perilously close
to becoming identified with *experiment.* The results of experiment,
what Peirce called special experience, great as their effect may
be on human life and welfare, are not what make up the substance
of a worthwhile personal existence. Dewey was not unaware of this
fact, as can be seen in his perceptive account of what he called
"an experience," to which I shall now turn.

Dewey's conception of having an experience points to the
depth and value of certain fulfillments and accomplishments which
are not only lasting in their significance but come to define our
being as individual persons. Experience, says Dewey, is often
inchoate and dispersed, lacking in any definite unity or form. By
contrast, an experience, the sort of event or episode of which we
say, "That *was an* experience," is marked by a consummation or
fulfillment, a completion rather than a cessation. A piece of work
satisfactorily finished, a vexing problem solved, an outstanding
dramatic performance, living through a violent storm at sea are
all, in Dewey's language, undergoings that have a unity because
they are pervaded by a quality and have a closure which bestows
upon them an inidividuality and self-sufficiency. Qualities which
hold together many elements in a unity - joy, sorrow, hope, fear,
anger - are not to be regarded as isolable "emotions" set over
against thought and action, but rather as the significance of what
is for us an experience. Taking an experience of thinking as an
example, Dewey says that it is unified by the intent so that the
conclusion when finally reached is not something separate but is
the consummation of the process, an indication that thinking has
its own esthetic character. Unfortunately, as Dewey well knew,

experience is impoverished and becomes superficial when the pressures of events, our desire to be doing something coupled with
impatience, lead to an unwillingness to let experience complete
itself. The result is many experiences and the experience of many
things, but little that attains the quality of an experience. The
upshot of Dewey's account is that the esthetic dimension is no
intruder in experience, nor is it a mere layer of refinement
externally added to the ordinary and mundane; it is instead the
essential character of complete experience - an experience. Dewey
sums up the point in these words: "In short, art, in its form,
unites the very same relation of doing and undergoing, outgoing
and incoming energy, that makes an experience to be an experience."[9]

Given the extent of the ground to be covered, I could not
attempt to correlate the views expressed with developments in the
field of phenomenology. It should, nevertheless, be clear what the
main points of contact are between the phenomenological approach
and the efforts of Peirce, James and Dewey to arrive at a new
conception of the nature of experience. There is first the emphasis on actual experiencing for the purpose of gaining a more
accurate grasp of the intricacies and nuances; secondly, the
broadening and deepening of the scope of experience and the refusal to identify it with atomic sensory data; thirdly, there is
the concern to understand experience not only as material for
knowledge but as the medium through which the individual person
lives and develops; finally, there is the rejection of the spectator stance in favor of a self participating and acting throughout
the entire range of what is there to be encountered in whatever
way.

NOTES

This essay has been previously published in *The Monist*, Vol. 68 (1985), pp. 538–554.

1. Charles S. Peirce, *The Collected Papers of Charles Sanders Peirce*, Vols. I–VI, ed. Charles Hartshorne and Paul Weiss (Cambridge, MA: Harvard University Press, 1931–1935); vols. VII–VIII ed. Arthur Burks (Cambridge, MA: Harvard University Press, 1958), 2.138–139. All further references to this work, which follow the standard form of volume number followed by a period and paragraph number, will be incorporated into the text of my essay.

2. William James, *Essays in Radical Empiricism* (New York: Longmans, Green & Co., 1912), p. 10.

3. John D. Wild, *The Radical Empiricism of William James* (Garden City, N.Y.: Doubleday & Co., 1969), p. 361.

4. Ralph Barton Perry, *The Thought and Character of William James* (2 vols.; Boston: Little, Brown & Co., 1936), II, 385.

5. William James, *The Principles of Psychology* (2 vols.; New York, Dover Publications, 1950 [authorized reprint of the original edition of 1890]), I, 226.

6. James, *Essays in Radical Empiricism*, p. 218.

7. It is an interesting question whether and to what extent one can speak of someone as being "experienced" in languages other than English.

8. John Dewey, *Art as Experience* (rpt., New York: Capricorn Books, 1958), p. 19.

9. Ibid.

CHAPTER IV

SIGNS, INTERPRETATION, AND THE SOCIAL WORLD [1]

Beth J. Singer (Brooklyn College)

In this paper I shall utilize concepts drawn primarily from two sources. One, the work of Justus Buchler, is neither pragmatist nor phenomenological but nevertheless has roots in Buchler's confrontation with the work of Peirce, Mead, Dewey, and Royce (an idealist who called himself an "absolute pragmatist"). The other is the work of Alfred Schutz, a phenomenologist who drew on James, Dewey, and Mead as well as Husserl (and also Leibniz, Bergson, and Whitehead). While my own outlook is based primarily on Buchler, I am reinterpreting his concepts as well as those that I derive from Schutz, and I shall also draw directly upon and similarly reinterpret Peirce. [2]

The expression 'the social world' in my title is deliberately ambiguous. It refers not only to society as such, communities of human individuals, but also and primarily to what Schutz calls "the common sense world of every day life," the world we perceive ourselves to inhabit in common and which we take for granted in our ordinary dealings. "The world," Schutz says,

> existed before our birth, experienced and interpreted by others, our predecessors, as an organized world. Now it is given to our experience and interpretation. All interpretation of this world is based on a stock of previous experiences of it, our own or those handed down to us. . .[3]

My primary thesis is that this organized, socially shared world is an order of complexes that have come to function as signs. Thus much of this paper will be devoted to an analysis of the concept of sign. In developing this analysis I will propose new definitions for ther terms 'interpretation', 'meaning', and

Robert S. Corrington, Carl Hausman, & Thomas M. Seebohm, eds., *Pragmatism Considers Phenomenology*, Washington, D.C.: Center for Advanced Research in Phenomenology & University Press of America, 1987.

'communication'. I will also try to show that the diverse "worlds" of the arts, science, religion, and other social institutions are orders of signs in the same sense.

The Need for a Sufficiently General Definition of 'Sign'

> Semiotics can be informally defined as a science that studies all possible varieties of signs, the rules governing their generation and production, transmission and exchange, reception and interdepen dent aspects: communication and signification. [4]

I am not concerned here with the nature of semiotics but with the interdependent aspects of signs named by Sebeok: signification or meaning, and communication. The concept of sign has a long history stretching back at least as far as Parmenides and Hippocrates. The pivotal figure in the recent history of sign theory is C. S. Peirce. As Douglas Greenlee points out, Peirce's sign theory was a general theory of meaning, "equally a theory of meaning and of meaning bearers."

> Peirce's approach to sign theory was to seek the primary elements of a general theory of signs in the properties of various kinds of things which are said to have meaning (cf. 8.119). . . Thus. . . [we can] regard anything which has meaning as a sign. [5]

In what follows, anything which has meaning will be so regarded.

In his early book on Peirce, Buchler points out that for Peirce, since the very concept of a sign involves a rule esta- blished by a community, "the very concept of a sign, in- volves . . . a mind in communication with other minds." [6] In a similar vein, Buchler states in *Nature and Judgment*, that the general theory of signs "grounds the property and activity of meaning in communication, and communication itself in the sign- relation." [7] Thus Peirce's theory of signs is also a general theory of communication. Buchler himself gradually ceased to work within the framework of sign-theory, but in those contexts where he still utilizes this concept, the sign function is also an intrinsically communicative one. The communication involved, however, is first of all not between minds and, second, not necessarily or primarily social or interpersonal. A sign communicates to, and has meaning for, integral human beings, doers and makers, not merely thinkers; beings that can communicate by acting and contriving as well as by linguistic or quasilinguistic behavior. A complex that functions

as a sign for someone is taken up into a process of communication
of that individual with himself, a process of "reflexive communication" in which its meaning is established or revealed. Only
among individuals for whom something is a sign in this sense can
it also serve as a sign in social communication.

If anything that has meaning is a sign, an analysis of what
it means to be a sign must encompass all kinds of meaning, without
exception. I do not find Peirce's analysis general enough, although I shall build upon some of its elements. Like most semiotic
theories, that of Peirce takes the word 'sign' in the broad sense
of 'sign *of*'. Signs are said by most writers in the field to stand
for, represent, refer to, denote, substitute for, intend, or
implicitly infer something other than themselves. Eco, for
example, speaks of a sign as "a certain object, be it an artifact
or a natural event, which refers back to something that is not
itself." The rule, convention or attitude that governs any instance of the sign-function "allows one to correlate a given
presence with a supposed concept or object."[8] Schutz, reviewing a
number of important discussions of signs, including those of
Whitehead, Cassirer, and Susanne Langer, can appropriately classify them all as having to do with "the problem of significative
reference" (p. 290).

But not everything meaningful refers; not every sign is a
"sign of," and in the case of a sign that does refer or represent
or denote, this may not exhaust its significative function or
meaning. For example, the word 'and' in a sentence does not refer
to or stand for a connection between terms or phrases; it connects
them additively. Its meaning is its performance of this function.
In the sentence, 'and' does not refer to the connected terms
either. We could say it is meaningful only "with reference to" the
terms, but then, by 'with reference to' we would mean 'in relation
to', and the relation must be analyzed. In this relation, 'and'
functions as a logical operator, and to do so it requires terms.
This requiring might be thought of as a type of referring: the
word 'and' could be said to point or refer to the places on either
side of it which, as a sign, it defines as requiring to be filled
by objects of a particular sort. But 'or' "refers" in the same
way. We could say that, as a meaningful sign, 'and' is incomplete;
the complete sign is 'x and x'', where the x's are variables of
certain types, so that 'and' stands for 'x' *and* 'x'. But this
merely sidesteps the issue, for the meaning of the complete sign
must still be shown. This meaning is the way the variables are
connected. In a sentence, words are substituted for the variables,
and are thereby connected additively.

As another example, if someone shouts, "Stop!" the shout is a sign. This sign does not stand for or refer to stopping: it commands it. The shout imposes an imperative, a role very different from merely standing for it. Again, if a sign is something that has meaning, what is the meaning of a musical sign, say a particular note? A musical note or tone is not merely a distinguishable sound; it is a sound that has meaning -- musical meaning -- in a system of sound-interpretation. By anyone with an "ear" accustomed to this system, it will be perceived (interpreted) as a tone in a scale or scales.[9] As so interpreted, it calls for certain kinds of treatment. It sounds right in some settings, wrong in others. In accordance with the rules of the system it can be used, in chords or phrases, in some ways but not in others. This is its meaning; a meaning that is not referential and may not be conceptually understood by one who sings or plays or dances to or appreciates music but who hears as the system determines nevertheless.

The example of a musical note suggests a model for the analysis of the sign-function that may be more adequate than representational models. In order to describe it, I must introduce some basic concepts, drawn from Buchler's writings, which may not be familiar to all readers.

Complex, Order, Ordinality

I shall use the word 'complex' as a generic term of reference. A complex is an *order* of related traits or constituents. Anything we can identify is a complex, distinguishable because it has an organized constitution.[10] A color, a rock, a person, a concept, a relation, a situation, the atmosphere in a room, all are complexes, orders. The constituents of each complex are also complexes: the intensity of a color, the molecular composition of a rock, the symmetry or asymmetry of a relation, each has a constitution of traits. So, in turn, do the factors that compose it. Reciprocally, every complex is a trait of other complexes, a constituent of other orders: a rock is a constituent of a landscape, of a geological stratum, of a system of gravitational relations, and so on. That every complex is an order of orders and belongs to other orders is Buchler's *principle of ordinality.* It will be shown to apply to signs and to the orders they constitute.

To belong to an order (to be a trait or constituent of a complex) is not to be enclosed within it or totally encompassed by it: a complex may belong to an indefinite number of orders, each in a different respect. The color of a blue sphere, for instance, belongs not only to that sphere but to a system of light rays, and also to the linguistic order in which the name 'blue' is defined. It belongs to each of these orders in virtue of a different aspect of its constitution, a different *integrity* or pattern of traits.

Judgment

Any complex may come to function as a sign, and this function will be defined in terms of the concept of judgment.[11] While in a given instance it may not be clear which is the case, we commonly distinguish between what we do and what happens to us. When we can be said to "do" something, we are actively responding to some complex, selective discriminating it and dealing with it in a way that embodies an appraisive attitude or stance. In the sense of 'judgment' defined by Buchler and adopted here, we are judging the complex.

Judgment is not limited to mental or intellectual or propositional activity. Conduct and the manipulation of materials and instruments are as much ways of judging as are speaking and reasoning. Judgment may be spontaneous or habitual as well as methodic, and it may occur without conscious awareness, as when we absently follow a familiar routine. It may be momentous or trivial, overt or subliminal. Even the act of attending to a complex, looking at it, listening to it, feeling it, is judging it.

We use the name 'judgment' for both an instance of judging and its product or outcome.[12] Judgments can be classified in terms of three broad categories or modes: assertive (roughly, discourse); active (action or conduct); and exhibitive (organizing materials into a pattern, structure, or contrivance). Judgments are assignable to the three categories, not on the basis of their descriptions, but on functional or circumstantial grounds. The same bodily movement, for example a nod of the head, may serve as a mark of assent or agreement to a statement or proposition (assertive), as a gesture of greeting (active), or as a motif in dance (exhibitive), and a given judgment may serve in more than one way at the same time.

To judge is to deal with complexes of any sort. The "dealing" may take the form of doing something with the complex, doing something to it or about it, using it, making it the subject-matter of discourse, or treating it in any other way. Talking about a complex and lifting it up are equally ways of judging it. Arranging flowers is no less judging them than identifying their genus and species.

Judgment, dealing with complexes, does not occur in a mind but in the world; in some situation or order of circumstances, an order of complexes in which a judging being is involved. More than one judging individual may be involved with and deal with the same complexes, whether in the same or in different ways, and individuals may coordinate their judgments of the same complex. Some judgments, often products of such coordination, are communicated to others and adopted by them as ways of dealing with the complexes in question. Any judgment may become habitual for an individual or institutionalized in a social group. Such habits and institutions are ordinarily taken for granted, but they govern the way we judge and, in so doing, play an important role in shaping our experience. They serve as interpretations in the sense to be defined below. The institutionalized ways of judging in all three modes that are common to the members of a society comprise its culture. Most of the ways an individual judges are derived from the culture, communicated to him by others who have already assimilated them and with whom he interacts and communicates.

In judging, we take a position toward the complexes we deal with; we treat them selectively and differentially. In so doing, we put our judgments forth as at least applicable and, at best, as requiring no alteration. We thereby call for them to be validated.[13] All judgment calls for, though it does not always receive, validation, confirmation, justification by further judgment. Since this holds also for validating judgments, no judgment is ever perfectly secure. Validation is ubiquitous, if not continuous, in the human process. Like judgment in general, it can occur in any mode or combination of modes and can be a social as well as an individual enterprise. For judgments in each mode there are various types of validation, and among the modes the conditions of validity differ. Assertions may be verified, falsified, questioned; devices may be shown to work well or poorly; actions may be judged successful or unsuccessful, right or wrong.

I shall now apply these terms in an analysis of the concept of sign and other, related concepts.

Sign, Interpretation, and Meaning

Nothing has meaning in and of itself. It can mean something only if it is judged, and it may have different meanings when judged in different ways or in different situations or perspectives, different orders of judgment. Even the meaning of a judgment is a function of the way it is judged and is relative to the perspective in which it is judged. However, not every judgment establishes or reveals the meaning of what it judges. In a sense of 'interpretation' I shall define, to have meaning a complex must be interpreted, and not all judgment is interpretation. And if anything that has meaning is a sign, not every complex judged is a sign.

It is hard to conceive a situation in which judgment occurs but in which no signs, no meanings, at all are involved. What is meaningless in one respect is likely to have meaning in another. We may not understand words in a foreign tongue: as linguistic communication they may be meaningless to us. Still, if we recognize them as words, they are in that respect meaningful, their meaning being that they call for interpretation *as* words. It is important to recognize, however, that even if this is the case, they remain meaningless words. It may be objected that to recognize this fact is to give the words meaning. But this meaning is not the meaning of the words as words; it is their meaning in relation to our non-significative judgment of them. The sounds are interpreted as words; but as words they are something more than the bare sounds and call for further interpretation, which we do not possess. The complexes that are signs in the first order of judgment have acquired a new integrity in the second order of judgment and in this second order they are not functioning as signs.

Suppose you are unexpectedly struck on the back. For a moment, you may not judge at all, and the event will be meaningless. Now suppose you focus awareness on what has happened, attend to it. You are judging it: Your paying attention is not only awareness of the event but selectively discriminating it and adopting an interrogative stance toward it. Yet even when you attend to it, you may not recognize what has happened to you. You may not realize that something or someone has hit you. If you do not, you will be unable to respond further to what has occurred, unable to do or say anything about it. As long as this is the case, the complex you are judging is without meaning; it is still not functioning as a sign.

While he sometimes uses the word 'sign' in the sense of something that represents something else, in *Nature and Judgment* Buchler suggests that we construe this term more broadly as "a means of further judgment"[14] or "an instrument fostering judgment."[15] Building on this idea, let me suggest that a complex which functions as a sign is one that is judged in such a way as to direct continuing judgment. To recognize what has happened to you is to define a response or a range of possible responses to it. The judgment that a friend has clapped you on the back calls for one sort of response; the judgment that you have been attacked

calls for a response of a different sort. To know the meaning of a
word is to have a judgment or set of judgments of it that directs
the ways we may use it. In each case, the complex judged acts as a
sign, calling for further judgment of a determinate kind or kinds.
To use an expression of Peirce, the complex has an *interpretant* or
a range of interpretants.

In Peirce's well-known analysis of the concept of a sign,
three elements are central: the sign, its object, and its
interpretant, joined in an irreducible triadic relation. The sign
is said to represent its object (to someone) and to "determine"
its interpretant, which is "an equivalent sign, or perhaps a more
developed sign" and stands in the same relation to the object as
the sign itself.[16] Peirce also speaks at times of the sign as
being "determined (i.e., specialized, *bestimmt*)" by its object,[17]
and he sometimes describes the interpretant as being in the mind
or as being a determination of a mind.[18]

In other passages, Peirce speaks of the interpretant of a
sign as the "proper significate effect" or "proper significate
outcome" of the sign[19] – "proper" in the sense of being produced
by the sign *qua* sign rather than *qua* mechanical cause. Peirce
names three general classes of proper significate effect. An
emotional interpretant is a feeling produced by a sign. (His
example is feelings produced in us by a piece of music.) An
energetic interpretant is an effort, muscular or mental (the
former illustrated by the response to the command to ground arms).
A *logical interpretant*, the kind intellectual concepts have, is
not itself a concept or idea but a habit-change ("a modification
of a person's tendencies toward action").[20] ("An idea is a plan of
action.")

For the reasons stated above, I do not think every sign must
stand for an object. But a complex that has no interpretant is not
functioning as a sign. It has no meaning. Peirce suggests that the
interpretant of a sign need not be a judgment of the assertive
kind. Let me define an interpretant as a judgment – active,
exhibitive, or assertive – that is called for by a sign. Obedience
is an interpretant of a command; the use of a musical note in a
melodic or harmonic sequence is an interpretant of the note; use
of the word 'and' in a linguistic expression is an interpretant of
this word.

A complex does not determine its own interpretants. Nothing,
that is, is inherently a sign. Determination of interpretants is a
function that must be performed by judgment, and this
determination is always relative to some set of conditions, some
order of judgment. That a stick of wood is to be used for hitting

a spherical object (its meaning as a bat) is an interpretant it would not have in connection with building a fire.

So-called "natural signs" are no exception to the principle that signs do not determine their own interpretants. Clouds and rain may be causally related, but to be a sign of rain is to be judged as a portent of rain: the expectation of rain is an interpretant of the clouds in a given set of circumstances. Similarly, a sign that stands for or represents another complex, whether or not the two are causally connected, is one that is judged as calling for the inference of the second as represented.

All this is to say that, in addition to the interpretant, the sign-function involves another judgment that mediates between the interpretant and the sign. This judgment appraises the complex in such a way as to direct further judgment of it; it determines the interpretant or interpretants. A habit is one kind of judgment that does this. It will be convenient to call this mediating judgment and the entire process by the same name, *interpretation*. An interpretation is a judgment that determines an interpretant. A sign is a complex interpreted, a complex in so far as it has an interpretant. An interpretant is a judgment determined by interpretation to be called for by a complex in some order or orders.

The sign-relation, then, is triadic, as Peirce maintained, and irreducibly so, although its constituents are not those named by him. Instead, they are the sign, an interpretation, and an interpretant. All three are essential. Peirce states, "A sign is something by knowing which we know something more."[21] In the framework I am employing here, a sign is a complex, by judging which we are enabled to judge it further. The sign may be determined to have (be eligible for) a range or selection of interpretants rather than a single one, as do linguistic and musical signs. Also, an interpretant may determine still further interpretants and so function also as an interpretation. For instance, having initially failed to recognize something, I may judge it in some way (say, turn it around) that results recognition. The recognition is an interpretant which in turn determines the complex to be eligible for certain other judgments. Judged in this way, the complex calls for certain interpretants in particular respects and particular circumstances. But recognition is not the only kind of judgment that can determine an interpretant. In riding a bicycle, for instance, determination of the shifts in weight called for to maintain one's balance is kinesthetic, a form of active judgment that may not even enter into awareness. Not all interpretation is conceptual. The discovery that clay could be modelled and shaped was an exhibitive interpretation, not an assertive one, even though it can be translated and communicated by assertions. Every instance of clay modelling is an interpretant of clay so interpreted, and so is the resulting piece of pottery.

A process of interpretation may be consciously and deliberately thought out, it may be spontaneous, or it may be habitual. It may require time or occur instantaneously. Most interpretation is habitual, so that meanings and the fact of meaningfulness are taken for granted. But the process of interpretation is complex nevertheless and has distinguishable phases even when these are not temporally separated.

Like any judgments, interpretations call for validation and are made more or less secure, reinforced or undermined, by subsequent judgments. And as with all judgments, those that play a part in the validation of interpretations may be in any mode or combination of modes and call for validation themselves. To be found valid is not necessarily to be correct, and validation is never final or definitive. Signs, moreover, can be reinterpreted; they can acquire new meanings and cease to be used with older meanings. Meaning, as Buchler points out, is never fully fixed or determinate. Not only texts, but all signs, are perpetually subject to reinterpretation.

Schutz's Semiotic Theory

In a later section of this paper I shall utilize what I take to be an important concept developed by Alfred Schutz, the concept of a province of meaning. This concept is integral to the semiotics elaborated by Schutz in his monograph, "Symbol, Reality, and Society," aspects of which are also touched upon in the related papers included in Volume I of his *Collected Papers*. In employing Schutz's concept I shall have to reinterpret it in terms of my own analysis of the sign-function. Schutz bases his theory on Husserl's concept of 'appresentation' or 'appresentational reference', which he takes to be the general form of all significative and symbolic relations (p. 297). I believe that appresentation (the kind of signification typified by our perception of a square surface as the side of a box even though we do not perceive the rest of the box) is an important kind of meaning, but I do not find it adequate as a model for all of the diverse kinds of sign.

What Schutz is concerned with is, first, the way the common sense world of everyday life is experienced, shaped by interpretation, and second, the way the worlds of science, religion, imagination, dream, and so on, are cognized and related to the everyday world. Appresentational reference plays a part in each. Schutz's general thesis concerning the former is that we immediately perceive only some aspects of everyday objects, processes, and events, but their "hidden" aspects, which transcend immediate experience, are apprehended "analogically," in ways guided by constructs (typifying constructs or types) that belong for the most part to our social heritage. Objects of religious belief, of scientific theorizing, of dream, fantasy, fiction, transcend the world of experience itself. They are not immediately apprehended at all, but are appresented in the everyday world by the kind of appresenting objects Schutz calls 'symbols'.

Appresentational reference, on this view, is a way of coming to grips with "transcendent experiences" (p. 326). In every appresentational situation, "we experience intuitively something as indicating or depicting significantly something else" (p. 296). Whether the appresenting object or the object appresented be "a perception, a recollection, a fantasm, or a fiction," "apprehension of a present element of a previously constituted pair 'wakens' or 'calls forth' the appresented element" (pp. 296-7). Schutz classifies what I am calling signs as either 'marks', 'indications', 'signs', or 'symbols'. He uses the name 'symbol' for an appresenting object that appresentationally refers to one that transcends the world of daily life (p. 343), and reserves the word 'sign' for "designating objects, facts, or events in the outer world [of daily life and work], whose apprehension appresents to an interpreter cogitations of a fellow-man" (p. 319). In any instance of appresentation, he says, "an object, fact, or event is not experienced as a 'self', but as standing for another object which is not given in immediacy to the experiencing subject" (p. 297). I have tried to show that signification may take other forms, that there are other types of meaning. A stroke of paint in a nonobjective painting, for example, is meaningful only in so far as it is "given in immediacy" together with the other elements in the painting, in relation to which alone it is significant.

An important feature of the Husserl-Schutz concept is that appresentational reference is not inferential. "In the appresenting immediate experience," on this view, "a unity of intuition is constituted" (p. 297). The sign is not, as it would be for, say, Hobbes, the antecedent of a consequent or vice-versa. What Hobbes would take to be the consequent (or antecedent) of the sign is given, although appresentationally rather than "immediately," together with the sign. The side of a box is perceived as part of the box; the box is not inferred. However, Schutz overlooks the fact that the meaning of some signs is inferential, as when the smell of smoke is taken to be a sign of fire. Not all signs are of this type, and active and exhibitive interpretations cannot be or determine inferences, but an adequate analysis of signification cannot exclude signs whose meaning is their calling for an inference.

As an analysis of the sign-relation, the concept of a unity of intuition is problematic in another respect. While Schutz is concerned with the world in which we act and interact and work, he describes appresentation always in terms that apply only to perceiving or remembering or imagining or dreaming – apprehending – objects, facts, or events. That these ways of judging affect action, affect the way we use materials and implements, the ways in which we relate to one another, is unquestionable. But conduct and the manipulation of materials are not themselves ways of apprehending. Signs are interpreted by active and exhibitive judgment, not as members of perceived or conceived pairings, but as compelling further action of a certain sort or further shaping or contriving. We may perceive a brick as part of an appresented wall, but by the mason who is building the wall, the brick is also interpreted actively and exhibitively in his employment of the techniques of masonry. Its interpretants are the ways it is to be handled in the ongoing process of construction. This is the case even if, in addition, the mason perceives or conceives the bricks as appresentationally referring to the emerging structure. The active-exhibitive interpretation does not determine a conception of the brick but a physical manipulation of it; a judgment Peirce would call an "energetic interpretant."

Schutz suggests the role of active judgment in interpreting the everyday world, for instance when he says that the "texture of meaning. . . originates in and has been instituted by human actions" (p. 10), and that

> what is supposed to be known in common by everyone who shares our system of relevances is the way of life considered to be the natural, the good, the right one by the members of the "in-group"; as such, it is at the origin of the many recipes for handling things and men in order to come to terms with typified situations, of the folkways and mores, of "traditional behavior," in Max Weber's sense. . . (p. 13)

But what he seems to mean is that action and motivation give rise to assertive judgments which in turn shape our interpretations. When he speaks of "typified situations," he means situations interpreted as typical by means of constructs (pp. 6-7), ideal types (p. 61), that arise out of (prepredicative) experience as a function of interest (pp. 280-1) or, as is the case with the great

preponderance of our typifications, are socially derived, handed
down to us by others (e.g., p. 13).

Appresentational reference is the way we interpret what we
immediately apprehend. In opposition to the tradition of classical
empiricism, Schutz maintains (and I concur) that what we perceive
is not sense-data or their equivalents, but interpreted objects
located in a field of related objects (p. 298). Experience, in his
view of it, is organized, its organization largely inherited and
socially shared. (By 'experience', Schutz means conscious
perception of objects and events in the everyday world.) The
organizing factors in experience are "constructs; a set of
abstractions, generalizations, formalizations, idealizations
specific to the respective level of thought organization" (p. 5;
see also p. 316). Discussing the intersubjective character of
common-sense knowledge and of the common-sense world of everyday
experience, Schutz says concerning "the apprehension of objects
and their aspects":

> We must interpret the terms "objects" and "aspects of
> objects" in the broadest possible sense as signifying objects
> of knowledge taken for granted. If we do so, we shall
> discover the importance of the constructs of intersubjective
> thought objects. (p. 12)

Over and above the question whether objects as such are all
thought-objects or constructs (which considerations of space force
me to set aside), to take objects and events to be interpreted
solely by constructs, by abstractions, generalizations, formalizations, idealizations of the sort Schutz defines, is to make their
interpretation always assertive and to overlook the fact that
complexes may also be interpreted by judgment in other modes. We
interpret complexes in and by our conduct relating to them, and by
using them as materials or as tools or implements, whether or not
we also interpret them by means of constructs or conceptions. Our
experience is shaped by these interpretations as well as by the
typifications in terms of which objects are apperceived and appresented. (This implies that experience includes more than
perception, but I must postpone discussion of this issue to
another paper.)

Interpretive Scheme

Peirce states that a sign or "representamen" stands for its object
in some respect, or "in reference to a sort of idea, which," he
notes, "I have sometimes called the *ground* of the

representamen."[22] Whether or not a sign is one that stands for an object, its meaning, its calling for the interpretant that it does, is similarly relative and requires a ground. A sign means what it does in some respect. But rather than being grounded in an idea, its meaning in that respect is relative to an order of judgments in which the complex is given a location and a role. (This is not to deny that a given order of judgment may be an order of ideas.) In its role in this order, a certain interpretant or certain interpretants apply to it. A stick of wood calls for use as an axe-handle or as a rolling-pin only in an order of activities in which such a use has a place, an order to which it is relevant and in which it is available to serve as an interpretant. I will call such an order an *interpretive scheme.* An interpretive scheme is an order of judgments that determines an interrelated set (an order) of interpretants. That is, it is an order of interpretations. By the interpretants it determines, this order selects complexes, actual or potential, to which it is relevant and applicable. These complexes are signs, interpreted by the order.

Relevance, as James, Bergson, and Schutz all note, is a function of interest. Schutz takes this interest and the system of relevances governed by it to be determined by the "purpose at hand." "It is [the] purpose at hand which defines those elements among all the others in. . . a situation which are relevant for this purpose" (p. 9). I do not disagree, but the respects in which complexes *may be* relevant in a given situation, and also the purposes that are relevant, are themselves defined by a prior and wider order of interpretations, that is, by an interpretive scheme. Interpretive schemes may be evolved by individuals or developed and institutionalized by a group or a society. What we call 'common sense' consists in the interpretive schemes that have been established in our culture as ways of dealing with recurrent circumstances.

Within the framework of a given scheme, interpretation may determine a sequence of interpretants of a complex, each a reinterpretation of it. Or the scheme may provide a range of possible interpretations for the complex, as a musical tone has indefinitely many possible interpretations within a harmonic system. In addition, different aspects of the same complex may have interpretations (hence interpretants) in more than one scheme, as, for example, human behavior may be interpreted in literature, in the discipline of psychology, in political life. Interpretive schemes are orders of judgments, and the principle of ordinality applies to them. A scheme may be a constituent of a more inclusive scheme and may encompass schemes that are narrower

in scope; it may have constituent interpretations that also belong
to other schemes or that interpret aspects of complexes interpreted by others. Mathematics is a constituent of physics, chemistry, and biology. In the study of nutrition, interpretations belonging to both chemistry and biology are brought to bear in
interpreting the requirements of an organism.

Province of Meaning

An interpretive scheme delimits an order of complexes, actual
or possible, interpreted as eligible for judgment by the interpretants provided by the scheme. I have defined a sign as a complex
interpreted, a complex having an interpretant or a series or range
of interpretants. An interpretive scheme, therefore, delimits an
order of signs. An example of such an order is the set of natural
numbers. Another is the variety of fibrous materials that can be
employed in weaving. The world of everyday experience is a highly
ramified order of signs. Its organization reflects the overlapping
and intersecting interpretive schemes which govern the ways in
which we maintain ourselves and relate to one another. These
include practical, technological, and moral interpretations,
active and exhibitive as well as conceptual ones, determining the
ways of doing and making as well as ways of perceiving and
conceiving.

A sign is a complex that has meaning. Adapting a term used by
Schutz, I will call the order of signs delimited by an interpretive scheme a *province of meaning.* Schutz's own expression is
'finite province of meaning', and he also speaks of finite provinces of meaning as 'worlds' or 'realities'. (See pp. 229-30) A
finite province of meaning, for him, is an order of experiences or
of intentional objects. Its organization is provided by the constructs which govern appresentation. A province of meaning, as he
defines it, is finite in the sense that while all the objects
within each province are consistent and compatible with one another, characterized by a particular "cognitive style" and "accent
of reality" (p. 230), they are not compatible with objects in
other provinces. "There is no possibility of referring one of
these provinces to the other by introducing a formula of transformation" (p. 232). In other words, they are not commensurate.
Thus, according to Schutz, provinces of meaning cannot intersect
or overlap.

The common-sense world of daily life is said by Schutz to be
the "paramount reality" (pp. 226 ff; 341 ff). It is only in this
world that objects are immediately apprehended; only this world
that we "gear into. . . by bodily movements" (pp. 211-212). Thus

only this world is the world of work (p. 212). Objects in provinces of meaning that transcend the world of daily life and work, the objects of scientific contemplation as well as those of religion, dream, and fantasy, can only be appresented by symbols. And it is only in the everyday world that communication can occur, because communication requires a material vehicle, a vehicle in the "outer" world of physical objects (p. 322). While he speaks of the diverse worlds (James's 'subuniverses') as "multiple realities" (p. 229) and holds that we bestow upon each a specific "accent of reality" (pp. 230, 341), it turns out that they are not all equally real. "Seen from [any province of meaning] P, supposed to be real, [any other province] Q and all the experiences belonging to it would be merely fictitious, inconsistent and incompatible and vice versa" (p. 232). However, Schutz also says that all worlds but the everyday have only "quasireality" (p. 233), "quasibeing" (p. 325), and our experience of them is "quasiexperience" (p. 238).

As I view it, a province of meaning is an order of complexes; it is not, as such, an order of experiences or an order of intentional objects (even though these would be provinces of meaning), but an order of complexes of whatever sort functioning as signs. A province of meaning is finite in that it is delimited, but it is not inherently incommensurate with other provinces. Any set of interrelated interpretations defines a province of meaning, and provinces defined by interpretive schemes that are related to one another are thereby related as well. As with the interpretive schemes that define them, provinces of meaning may include or exclude others, may be constituents of others and constituted by others, may intersect with others. And just as a complex may be interpreted and have interpretants in more than one interpretive scheme, it may belong to more than one province of meaning.

As Schutz implies, "reality" is a judgment. We do indeed encounter complexes that we characterize by such expressions as "unreal" or "not really real": dream objects, characters in literary works, optical illusions. But philosophically, such distinctions are questionable. A complex that belongs to one province of meaning in a given respect (in virtue of a given integrity) may in other respects belong to different orders. A figure in a dream may exercise a genuine and powerful influence on our waking life. Hamlet on stage, a fictional character in the drama, is nevertheless a physical presence; he belongs to what Schutz characterizes as the outer world of physical things including our bodies (pp. 226-7). He belongs to both provinces of meaning concurrently, even though in different respects. The "accents of reality" of the two provinces differ, but in kind, not degree. The difference lies in the meaning the complex has for us in each order. The ordinality of signs entails their ontological parity (a parity Buchler extends to all complexes and all ways of being).[23] In his doctrine of 'multiple realities' Schutz suggests such a principle, but he backs away from it.

Complexes belonging to a province of meaning are not totally encompassed by it and are not "things-in-themselves." They are complexes for which interpretant judgments are provided by an interpretive scheme, and they are "in" the province delimited by that scheme only in so far as they are interpreted in the relevant ways, have meanings relevant to the scheme. Any complex may have interpretations in more than one order and belong to more than one province of meaning. A good example of this is salt, which has interpretants in cookery, in the feeding of cattle, and in the discipline of chemistry, *inter alia*. The behavior of an electron is another example. It is interpretable by formulae of theoretical physics and also by means of the visible traces it leaves in a cloud chamber. Each kind of interpretant, in turn, applies to the other.

A province of meaning is not an order of ideas, although there are such provinces. But a province of meaning as such is an order of complexes interpreted or preinterpreted, signs, calling for judgment in determinate ways. A universe of discourse is a province of meaning, but not every province of meaning is a universe of discourse. What we call 'a world' is a province of meaning delimited by an order of interrelated interpretive schemes. It is an order of signs, complexes that have meanings (interpretants) in that inclusive order of interpretation; the business world, the world of science, the world of sport, worlds of fiction and imagination, all qualify. In so far as it is an order of complexes that have meaning for us, even the natural world is a province of meaning, an order of signs in the same sense as the others.

Communication and the Social World

I have been using the word 'sign' as a name for anything that has meaning, and I have said that anything that communicates is a sign. Let me show how the two are related.

I have defined a sign as a complex interpreted – judged in such a way as to direct continuing judgment. This is to say that the interpretation of a complex is, at least potentially, initiating a sequence of judgments. According to Buchler, "anything. . . communicates to an individual if, in consequence of its impact, he directly begins to communicate with himself about it."[24] He speaks of such a situation as a "sign-situation."[25] In interpreting a complex, I suggest, we are communicating with ourselves in the sense that in making a judgment we are directing ourselves to make another judgment relating to the same complex. This "reflexive communication," to use Buchler's term, may be thought of as the primary form of communication, since in social communication we communicate with ourselves as well as with one another. Yet in another sense, social communication may be viewed as primary, because most of our interpretations are inherited, acquired through social communication, so that reflexive communication presupposes and is conditioned by communication that is social.

Communication, in the most general and basic sense, may be defined as the process of interpreting complexes and thereby directing or controlling continuing judgment. That is, it is the process in which complexes function as signs. In reflexive communication one is directing one's own judgment by means of interpretations; in social communication (i.e., symmetrical or reciprocal social communication), there is conjoint and reciprocal sign-interpretation in which individuals participate together in directing their own and one another's ongoing judgment, active, exhibitive, or assertive. All social interaction, on this view, is communication. It need not take linguistic form or employ language in any way.[26] Two children on a seesaw communicate with one another (and with themselves) wordlessly, actively interpreting the motion of the seesaw by their bodily movements, each of which calls for a response (interpretant) on the part of the other.

I have noted that all judgment and interpretation calls for validation. Social communication requires mutual and reciprocal validation. It necessarily involves signs that are public, available to more than one interpreter and for which the interpreters can establish common interpretants. Signs that are not public, however, may be made available in some respects if public signs are employed as their interpretants. It is in this way that someone communicates a new and original idea or an inner feeling. I cannot communicate my sense of pain directly to you, but I can communicate by means of an interpretant of the pain. But whether the signs they try to communicate are public or private, individuals communicating with one another must coordinate their interpretations of these signs and must validate them jointly. They do so by offering successive interpretants, using each in turn as a sign, until they are confident that they are interpreting the sign in question as nearly as possible in the same way. This is the process in which socially shared interpretive schemes are built up. It is a process of communication and, like all communication, may employ active and exhibitive judgments as well as assertive ones (as anyone knows who has ever danced with a partner or made love).

Communication occurs within a province of meaning, and links to other provinces may be established by interpretation. A province of meaning is not a province of thought; it is an order of complexes, signs. It is not in a mind or minds. It is a sphere of interpretation in which one can operate as a judging being. Schutz, following Husserl, speaks of a "communicative common environment" (p. 315) or "common comprehesive environment" (p. 352 [where 'comprehensive' refers to understanding rather than inclusiveness]). Schutz maintains that, since it requires an immediately perceivable, material vehicle, communication can only take place in the physical world, the "outer" world of everyday, common-sense experience. Only this world is a "communicative common environment." Communication pertaining to other provinces of meaning is only possible, he contends, by means of symbols employed in the everyday, physical world. But if a province of meaning is an order of signs in the sense I have defined, every province of meaning is necessarily an environment of reflexive communication and potentially an environment for social communication, potentially a common communicative environment, delimited by interpretations in any mode or combination of modes of judgment.

Those who share a communicative environment constitute a community of interpretation, not in Royce's sense, but in the sense that they share in a common interpretive scheme and a correlative set of meanings. Each of us belongs to many communities.

I have defined the province of meaning delimited by a comprehensive order of interpretive schemes as a 'world'. In this sense of the term, there are social worlds, common to communities of interpretation, and there are also personal worlds, shaped by individual interpreters. But even the latter are not intrinsically private. Every individual belongs to many communities of interpretation, so that any interpretive scheme an individual can devise is likely to contain interpretations that are socially shared. In addition, as I have tried to show, all signs, and hence all interpretations, are potentially communicable.

There is a sense in which we can speak of "an individual's world." This is the order comprising all the orders of signs that are provinces of meaning for that individual. It is an order that evolves and changes through time. Because the individual belongs to communities of interpretation, and because a province of meaning is by its very nature a communicative environment, the individual's world, too, is an inherently social world. It is also a multidimensional one, a product of interpretation and communication in all the modes of judgment.

N O T E S

1. This paper has been revised as a result of discussions, both on the floor of the conference and afterward. In addition to those who raised questions at the meeting, I am grateful to Dr. Marjorie Miller and Dr. Armen Marsoobian for their criticisms.

2. One way I depart from Buchler is in my use of the concepts of sign and interpretation in explicating the concept of meaning. While Buchler utilized the concept of sign and eventually gave it a new and broadened sense, in treating the concept of meaning he came to dispense with it. The word 'interpretation' is used by him in a narrow sense, and his preferred term, 'articulation', has different connotations from 'interpretation' as I define it here.

3. Alfred Schutz, *The Problem of Social Reality*, Vol. I of *Collected Papers*, ed. by Maurice Natanson (The Hague: Martinus Nijhoff, 1962), p. 7. All further references to Schutz's writings are to this volume and will be incorporated into the text of my essay.

4. Thomas A. Sebeok, "Preface" to *Sight, Sound, and Sense* (Bloomington and London: Indiana University Press, 1978), p. viii.

5. Douglas Greenlee, *Peirce's Concept of Sign* (The Hague and Paris: Mouton, 1973), pp. 7, 14.

6. Justus Buchler, *Charles Peirce's Empiricism* (London: Kegan Paul, Trench, Trubner and Co., Ltd., 1939), p. 155.

7. Justus Buchler, *Nature and Judgment* (New York: Columbia University Press, 1955), p. 154.

8. Umberto Eco, "Semiotics: A Discipline or an Inter-disciplinary Method?" *Sight, Sound, and Sense*, p. 74.

9. As Peirce and Buchler contend, perceiving, unlike bare sensing, involves judgment. The word 'interpretation', used informally here, will be given a specific meaning below.

10. Buchler maintains in *Metaphysics of Natural Complexes* (New York: Columbia University Press, 1966), p. 1, "Whatever is, in whatever way, is a natural complex." That principle as such is not at issue here.

11. Cf. Buchler, *Nature and Judgment* and the earlier *Toward a General Theory of Human Judgment* (New York: Columbia University Press, 1951; second, revised edition, New York: Dover Publications, 1979).

12. In that it emerges from human life and experience, an act of judgment is itself a product and is so called by Buchler.

13. Buchler, *Toward a General Theory of Human Judgment*, Ch. VI, "Validation."

14. Buchler, *Nature and Judgment*, p. 156.

15. *Ibid.*, p. 157.

16. Charles S. Peirce, *The Collected Papers of Charles Sanders Peirce*, Vols. I–VI ed. Charles Hartshorne and Paul Weiss (Cambridge: Harvard University Press, 1931–35); Vols. VII–VIII ed. Arthur Burks (Cambridge: Harvard University Press, 1958), 2.228. All references to this work shall follow the standard form of volume number followed by a period and paragraph number.

17. *Ibid.*, 8.177.

18. *Ibid.*

19. *Ibid.*, 5.474.

20. *Ibid.*, 5.475.

21. *Ibid.*, 8.332.

22. *Ibid.*, 2.228.

23. See Buchler, *Metaphysics of Natural Complexes*, pp. 31–51.

24. Buchler, *Toward a General Theory of Human Judgment*, p. 30.

25. *Ibid.*, p. 31.

26. In this connection I question Habermas's concept of communicative action. Habermas seems to hold that to be communicative, interaction must involve speech as well as action. He says:

. . . the concept of *communicative action* refers to the interaction of at least two subjects capable of speech and action who establish interpersonal relations (whether by verbal or by extraverbal means). The actors seek to reach an understanding about the action situation and their plans of action in order to coordinate their actions by way of agreement. The central concept of *interpretation* refers in the first instance to negotiating definitions of the situation which admit of consensus. As we shall see, language is given a prominent place in this model.

(Jürgen Habermas, *Reason and the Rationalization of Society*, in *The Theory of Communicative Action*, trans. by Thomas McCarthy [Boston: Beacon Press, 1984], I, 86.) Interpretation, for Habermas, is linguistic, a matter of description or characterization (*Ibid.*, p. 107). Interpretation subserves action; acts alone are not judgments and do not interpret other acts. Communication, as he speaks of it, is the employment of symbolic expressions. (See, e.g., *ibid.*, p. 115.) "Actions regulated by norms, expressive self-presentations, and also evaluative expressions, *supplement constative speech acts* in constituting a communicative practice" (*ibid.*, p. 17; italics added). While this may occur, in my view it is not the sole form of communicative interaction, and there can be action that is inherently interpretive and communicative.

CHAPTER V

HEIDEGGER AND HUMANISM

Richard J. Bernstein (Haverford College)

Heidegger is a thinker who has taught us to be sensitive to mood (*Stimmung*). By attending to and reflecting upon moods, we can come to a deeper understanding of our being-in-the-world and our comportment with Being (*Sein*) itself. I want to begin (one of several beginnings in order to find a pathway into the thicket of Heidegger's thinking about humanism) by seeking to elicit a mood that is becoming increasingly pervasive in our intellectual, cultural, and everyday lives. To highlight what I mean, it is helpful to contrast the present mood with one that typifies so much of nineteenth century continental thought.

Consider the spirit that breathes through such diverse thinkers as Hegel, Marx, and Nietzsche. The mood I want to identify is beautifully exemplified by the passage from the Preface to Hegel's *Phenomenology of Spirit* when he writes about his age as a birth-time and a period of transition. Spirit, which is always restless and moving forward, is about to burst forth into a new qualitative stage of development – a happening that he metaphorically characterizes as the birth of a child. "But just as the first breath drawn by a child after its long quiet nourishment breaks the gradualness of merely quantitative growth – there is a qualitative leap, and the child is born – so likewise the Spirit in its formation matures slowly and quietly into its new shape, dissolving bit by bit the structure of its previous world. . . ."[1] We find variations on this same metaphor throughout the writings of Marx, especially in his early writings. The mood is one of expectation, hope, of being on the verge of a radical qualitative transformation, a new beginning that emerges out of the womb of an old and dying order – a beginning that at once presupposes what has been, breaks with it, and fulfills and redeems it.

Even Nietzsche – who philosophizes with a hammer, who is the great unmasker, the supreme practitioner of the hermeneutics of suspicion, the penetrating critic of the disease of nihilism which he sees as spreading throughout European Culture – tells us that

Robert S. Corrington, Carl Hausman, & Thomas M. Seebohm, eds., *Pragmatism Considers Phenomenology*, Washington, D.C.: Center for Advanced Research in Phenomenology & University Press of America, 1987.

pregnancy is also a disease. There is a mood of exuberance, affirmation, and yea saying. These are thinkers of *Aufhebung* and *Überwindung* where there is at once negativity and destruction, but where there is also "determinate negation," affirmation, the expectation of a new and higher "form of life." Indeed it is this mood that underlies and nourishes the explicit conceptual forms of teleology that inform their writings.

Contrast this mood with what appears so prevalent and pervasive in our time. There is a sense of entropy, of almost inescapable decline where suspicion, unmasking, and destroying of illusions have been carried so far that there is even an inability and anxiety to "name" what we are living through. We speak of "post-modernity," "post-subjectivism," "post-structuralism," etc., but no one seems to be able to satisfactorily fill in the content of the "post." We hear from all sides about the end of metaphysics, the end of philosophy, and even the end of Western Civilization – but "end" here no longer has any resonances of a *telos*, a fulfillment, accomplishment or consummation –- except in the bitter ironic sense that what has "finally" been revealed is the nihilism that has always been implicit in Western Civilization. This mood is epitomized by Heidegger when he writes:

> The decline of the truth of beings occurs necessarily, and indeed as the completion of metaphysics.
>
> The decline occurs through the collapse of the world charac terized by metaphysics, and at the same time through the desolation   of the earth stemming from metaphysics.
>
> Collapse and desolation find their adequate occurence in the   fact that metaphysical man, the *animal rationale*, gets fixed as the   laboring animal.
>
> This rigidification confirms the most extreme blindness to the   oblivion of Being. But man wills *himself* as the volunteer of the will to will, for which all truth becomes that error which it needs in order to be able to guarantee for itself the illusion that the will to will can will nothing other than empty nothingness, in the face of which it asserts itself without being able to know its own completed nullity . . . .
>
> . . . .
>
> The decline has already taken place. The consequences of this   occurence are the events of world history in this century. They are merely the course of what has already ended. Its course is ordered historio-technologically in the sense of the last stage of metaphysics. This order is the

last arrangement of what has ended in the illusion of a
reality whose effects work in an irresistible way, because
they claim to be able to get along without an unconcealment
of the *essence of Being*. They do this so decisively that they
need suspect nothing of such an unconcealment. . . .
         The still hidden truth of Being is withheld from meta-
physical   humanity. The laboring animal is left to the giddy
whirl of its products so that it may tear itself to pieces
and annihilate itself in empty nothingness.[2]

It is difficult to imagine a more devastating condemnation of the
destiny of "metaphysical humanity," or a more bleak portrait of
the modern age – although we must not forget that Heidegger
frequently cites the evocative lines from Hölderin: "But where
danger is, grows the saving power also. . . ." (I will return to
Heidegger's interpretation of these lines later in this essay).
        The mood that I am seeking to elicit discloses itself in what
might be called the "rage against Humanism." "Humanism" seems to
have become the signifier that names everything that is ominous,
dark, and nihilistic in the modern age – and if Heidegger is
right, "metaphysical humanism" has its origins already in the
classical Greek *philosophy*, when "original thinking comes to an
end." We shall see, however, that discerning what is meant by
"Humanism" and discriminating the sense (senses) in which
Heidegger condemns humanism (which can even be read as opening
vistas for thinking about a "new" humanism) requires a complex
task of unraveling. But before pursuing the question of humanism,
let me try out another *Holzwege* into the labyrinth of Heidegger's
thinking.
        For all of Heidegger's erudition there is no evidence that he
ever seriously read or thought about the American pragmatic
thinkers. His occasional remarks about "pragmatism" and "America"
illustrate what he himself has perceptively characterized as
"chatter" (*Gerede*). He would probably shudder at even calling them
"thinkers" – if by thinking we mean the type of "original,"
"meditative," "poetic" thinking that he seeks to elucidate in his
later writings.[3] On the contrary, they exemplify the type of
calculative, technological thinking that is revealed in the last
stages of the decline of "metaphysical humanity." But for someone
who has studied and listened to these philosophers, the encounter
with Heidegger is at once perplexing and troubling. For one is
stuck by the deep affinities and resonances, especially with the
Heidegger of *Sein und Zeit*. We can witness this most vividly by

comparing the critiques of Cartesianism that Heidegger and the pragmatists took to be at the heart of so much of modern philosophy and culture. Almost every point that Peirce makes in his brilliant attack on Cartesianism in 1868[4] (and which is reiterated by later pragmatic thinkers) is echoed in *Sein und Zeit*: the radical critique of modern subjectivism; epistemological foundationalism; the dubious quest of certainty; the "spectator theory of knowledge;" the suspicion and de-structuring of the dualisms and dichotomies of modern thought; the decentering of the very idea of autonomous consciousness; the claim that we never fully escape from our prejudices and prejudgments – all of these themes are shared by Heidegger and the pragmatists. Even more important, the sense of our historicity, that we are beings "thrown" into the world, that we are always already *in medias res* that it is more revealing to understand our *Dasein* by attending to our pre-reflective practices and to what is ready-to-hand (*zuhanden*) are motifs common to Heidegger and the pragmatists. Together they share a heroic effort to break with the excesses of subjectivism, individualism, and the false sense of human beings as the sovereign and "lord of beings." But despite these similarities and affinities, one is also struck by the differences of tone, emphasis, and concern. Whatever one makes of Heidegger's famous *Kehre*, there is ample evidence in *Sein und Zeit* that the analysis of *Dasein* is preparatory for encountering the *Seinsfrage*. And in his subsequent writings, Heidegger warns us against a distorted anthropological, humanistic, or existential misreading of *Sein und Zeit*. The one theme – the single thought – to which Heidegger returns again and again is the question of Being itself, and the ontological difference of beings and Being. From Heidegger's perspective, the pragmatists are only further evidence of the oblivion and forgetfulness of Being – at best a minor footnote to the last great "metaphysical" thinker, Nietzsche. The pragmatists might object that despite Heidegger's efforts to think through and beyond metaphysics, to overcome metaphysics, he is still entrapped and inscribed in the tradition he seeks to overcome. One way of putting the issue forcefully is to ask where Heidegger and the pragmatists "stand" on the question of humanism, or as Heidegger prefers to phrase it, "the *humanitas* of *homo humanus*." For Heidegger, "the essence of man consists in his being more than merely human, if this is represented as 'being a rational creature'. . . . Man is not the lord of beings. Man is the shepherd of Being."[5] As the "shepherd of Being," man's "dignity" is to be found in being called by Being itself into the preservation of Being's truth. But the pragmatists would certainly be critical of this fateful dichotomy of man as "lord of beings" or "shepherd of Being." What is left unsaid, what seems to pass into the shadows of the background is what Aristotle called *praxis* - the distinctively human form of activity manifested in *ethos* and the life of the *polis*. The type of "action" that becomes dominant in Heidegger's later writings - indeed it is almost obsessive - is the *activity* of thinking itself; thinking which "concerns the relation of Being to man"; the "thinking that is to come [which] is no longer philosophy, because it thinks more originally than metaphysics - a name identical to philosophy"; thinking which is a deed "that surpasses all *praxis*," which "towers above action and production, not through the grandeur of its achievement and not as a consequence of its effect, but through the humbleness of its inconsequential accomplishment."[6]

The mention of *praxis*, which is intended to call to mind Aristotle's meaning and more generally the tradition of practical philosophy that he helped to initiate, brings me to my third beginning - a pathway that brings us even closer to the heart of Heidegger's attack on metaphysical humanism. In the early 1920s, before the publication of *Sein und Zeit*, when Heidegger was still teaching at Marburg, he gave a famous seminar on Aristotle's *Nicomachean Ethics*, focussing on the discussion of *phronesis* in Book Six. We know a great deal about that seminar, at least indirectly, because Gadamer frequently refers to it as a decisive event in his own intellectual development.[7] And we know what Gadamer appropriated from Heidegger's *phronesis* interpretation. For at a crucial stage in *Truth and Method*, Gadamer tells us that "if we relate Aristotle's description of the ethical phenomenon and especially of the virtue of moral knowledge [*phronesis*] to our own investigation, we find that Aristotle's analysis is in fact a kind of model of the problems of hermeneutics."[8] It is not just that hermeneutical understanding is a form of *phronesis*, but the theme of *phronesis* becomes increasingly prominent in Gadamer's own thinking - so much so that he tells us:

> I think, then, the chief task of philosophy is to justify this way of reason against the domination of technology based on science. That is the point of philosophic hermeneutic. It corrects the peculiar falsehood of modern consciousness: the idolatry of scientific method and the anonymous authority of the sciences and it vindicates again the noblest task of the citizen - decision making according to one's responsibility - instead of conceding the task to the expert. In this respect, hermeneutic philosophy is the heir of the older tradition of practical philosophy.[9]

But I do not think that we find anything comparable to this eloquent claim in the writings of the later Heidegger. On the contrary, Heidegger tells us that "philosophy is over" and in his *Der Spiegel* interview, which was published posthumously, he declares:

> Philosophy will not be able to effect any direct transformation on the present state of the world. This is true not only of philosophy but of any simply human conception and striving. Only a god can save us now. We can only through thinking and writing prepare to be prepared for the manifestation of god, or the absence of god as things go downhill all the way. [10]

It is *almost* as if Heidegger has completely "given up" on the *humanitas* of *homo humanus*, despairing of even the possibility that man can come into the clearing of Being - although we shall later explore the ways in which this is not quite accurate. But the contrast with Gadamer (and in this respect Gadamer is much closer to the pragmatists) is dramatic. Gadamer does not think that we have reached a stage where "science has expanded into a total technocracy, and thus brings on the 'cosmic night' of the 'forget-fulness of Being.'" [11] As he tells us, in this respect, his "divergence from Heidegger is fundamental." [12] Gadamer's defense and explication of *phronesis* and the role that it can still play in fostering human solidarity is one of the most subtle and powerful statements of the type of humanism that Heidegger *appears* to condemn. How are we to account for Heidegger's virtual silence about *praxis* and *phronesis* in his later writings? Why is it that this "intellectual virtue" which also reveals *aletheia* seems to drop from our view? What does this mean for Heidegger's own understanding and critique of humanism? These are the questions that I now want to explore.

II.

So let me turn directly to Heidegger's *Letter on Humanism* - the *locus classicus* for his discussion of humanism. This is clearly one of Heidegger's most important texts. Let us recall the circumstances under which it was written and published, for these are relevant for what it says and leaves unsaid. The letter was written in response to a series of questions posed by a French colleague, Jean Beaufret - the first of which is: "*Comment re-donner un sense au mot 'Humanisme'?*" ("How can we restore meaning to the word 'humanism'?") Sartre's manifesto *Existentialisme est un Humanisme* had recently appeared, and this text is in the background of both Beaufret's questions and Heidegger's response. The *Letter* was an occasion for Heidegger to disassociate himself as strongly as possible from the existentialism propounded by Sartre – and more generally, from what Heidegger took to be the distorted reading of *Sein und Zeit*. But the *Letter*, which was published in 1947, was much more. It was an opportunity for Heidegger to reflect on his own thinking and writing since the publication of *Sein und Zeit* – especially his thinking about Nietzsche and Hölderin. In retrospect, one can also see that most of the themes of Heidegger's subsequent writings are mentioned in the *Letter*. We should also remember that the *Letter* was written at a time when Heidegger was forbidden to teach and when he was being severly attacked for his "role" in Nazi Germany. I mention this because in its style and content, the *Letter* can be read – in the classical sense – as an *apologia*. Finally, I do not think it is without significance that the original German publication of the *Letter* in 1947 appeared as an "appendix" or "supplement" to the second edition of *Platons Lehre von der Wahrheit*. But Heidegger does not begin the *Letter* by explicitly taking up Beaufret's questions. Let me cite the opening:

> We are still far from pondering the essence of action decisively enough. [One views] action as causing an effect. The actuality of the effect is valued according to its utility. But the essence of action is accomplishment. To accomplish means to unfold something into the fullness of its essence, to lead it forth into this fullness – *producere*. Therefore only what already is can really be accomplished. But what "is" above all is Being. Thinking accomplishes the relation of Being to the essence of man. It does not make or cause the relation. Thinking brings this relation to Being solely as something handed over to it from Being. Such offering consists in the fact that in thinking Being comes to language. Language is the house of Being. In its home man dwells. Those who think and those who create with words are the guardians of this home. Their guardianship accomplishes the manifestation of Being insofar as they bring the manifestation to language and maintain it in language through their speech. Thinking does not become action only because some effect issues from it or because it is applied. Thinking acts insofar as it thinks. Such action is presumably the simplest and at the same time the highest, because it concerns the relation of Being to man. [13]

The style here is typical of the writings of the later Heidegger with its deceptively simple staccato sentences – a style intended to provoke and call forth thinking, but which also can have and has had a mesmerizing effect on many of Heidegger's disciples. Before we even grasp what is being said here, the progression of key words signifies the pathway of Heidegger's own thinking – from "action," "accomplishment," "Being," "thinking," "Language," "dwells," "guardianship," to the completion of the hermeneutical circle with the claim that thinking is presumably the simplest and highest form of action. This is virtually a catalogue of the major themes of the later Heidegger, and – as I will try to show – without yet mentioning "humanism," this opening passage contains Heidegger's response to the question of humanism.

But let us go over carefully the flow of Heidegger's thinking here and arrest it. The second sentence in German reads: "*Man kennt das Handeln nur als das Bewirken einer Wirkung.*" Who is Heidegger speaking about when he writes: "*Man kennt. . .?*" One might speculate that what he means here is the same as what he means when he speaks of "*Das Man*" in *Sein und Zeit.* But why is this so important? Because Heidegger here already passes over in silence a crucial distinction concerning action. Heidegger is certainly correct in identifying a pervasive and deeply entrenched way of thinking about action in the modern age. We might even label this the "technical" understanding of action – where action is exclusively thought of as making something happen, as effecting a means to achieve a predetermined end. But this is certainly not the way in which Aristotle, and those who identify themselves with the tradition of practical philosophy that traces itself back to Aristotle's ethical and political writings, think of *praxis.* Heidegger is certainly aware of the distinctions between *poiesis* and *praxis*, *techne* and *phronesis*, but in this context when he speaks of action (*Handeln*) he passes over these distinctions in silence. The point is not merely of philological or historical interest, for it stands at the very center of contemporary concerns with the character and different modes of action[14] It is, for example, central for two of Heidegger's most prominent students, Gadamer and Arendt, as well as being central for Habermas and the pragmatists. For all of them – in very different ways – have sought to expose what is at stake in collapsing all of human activity into the technical sense of action – a sense of action that departs radically from what Aristotle meant by both *poiesis* and *praxis*. They would all endorse the claim of Habermas when he seeks to distinguish the technical and practical senses of action and power:

The real difficulty in the relation of theory and praxis does not arise from this new function of science as a technological force, but rather from the fact that we are no longer able to distinguish between practical and technical power. Yet even a civilization that has been rendered scientific is not granted dispensation from practical questions, therefore a peculiar danger arises when the process of scientification transgresses the limit of technical questions, without, however, departing from the level of reflection of a ra tionality confined to the technical horizon. For then no attempt is made to attain a rational consensus on the part of citizens con cerning by practical control of their destiny. Its place is taken by the attempt to attain technical control over history by perfecting the administration of society, an attempt that is just as impractical as it is unhistorical.[15]

But this is not the way in which Heidegger understands our contemporary horizon. Indeed he sees the seeds of the technical sense of action and calculative thinking already implicit in Plato and Aristotle. (This is just the thesis that he develops in *Platons Lehre von der Wahrheit*).[16] In what might be called Heidegger's "strong" reading of the history of philosophy which reveals the history of Being, there has been a relentless, ineluctable drive toward making manifest the concealed technical thrust implicit in the history of metaphysics. What emerges in Heidegger's writings after *Sein und Zeit* is a reiterated series of hidden indentities: philosophy = metaphysics = humanism = nihilism = enframing [*Gestell* – the "essence of technology"] culminating in the last stage of metaphysics where there is "the consumption of all materials, including the raw material 'man.'"[17]

If we are to be "saved" from this destiny, if man is to find again a dwelling – an *ethos* – so that he can escape from his homelessness, a homelessness which has become so radical in the modern age, it is only by answering the call of thinking – meditative, poetic, original thinking; thinking which does not come to an end with the end of philosophy, but is "in transition to another being."[18] "Where enframing reigns," as it does in the modern age, "there is danger in the highest sense." "But where danger is, grows the saving power also."[19] It is not technology itself that is the supreme danger, but the essence of technology – *Gestell.* In this respect there is a point of analogy with the passage we cited from Habermas when he suggests that the danger does not come from the new function of science as a technological force, but rather from our being "enframed" in a technical horizon. But where Habermas (and this move is also characteristic of Gadamer, Arendt, and the pragmatists) emphasizes the difference between a technical and practical horizon, Heidegger appeals to a "poetic revealing." Being is always near and distant. He concludes *The Question Concerning Technology* by *asking* whether a poetic revealing "may expressly foster the growth of the saving power, may awaken and found our vision of that which grants and our trust in it," and by declaring, "The closer we come to the danger, the more brightly do the ways into the saving power begin to shine and the more questioning we become. For questioning is the piety of thought."[20]

Heidegger at once portrays our extreme "spiritual decline" -- "the darkening of the world, the flight of the gods, the destruction of the earth, the transformation of men into a mass, the hatred and suspicion of everything free and creative," where the "childish categories of pessimism and optimism have long since become absurd,"[21] - and yet affirms the possibility of the growth of the saving power through the highest form of action: thinking which concerns the relation of Being to man.

This is why I have said that Heidegger's response to the question of humanism is already implicit in the opening sentences of the *Letter*. If we think of humanism as identical with metaphysics and *Gestell*, which is itself the manifestation of the oblivion and forgetfulness of Being, then Heidegger is opposing such humanism in the strongest possible manner. If humanism in the modern age "is nothing but a moral-aesthetic anthropology, that philosophical interpretation of man which explains and evaluates whatever is, in its entirety, from the standpoint of man and in relation to man"[22] then all of Heidegger's pathways are intended to expose, reject and exorcise this modern "world picture." This is why the distinctions between *poiesis* and *praxis*, *techne* and *phronesis* are so insignificant in the writings of the later Heidegger. "No mere action will change the world," for all *human* action collapses into the "will to will." Our only hope - and it seems to be a feeble hope - is by answering the silent call of Being.

But I want to argue that such a response to the question of humanism is not only totally inadequate, but is itself extremely dangerous - dangerous because it seduces us into thinking that all human activity (other than the activity of thinking) reduces itself - flattens out - into *Gestell*, manipulation, control, will to will, nihilism; dangerous because it virtually closes off the space for attending to the type of thinking and acting that can foster human solidarity and community. Rorty's casual remark may seem tendentious and offensive: "Heidegger decides that since the

Nazis didn't work out, only a god can save us now,"[23] but it contains a kernel of "truth." For the focal point of so much of Heidegger's writings after the publication of the *Letter on Humanism* leads us to an Either/Or: *either* we are condemned to metaphysical humanism, whose last stage is where "the laboring animal is left to the giddy whirl of its products so that it may tear itself to pieces and annihilate itself in empty nothingness," *or* we can be "saved," return to an *ethos* – a dwelling – through a poetic revealing and meditative thinking.

Let me try to show this by attending to Heidegger's explicit remarks about humanism. When Heidegger takes up the question, "How can we restore meaning to the word 'humanism'?", he begins by wondering whether we should even retain the word "humanism." "Isms" are notoriously misleading and tend to obscure more than they illuminate, "but the market of public opinion continually demands new ones."[24] He briefly reviews the variety of forms of Western humanism, mentioning Roman, Christian, and Marxist humanism. But Heidegger is not concerned with a historical survey of the varieties of humanism; he seeks to "bring forth" the essence of humanism. What then is this essence?

> Every humanism is either grounded in metaphysics or is itself made to be the ground of one. Every determination of the essence of man that already presuppposes an interpreta- tion of being without asking about the truth of Being whether knowingly or not, is metaphysical. The result is that what is peculiar to all metaphysics, specifically with respect to the way the essence of man is determined, is that it is "humanistic."[25]

So humanism and metaphysics are inextricably linked together. What then is the essential character and limitation of "metaphysical humanism"? "In defining the humanity of man, humanism not only does not ask about the relation of Being to the essence of man; because of its metaphysical origin humanism even impedes the question by neither recognizing nor understanding it."[26] And what then is the concealed essence of metaphysics? It is itself techno- logy – or more accurately, the essence of technology, *Gestell*. "The name 'technology' is understood here in such an essential way that its meaning coincides with the term 'completed meta- physics.'"[27] And lest we think that Heidegger is dealing with "mere words," let us remember that already in *An Introduction to Metaphysics*, Heidegger asks: "Is 'being' a mere word and its meaning vapor or is it the spiritual destiny of the Western world?" his response is unambiguous:

> This Europe, in its ruinious blindness forever on the point of cutting its own throat, lies today in a great pincers, squeezed between Russia on the one side and America on the other. From a metaphysical point of view, Russia and America are the same; the same dreary technological frenzy, the same unrestricted organization of the average man.[28]

I know that there are many sympathetic interpreters of Heidegger who take such statements as unfortunate lapses, but Heidegger's claims about the consequences of the oblivion and forgetfulness of Being are by no means untypical. Over and over again he seeks to reveal the ineluctable progression from philosophy to metaphysics to the devastating power of the essence of technology – all of which reveal the essence of metaphysical humanism.

Thus far I have been emphasizing and seeking to clarify Heidegger's anti-humanism. But there will be those who say that to leave the matter here is to leave one with a distorted interpretation of Heidegger. It is to miss the point of his critique of metaphysics and humanism. Heidegger is not totally rejecting humanism, just as he does not totally reject metaphysics. His project is one of overcoming (*Uberwinden*) where he seeks to think *through* the very grounds and origins of metaphysical humanism. Even in the *Letter*, he tells us "the essence of man consists in his being more than merely human" and that metaphysical humanism fails to do justice to man's dignity. To understand Heidegger we must realize that he is leading us to a more primordial way of understanding the *homo humanus* It is true that what Heidegger opens up for us "contradicts all previous humanism" and seeks to make a radical break with metaphysical subjectivism, but he does this in order to shock us into thinking about the meaning of the *humanitas* of *homo humanus* in a new (or very old) way.[29] He seeks to awaken a reflection "that thinks not only about man but also about the 'nature' of man, not only about his nature but even more primordially about the dimension in which the essence of man, determined by Being itself, is at home."[30] Furthermore, it may be argued that we need to realize that Heidegger is dealing with questions in a more "primordial," "radical," "fundamental" manner. What he sees so clearly is that modern attempts to "solve" problems turn out to be variations on the same theme – the theme of *Gestell*. They are part of the problem of modernity and its metaphysical humanism. Only if there is some fundamental conversion in our thinking, a thinking that transcends *praxis* and *poiesis*, a thinking that "is neither theoretical nor practical, nor. . . the conjunction of those two forms of behavior"[31] can we be "saved." Read in this way, after we sort out precisely what he is seeking to destroy and overcome, we can interpret Heidegger as opening vistas for a new way of thinking about humanism, as pointing to what might be called a "meta-humanism."

Let me first emphasize that I do think that this is certainly Heidegger's primary intent – and there is plenty of textual evidence to support such as reading. But my questioning and skepticism concerns the content (*Inhalt*) of this new/old meta-humanism. Following the hermeneutical principle of seeking to give the strongest possible interpretation to what one seeks to understand, I want to proceed with the help of two guides who do read Heidegger this way: Fred Dallmayr and John Caputo. Neither is uncritical of Heidegger, but both, in different ways, sensitively and perceptively try to show how Heidegger "delineated a new version of humanism"; how his thinking leads to a "recovery of man."

III.

There are many virtues in Dallmayr's discussion of Heidegger.[32] As a political theorist he is particularly sensitive to the relevance of Heidegger's writing for rethinking the social and political character of human beings. He carefully reconstructs Heidegger's radical critique of subjectivity. He reviews – and clearly shows – what is misleading about the appropriation and commentary on Heidegger that construes *Dasein* "egologically" as an existential adaptation of Husserl's phenomenology, and in particular Husserl's theory of intersubjectivity. He reminds us of the the central role of care (*Sorge*), solicitude (*Fürsorge*), co-being (*Mitsein*) and Dasein's being-with (*Mitdasein*) in *Sein und Zeit*.[33]

He tells us that the crucial experiential trait of *Dasein* is "neither rationality nor will to power but *care* – a term denoting both the anxiety deriving from the lack of a fixed behavioral structure and the capacity for genuine attentiveness reaching behind subjectively-instrumental pursuits."[34] *Dasein*, as care, is "intrinsically permeated by *world* and others." "Everyday existence, although regularly inauthentic, is not only a defect to be remedied, but a mode of being-in-the-world. As such it is implicitly open to Being and thus contains at least the anticipation of authentic co-being."

Dallmayr's reading of Heidegger, insofar as it pertains to the question of humanism, is eloquently summed up when he writes:

Emancipatory solicitude - also called anticipative-emancipatory solicitude -- is introduced in the section delineating different types of care, especially as a counterpart to managerial solicitude. In contradistinction to the latter's manipulative thrust, Heidegger writes, "there is the possibility of a kind of solicitude which does not so much displace the Other as anticipate him in his essential potentiality for Being - not in order to take 'care' away from him but in order to restore it to him in a genuine fashion. Involving the dimension of authentic care, that is, the very existence of the Other and not merely the affairs with which he is concerned, this type of solicitude helps the Other to become transparent to himself in his care and to become *free for* it."

And Dallmayr goes on to claim:

As is apparent, Heidegger's observations carry important normative implications; in fact, his conception of authentic existence and co-being can in my view be seen as a reformulation of the traditional notion of the good life and in particular of the Kantian postulate of the kingdom of ends. Compared to the latter principle, Heidegger's conception has the advantage not only of increased realism or concreteness but also of greater moral adequacy. Despite its anti-utilitarian intent, the postulate to treat others as ends rather than means contains instru mentalist traces, in the sense that the ego tends to function as a means for others who, in turn, appear as values "for me" or as "my" ends. Authentic co-being, on the contrary, is distinguished by respect for others in their *Dasein* and their "potentially for Being," rather than in their role as moral goals.[35]

Dallmayr epitomizes this reading of Heidegger - this "new version of humanism" - when he says: ". . . authentic *Dasein* does not rule out co-being, but only efforts of interhuman management. Forsaking manipulation and mastery, genuine solicitude manifests itself in *letting be*, in the willingness to let others live their lives and anticipate their deaths -- an attitude which is far removed from indifference."[36]

Although Dallmayr bases his interpretation of Heidegger on a careful analysis of *Sein und Zeit*, it becomes clear that he does not think that Heidegger abandons or retracts this understanding of *Dasein*. Rather Dallmayr's understanding of Heidegger's development is one where these themes are deepened and illuminated.[37] But despite the apparent persuasiveness of Dallmayr's attractive interpretation, I do not find it fully convincing.

First, as Dallmayr himself indicates, the "normative implications" that he draws from Heidegger's analysis of *Dasein* are his – not Heidegger's. On the contrary, Heidegger warns us against a "moral-philosophical" or "moral-existentiell" interpretation of such terms as "authenticity" and "inauthenticity." It is almost as if Heidegger fears that any such normative interpretation must be "anthropological" in its perjorative sense, and contaminates the purity of "an 'ecstatic' relation of the essence of man to the truth of Being."[38]

Secondly, even such rich and evocative terms as "care" and "solicitude" undergo a subtle but decisive turn in Heidegger's writings. For it is not the authentic care and solicitude of other human beings that is his major concern, but the care of Being and Language itself.

Thirdly, *Mitsein* and *Mitdasein* also seem to recede into the background. Heidegger is less and less interested in delineating the types of sociality and community – or even in suggesting how "authentic community" might be achieved. Ethics (and politics too) arise as disciplines only when "thinking waned." In the typical Heideggerian move which is always seeking to take us back to what is presumably "primordial," Heidegger tells us that to understand *ethos*, we need to go beyond (and behind) Aristotle, to the tragedies of Sophocles, and ultimately to Heraclitus' three words *ēthos anthrōpos daimōn*, for the essence of *ethos* to come into a clearing. Despite Heidegger's brilliant and imaginative interpretation of this fragment[39] it is difficult to see that it brings us very far in understanding what *ethos* means for our being-in-the-world. Indeed, as Heidegger interprets the fragment "Man dwells, insofar as he is man, in the nearness of god," it brings us back to thinking, not *praxis*.

Fourthly, despite Dallmayr's claims about Heidegger's "increased realism or concreteness" and his "greater moral adequacy," this is precisely what Heidegger's pronouncements seem to lack. I fail to see how for all its metaphoric power, Heidegger's "poetic" remarks about dwelling, *ethos*, and letting be provide any determinate orientation or guidance for how we are to lives in "authentic community" – or what such an "authentic community" even means. Typically, when Heidegger speaks of public life or the public realm, he speaks of it in a disparaging tone; for example, when in the *Letter* he mentions "the peculiar dictatorship of the public realm"[40] in the modern age. Once again, what seems to be lacking is any attention to a discrimination of the mode or types of public or communal life. One may even question whether terms like "care," "solicitude," and "authenticity" are the most illuminating for analyzing communal ethical and political life. For they do not "bring forth" the dialogic and communicative dimensions of ethical and political life.

Finally, I think one must be wary of Heideggerian claims about what is truly primordial and concrete when we realize that the reading that Dallmayr gives of *Sein und Zeit* appears to be compatible with the aggressive – almost nationalistic – call for spiritual regeneration characteristic of *An Introduction to Metaphysics* – where terms like "courage," "decision" and "destiny" are so prominent, and the much more resigned (but still active) language of *Gelassenheit* and the *Der Spiegel* interview.[41]

Caputo too has no hesitancy in speaking of Heidegger's *Letter* as presenting us with a "species of humanism," albeit a "humanism of a higher sort." And the title of his essay from which these phrases are cited is intended as a direct challenge to those who speak so facily of the "end of man": "Hermeneutics as the Recovery of Man."[42] In this essay, and in Caputo's defense of Heidegger against what he takes to be the distortive, reductionist misreading of Heidegger by Derrida and Rorty, he argues passionately for reading Heidegger as providing new insight about the *humanitas* of *homo humanus*. Caputo's thesis is that there are "two philosophies of recovery or retrieval which feed into the hermeneutic strategy of *Being and Time* – the Kierkegaardian notion of existential 'repetition,' and the phenomenological return to beginnings in Husserl."[43] According to Caputo, it is "Kierkegaardian repetition that controls and decisively modifies the phenomenological element in *Being and Time*, and hence the hermeneutics which is at work in this book has broken with metaphysics."[44] Contrary to Derrida's (and Rorty's) reading of Heidegger, this type of recovery of origins has nothing to do with a "nostalgia for presence." I cannot go into the details of Caputo's perceptive analysis of these two philosophies of recovery, and the ways in which he argues that Heidegger shows that they belong together. But Caputo's point becomes clear when he writes:

> But authentic *Dasein* which has the courage for anxiety, recovers the absence which underlies its presence; it breaks the grip of the actual upon its Being and, in so doing, recovers its freedom. The freedom of *Dasein* is that it is no longer held fast by the actual; it is a transcendence beyond things which stretches out into the Nothing.[45]

Similar theses are at work in Caputo's spirited critique of what he takes to be Rorty's distorted interpretation of Heidegger. Rorty "has taken up only the 'deconstructive' side of Heidegger, the critique of metaphysics. . . but. . . he remains quite hostile to Heidegger's project of retrieval (*Wiederholung, Andenken*)."[47] For the purposes of this essay, I want to bracket the issue of whether Caputo is right in arguing that the "deconstructive" interpretation of Heidegger by Derrida and Rorty is one that "can only come to grief." Rather I want to concentrate on his portrait of Heidegger and hermeneutics which he wants to distinguish and defend against the deconstructive misappropriation of Heidegger. Caputo epitomizes this when he writes:

> In my view, the point that the continental philosophers have been making, first under the name of "existentialism," then of "phenomenology," and nowadays of "hermeneutics" – all of which, to use Rorty's term, is "edifying" philosophy – is to make of philosophy a concerted effort to put man back in touch with himself. Their attack upon metaphysics has been aimed at reawakening a sense of the human drama, at recovering the lived quality of our experience and the historicity of the dialogue into which we have all been entered. On this account, everything turns on what Heidegger, following Kierkegaard, called "repetition" or "retrieval" (*Wiederholung*) of a primordial but latent pre-understanding in which we all always and already stand.[48]

I do think that Caputo is right in seeking to recover and retrieve a deep underlying theme in Heidegger's thinking. But we need to turn our attention to what such phrases as "a sense of the human drama" and "recovering the lived quality of our experience" really mean - if these are to be more than mere rhetorical gestures. If a concerted effort is to be made to "put man back in touch with himself," don't we have to recognize that *one* vital dimension of what we truly are is beings of *praxis*? Willy-nilly, we are beings compelled to act in this world. We are, as even Heidegger tells us, inextricably bound up not only with other beings, but with other human beings. If we are "thrown" into this world then ethical and political action is inescapable. What Caputo has not shown us, has left unsaid, is *how* repetition and retrieval illuminate our *praxis* here and now. Ethics and politics need not be inter- preted as asking for blueprints, specific rules of action, methodical procedures to follow in order to "solve" our ethical and political problems. But a "higher" or more "primordial" sense of humanism that does not help to provide any orientation toward our *praxis* comes very close to being empty. Not only is it empty, but it can also be dangerous because it can mystify the *contents* of such repetition.

We should not forget that one of the most infamous contexts in which Heidegger calls for repetition is in 1935 when, he calls for spiritual regeneration of the German nation.

> All this implies that this nation, as a historical nation, must   move itself and thereby the history of the West beyond the center of   their future "happening" and into the primordial realm of the powers of being. If the great decision regarding Europe is not to bring annihilation, that decision must be made in terms of new spiritual   energies unfolding historically from out of the center.
>
> To ask "How does it stand with being?" means nothing less than   to recapture, to repeat [*wieder-holen*], the beginning of our histori   cal-spiritual existence, in order to transform it into a new beginning. This is possible. It is indeed the crucial form of history, because it begins in the fundamental event. But we do not repeat a beginning by reducing it to something past and now known, which need merely to be intimated; no, the beginning must be begun again, more radically, with all the strangeness, darkness, insecurity that attend   to a true beginning. [49]

This too presumably requires "courage" and the imperative to become what we truly *are*. What I find lacking in Caputo's explication and defense of Heidegger's "humanism of a higher sort" is the same thing that I find lacking in Dallmayr's explication. Both leave us just where we need to begin serious questioning. Both are extremely persuasive in clarifying what underlies Heidegger's critique of "metaphysical humanism" and of the ways in which he seeks to overcome it. But neither is very helpful in revealing the determinate content of this so-called higher humanism. And both seem to sidestep Heidegger's increasing skepticism about any positive role that *praxis* and *phronesis* might play in putting us back in touch with ourselves. [50]

IV.

Except for my brief remarks at the beginning of this essay, I have not explicitly discussed the pragmatic thinkers, but they have not only been in the background of my probing of Heidegger's anti-humanism and his "meta-humanism," but in the foreground. I indicated that there is a great deal that is shared by the

pragmatists and Heidegger. Both share a radical critique of the
metaphysics of subjectivity. Both seek to undercut the dichotomy
between subjectivism and objectivism that provides the framework
of so much of modern thought. Both have a profound sense of our
finitude and historicity. Both reject the conception of man as
"lord of beings." The pragmatists – especially Dewey – are aware
of the danger of limiting ourselves to a technical horizon – of
the genuine threat of what Heidegger calls *Gestell*. And the
pragmatists can also be seen as reawakening our sense of the human
drama and recovering the lived quality of our experience. But
there is a decisive *difference*. For the pragmatists turn our
attention to how we think about our *praxis*, and how we can foster
a sense of solidarity and community among human beings. This is
why the notion of a critical community without any absolute
beginning points or finalities is so fundamental for them – a type
of community in which there can be an overcoming of the "eclipse
of public life." Our dialogue and communicative transactions are
not only with Being itself, but with other human beings. And if we
are to understand this concretely and cultivate what Aristotle
called *phronesis* in *our* historical situation, then we must turn
our attention to the ethical and political questions – the
practical questions that Heidegger does not directly confront. One
need not denegrate what Heidegger has taught us about the
ontological difference of beings and Being, Language, and
Thinking. One can agree with much of Heidegger's analysis and
critique of calculative, manipulative thinking, where human beings
are only "human resources." But the dichotomy between "two kinds
of thinking, each justified and needed in its own way: calculative
and meditative thinking"[51] is too undifferentiated. What is
paradoxical in Heidegger is that despite his enormous subtlety and
powers of discrimination, the pathways of his later thinking lead
us to a series of stark contrasts – contrasts that too easily lead
to a view of all "merely" human actions as only variations of
Gestell. What Gadamer, Arendt, Habermas, and the pragmatists
illuminate for us, try to bring into a clearing – is obscured and
left in darkness by Heidegger. For all of them are acutely aware
of the "deformation of praxis" in the modern age, and the
conceptual and material ways in which *praxis* is assimilated to a
fabricating, technical mentality. In this respect too, we can
become aware of the dangers of the mood that I sought to elicit at
the beginning of this essay and which is manifested in so much of
Heidegger's writings. For Heidegger's condemnation of the
nihilistic humanism implicit in Western metaphysics and his deep
skepticism about the modern age easily slide into a form of
"totalizing critique" that seductively leads us to the inexorable

conclusion that "we can only through thinking and writing prepare to be prepared for the manifestation of god, or the absence of god as things go downhill all the way." The primary issue is not one between "pessimism" and "optimism." It is rather an issue of bringing into a clearing, achieving an orientation concerning what we are to do, how we are to live our lives *together* – what "authentic community" means, and how it can be nurtured. If "questioning is the piety of thought," then this questioning cannot turn away from thinking about our *praxis*. Meditative thinking and poetic revealing may "foster the growth of the saving power," but a "higher species" of humanism or metahumanism that is silent about what human *praxis* means here and how in our concrete historical horizon will not "save" us – it will only obscure and conceal "the supreme danger."

N O T E S

1. G. W. F. Hegel, *Phenomenology of Spirit*, trans. A. V. Miller (Oxford: Oxford University Press, 1977), p. 6. I am not suggesting a "return" to the mood of the nineteenth century. The contrast is intended to highlight a present mood. After Auschwitz it would make no sense to speak of a return to the nineteenth century.

2. Martin Heidegger, *The End of Philosophy*, trans. Joan Stambaugh (New York: Harper & Row, 1973), p. 86. This passage is cited from Heidegger's text, "Überwindung der Metaphysik." The difference in mood that I am speaking about is reflected in the difference between Nietzsche's and Heidegger's use of *Überwindung*. For Heidegger's use of this term, see Joan Stambaugh's note on p. 84. Joseph J. Kockelmans has pointed out that this passage was written during the 1930's, and reflects the events leading up to World War II and what many people felt at that time. But there were others, including Heidegger's teacher, Husserl, who gave expression to very different sentiments. Compare what Heidegger says with Husserl's passionate plea (written at approximately the same time) for

> a philosophy with the deepest and most universal self-understanding of the philosophic ego as the bearer of absolute reason coming to itself. . . . that reason is precisely that which man *qua* man, in his innermost being, is aiming for, that which alone can satisfy him, make him 'blessed'; that reason allows for no differentiation into 'theoretical,' 'practical,' 'aesthetic,' or whatever. That being human is teleological being and an ought-to-be, and that this teleology holds sway in each and every activity and project of an ego. . . (Edmund Husserl, *The Crisis of European Sciences and Transcendental Phenomenology*, trans. by David Carr [Evanston, IL: Northwestern University Press, 1970], pp. 340–341.)

I do not think that what Heidegger says in the cited passage can be "localized" in a pre-World War II context. For similar thoughts are expressed in his later essays on technology and his *Der Spiegel* interview.

3. Throughout this essay, I speak of Heidegger's "later writings" to distinguish them from *Sein und Zeit*. I do not, however, agree with those who think that there is a total break or

reversal between *Sein und Zeit* and Heidegger's subsequent writings. Fred Dallmayr presents a more subtle and discriminating periodization of Heidegger's writings, distinguishing an early, middle, and late period. See Fred R. Dallmayr, "Ontology of Freedom: Heidegger and Political Philosophy," *Political Theory*, XII (May, 1984), 204-234. See also Reiner Schürmann, "Political Thinking in Heidegger," *Social Research*, XLV, 1 (Spring, 1978), 191-221.

4. See Charles S. Peirce, "Questions Concerning Certain Faculties Claimed for Man," "Some Consequences of Four Incapacities," and "Grounds of Validity of the Laws of Logic." These papers are included in Vol. 5 of *The Collected Papers of Charles Sanders Peirce*, ed. by Charles Hartshorne and Paul Weiss (Cambridge, MA: Harvard University Press, 1934), 5.213-263, 5.264-317, and 5.318-357 respectively.

5. *Letter on Humanism* in Martin Heidegger, *Basic Writings*, ed. by David F. Krell (New York: Harper & Row, 1977), p. 221. Page references to the *Letter* cited in this paper are from this translation. Heidegger typically speaks of "man" when referring to man and woman. For stylistic reasons, I have followed his use of the masculine term.

6. *Ibid.*, p. 239.

7. In my *Beyond Objectivism and Relativism* (Philadelphia: University of Pennsylvania Press, 1983), I have discussed the significance and appropriation of Aristotle's conception of *praxis* and *phronesis* by Gadamer. See also his "Letter" included as an Appendix to this book.

8. Hans-Georg Gadamer, *Truth and Method*, trans. by G. Barden and J. Cumming (New York: Seabury Press, 1975), p. 289.

9. Hans-Georg Gadamer, "Hermeneutics and Social Science," *Cultural Hermeneutics*, II (1975), 316.

10. "Only a God Can Save Us Now," trans. D. Schendler, *Graduate Faculty Philosophy Journal* (New School for Social Research), VI (1977), 16.

The German original reads:

Wenn ich kurz und velleicht etwas massiv, aber aus langer Besinnung antworten darf: Die Philosophie wird keine unmittelbare Veränderung des jetzigen Weltzustandes bewirken können. Dies gilt nicht nur von der Philosophie, sondern von allem blossmenschlichen Sinnen und Trachten. Nur noch ein Gott kann uns retten. Uns bleibt die einzige Möglichkeit, im Denken und im Dichten eine Bereitschaft vorzubereiten für die Erscheinung des Gottes oder für die Abwesenheit des Gottes im Untergang: dass wir im Angesicht des absesenden Gottes untergehen.

See also William J. Richardson's translation of this interview in *Heidegger: The Man and the Thinker*, ed. by Thomas Sheehan (Chicago: Precedent Publishing, 1981), pp. 45-73.

Many scholars of Heidegger object to relying on this interview in understanding his "serious" thinking. While nothing in my own argument is dependent on the use of this text (Heidegger expresses similar thoughts in many other places), I fail to see the rationale for not taking the interview seriously. Heidegger fully understood the importance of the interview, agreed to it on the condition it would be published posthumously, and even had the opportunity to edit his remarks.

11. Gadamer, *Truth and Method*, p. xxv.

12. See "A Letter by Professor Hans-Georg Gadamer" in *Beyond Objectivism and Relativism*, p. 264.

13. Heidegger, *Letter on Humanism*, p. 193. The English translation of the *Letter* by Frank A. Capuzzi translates the second sentence as follows: "We view action as causing an effect." But this translation fails to capture the difference between the first and second sentence, between "*Wir bedenken. . .*" and *Man kennt. . .*"

14. See the discussion of the issues raised by these distinctions in Bernstein, *Beyond Objectivism and Relativism*.

15. Jürgen Habermas, "Dogmatism, Reason, and Decision: On Theory and Praxis in Our Scientific Culture" in *Theory and Practice*, trans. by John Viertel (Boston: Beacon Press, 1973), p. 255.

16. In the *Letter on Humanism*, Heidegger writes: ". . . we must free ourselves from the technical interpretation of thinking.

The beginnings of that interpretation reach back to Plato and Aristotle. They take thinking itself to be a *techne*, a process of reflection in the service of doing and making. But here reflection is already seen from the perspective of *praxis* and *poesis*" (p. 194). For an excellent review and critique of Heidegger;s interpretation of Plato, see Robert Dostal, "Beyond Being: Heidegger's Plato," *Journal of the History of Philosophy*, 23 (January 1985).

17. Heidegger, "Overcoming Metaphysics," in *The End of Philosophy*, p. 106.

18. *Ibid.*, p. 96.

19. Heidegger, "The Question Concerning Technology," in *Basic Writings*, pp. 309-310.

20. *Ibid.*, p. 317. The tendency to pass over the distinctions between *poesis* and *praxis*, *techne* and *phronesis* is even more striking in this text, given as a lecture in 1949 and revised in 1953. For Heidegger explicitly mentions the chapter from Aristotle's *Nichomachean Ethics* in which these distinctions are drawn (and which was the basis of his seminar given in the early 1920's). But although Heidegger explicitly discusses the meanings of *poiesis* and *techne* and their relation to *aletheia*, he does not mention either *praxis* or *phronesis*. When this lecture reaches its climax -- when Heidegger speaks of the extreme or supreme danger of *Gestell* and the growth of the "saving power" -- Heidegger turns to *poiesis* and *techne*, not *praxis* and *phronesis*.

21. Martin Heidegger, *An Introduction to Metaphysics*, trans. by Ralph Manheim (New Haven: Yale University Press, 1959), p. 38.

22. Martin Heidegger, "The Age of the World Picture," in *The Question Concerning Technology and Other Essays*, trans. by William Lovitt (New York: Harper Books, 1977), p. 133.

23. Richard Rorty, "A Discussion" by Dreyfus, Taylor and Rorty, *The Review of Metaphysics*, XXXIV (1980), 52. I have not explicitly raised the tangled issue of "Heidegger and the Nazis" in this paper. I think that one of the most balanced summaries of the facts is presented by George Steiner in his sympathetic and perceptive book on Heidegger in the Penguin Modern Masters series. I fully endorse his own judgment when he writes: "But nauseating as they are, Heidegger's gestures and pronouncements during 1933-

34 are tractable. It is his complete silence on Hitlerism and the holocaust after 1945 which is very nearly intolerable." (*Martin Heidegger* [New York: Penguin Books, 1978], p. 123.) See also Fred Dallmayr's discussion in "Ontology of Freedom: Heidegger and Political Philosophy."

24. Heidegger, *Letter on Humanism*, p. 195.

25. *Ibid.*, p. 202.

26. *Ibid.*

27. Heidegger, "Overcoming Metaphysics," p. 93.

28. Heidegger, *Introduction to Metaphysics*, p. 37.

29. In the *Letter*, Heidegger writes: "With regard to this more essential *humanitas* of *homo humanus* there arises the possibility of restoring to the word 'humanism' a historical sense that is older than its oldest meaning chronologically reckoned. . of the word. That requires that we first experience the essence of man more primordially, but it also demands that we show to what extent this essence in its own way becomes fateful. The essence of man lies in ek-sistence" (p. 224).

30. Heidegger, *Letter on Humanism*, p. 225.

31. *Ibid.*, p. 240.

32. See Dallmayr's discussion of Heidegger in *Twilight of Subjectivity: Contributions to a Post-Individualist Theory of Politics* (Amherst: University of Massachusetts Press, 1981); *Language and Politics* (Notre Dame: University of Notre Dame Press, 1983); and in "Ontology of Freedom: Heidegger and Political Philosophy."

33. See especially chapter 2, "Intersubjectivity and Political Community," in Dallmayr, *Twilight of Subjectivity*.

34. Dallmayr, *Twilight of Subjectivity*, p. 31.

35. *Ibid.*, pp. 68-69.

36. *Ibid.*, p. 70

37. See especially the discussion of the meaning of "freedom" in Dallmayr's "Ontology of Freedom." Dallmayr is extremely perceptive in revealing what Heidegger means by "freedom." But here, too, I have critical reservations when he claims: "Instead of vouchsafing individual isolation and selfishness, freedom in this view is not merely an accidental ingredient, but the essential grounding of human solidarity (or socialism) – just as solidarity properly construed denotes a reciprocal effort of liberation or mutual 'letting-be.' (p. 228). Dallmayr at this point in his paper does not elaborate further on such implications, but turns to a discussion of Hannah Arendt. For all Arendt's indebtedness to Heidegger, I do not think her own original interpretation of freedom as coterminus with the open space of disclosure in the public realm of action (*praxis*) repre- sents "tentative steps in the direction sketched by Heidegger." Rather it is an attempt to bring into a clearing just what Heidegger obscures. Arendt tells us: "Men *are* free – as distinguished from their possessing the gift of freedom – as long as they act, neither before nor after; for to *be* free and to act are the same." (Hannah Arendt, "What is Freedom?," in *Between Past and Future* [New York: Viking Press, 1968], p. 153). See my discussion of Arendt in *Beyond Objectivism and Relativism*.

Just as Heidegger leads us to a misleading dichotomy between man as the lord of being *or* the shepard of being, there is a similar misleading dichotomy in his treatment of freedom. For Heidegger writes as if all modern treatments of freedom ultimately reduce themselves to conceiving of freedom as the (causal) property of autonomous subjects. It is against this subjective understanding of freedom that Heidegger elaborates his "alternative." But posing the issue in this manner obscures the various "modern" approaches to freedom that stress its intrinsically communal character and which do not assimilate freedom to a type of spontaneous causality by a self-sufficient subject. In addition to Arendt, see, for example, John Dewey, "Philosophies of Freedom," in *John Dewey: On Experience, Nature, and Freedom*, ed. by Richard J. Bernstein (New York: 1960).

38. Heidegger, *Letter on Humanism*, p. 212.

39. *Ibid.*, pp. 232–235.

40. *Ibid.*, p. 197.

41. Dallmayr shows that a close reading of Heidegger's texts reveals that already in the later 1930's he was extremely critical

of the abuses of "nationalism." This is frequently emphasized by those who claim one should not judge Heidegger *solely* on the basis of his writings between 1933 and 1935. My point, however, is to highlight the *gap* between the ontological and the ontic level of analysis; to point out the lack of mediation or determinate negation. So while I reject the claim of those who argue that there is an intrinsic or logical connection between Heidegger's philosophy and his misjudgments about the *Führer* and the Nazis, it is philosophically more troubling to see the compatibility of widely divergent ontic judgments with Heidegger's "fundamental ontology."

42. The essays by John Caputo that are especially relevant to the question of Heidegger and Humanism are: "Hermeneutics as the Recovery of Man," *Man and World*, XV (1982); and "The Thought of Being and the Conversation of Mankind: The Case of Heidegger and Rorty," *The Review of Metaphysics*, XXXVI (1983).

43. Caputo, "Hermeneutics as the Recovery of Man," p. 343.

44. *Ibid.*, p. 344.

45. *Ibid.*, p. 354.

46. *Ibid*, p. 360.

47. Caputo, "The Thought of Being and the Conversation of Mankind," p. 662.

48. *Ibid.*, p. 682.

49. Heidegger, *An Introduction to Metaphysics*, pp. 38-39.

50. Reiner Schürmann has offered a very different reading of Heidegger's "political thinking" - one which seems to be diametrically opposed to and flatly contradicts the interpretations of Dallmayr and Caputo. Schürmann speaks "the symbolic difference as subversion. "The symbolic difference, as the middle term that carries the phenomenological destruction into practical subversion, translates the 'turn' in thinking into an 'overturn' in action. The categories for understanding such action, as I see them, are at least five: (1) the abolition of the primacy of teleology in action; (2) the abolition of the primacy of responsibility in the legitimation of action; (3) action as a protest against the administered world; (4) a certain disinterest

in the future of mankind, due to a shift in the understanding of destiny; (5) anarchy as the essence of the 'memorable' requiring thought as well as of the 'do-able' requiring action." (Reiner Schürmann, "Political Thinking in Heidegger," *Social Research*, XLV [1978], 201.)

If one accepts this interpretation, then it would make good sense why the late Heidegger "abandons" *praxis*. But each of Schürmann's "categories" for understanding action is negative. Indeed his analysis of action is not only reminiscent of "negative theology" but entangles us in similar aporias. I do not see how the symbolic difference is "a middle term," how it enables us to understand what is the *determinate* character of political thinking or action. What kind of political action satisfies these five categories? For a critique of Schürmann, see Bernard P. Dauerhauer, "Does Anarchy Make Political Sense? A Response to Schürmann," *Human Studies*, I (1978), 369-375.

51. Martin Heidegger, *Discourse on Thinking*, trans. of *Gelassenheit* by John M. Anderson and E. Hans Freund (New York: Harper & Row, 1966), p. 46.

CHAPTER VI

ROYCE'S PRAGMATIC IDEALISM

AND EXISTENTIAL PHENOMENOLOGY

Charles M. Sherover (Hunter College)

In 1879, Josiah Royce, then just twenty-two, set forth in a diary he then kept a statement of motivating philosophic concerns. Some twenty years later, he gave these themes a mature development – first in the speculative metaphysic of *The World and the Individual*, and, again, twelve years later in *The Problem of Christianity*. Starting with an explicit phenomenological stance concerned with the underlying structure of individual life-experiencing, he pointed us to the presence of that which does not directly present itself in actual momentary experience and to the pervasiveness of time in the human outlook as the unity of any experiential present with its past and its future. From this beginning he saw that the speculative development of phenomenological questioning leads to some kind of philosophic idealism which sustains, enriches and broadens out its originating concerns.

Royce's key diary entry reads:

'The New Phenomenology'; Would this title be sacrilegious? And this for an opening: Every man lives in a present and contemplates a past and future. In this consists his whole life. The future and past are shadows both, the present is the only real. Yet in the contemplation of the shadows is the realm wholly occupied; and without the shadows the real has for us neither life nor value. No more universal fact of consciousness can be mentioned than this fact. . . . For it is in view of this that all men may be said to be in some sense Idealists.[1]

A few months later, a second entry says:

Robert S. Corrington, Carl Hausman, & Thomas M. Seebohm, eds., *Pragmatism Considers Phenomenology*, Washington, D.C.: Center for Advanced Research in Phenomenology & University Press of America, 1987 .

I see Kant as I never saw him before. But we must put
our problem differently. Thus says Kant: What is the relation
of knowledge to its object? Thus say we: What is the relation
of every conscious moment to every other? Our question may be
more fundamental, and can be made so only through study of
him.[2]

In other entries, Royce expresses explicit concern with the
question of 'being' and its temporal dimension,[3] and sees in the
relation of Kant's *ich denke* to its *Vorstellungen* or 'presentations' the consequence that "all past moments must have been
possibly knowable as present moments."[4]

These diary entries suggest that if one looks at Royce's
mature work from the vantage point of Heidegger's *Being and Time*,
one can reasonably assert that both Royce and Heidegger came to
philosophy with similar questions; though they finally travelled
in somewhat different directions, they shared many common outlooks
and common doctrines. Both found philosophic roots in Leibniz,
Kant and Hegel and joined in taking their lead from Kant. Each
developed a doctrine of the essential interrelationship of time
and being and of the import of futurity for the comprehension of
the experiential present; each commenced his prime work by
claiming to face an announced primacy of ontology; each insisted
on the import of individuality and the thesis that the individual
is always rooted in a world of other people and of things - in
Royce's case, the pervasive sociality of the individual, in
Heidegger's, of Being-in-the-world and Being-with - each insisted
on the forward-looking activity of human consciousness as animated
and focused by specific problematic concerns - in Royce's case by
the notion of selective attention, in Heidegger's by the notion of
Care - each urged that a careful concern for the structure of
human temporality intimates a new way to read its social manifestation as history; each tied individuality, temporality, and freedom together, not as accidental attributes, but as ontological
ingredients; each took the notion of causality as but one kind of
interpretational category and saw science as but one manifestation
of the structure of human practical concerns which both, following
Kant, regarded as more primordial than any theoretical understanding; both turned from a phenomenological ontology of human
experiencing to what Kant might have termed its 'noumenal reach' -
in Royce's case, continually to the question of God or the
Absolute, in Heidegger's case, finally to the quest for Being
itself.

These common phenomenological concerns, doctrinal themes, and
even their transcendent turns joined to yield a somewhat similar

result. Royce, in the end, turned in *The Problem of Christianity* to the fundamentality of what he called a 'community of interpretation.' Heidegger, in the end, has yielded a primacy of concern for hermeneutics – which, I think, must presuppose something like Royce's concept of community for its ground.

These similarities notwithstanding, Royce and Heidegger manifested pervasively radical differences of philosophic mood. Heidegger, somewhat taking up Kierkegaard's consuming *angst* and Nietzsche's 'transvaluation of all values,' often focused on 'fear' and 'dread' and in the end voiced a fundamental kind of alienation from being.

Royce shared with both Heidegger and American pragmatism the heritage of German Idealism. But he was also a prime exemplar of that American mind which, as Dewey once noted, Emerson had formed when it was still in the making. Royce was an heir of Emerson, who instilled a deep moral idealism into the American conscience and whose supreme admonition was "Honor truth by its use"; he was a student of Peirce and a colleague and friend of James. These associations conspire to suggest that strong pragmatic tenets helped to shape Royce's thinking. Indeed, Aiken has perceptively suggested that along with Santayana, Royce should be recognized "as speaking in one sense for a pragmatism wiser, more liberal, and more comprehensive than that of Peirce or James or even Dewey."[5]

However this evaluation may be, it does seem clear that Royce brought together into his own vision both basic phenomenological concerns and pragmatic orientations. Melding these with his own education in the heritage of German Idealism, his philosophic statement repudiated any notion of alienation, urged the constructive utilization of tragic situations, called philosophy back to its responsibility as moral educator and stand as a bold affirmation of what Leibniz once termed our 'common citizenship in this cosmic republic.' Effectively repudiating any existential alienation and explicitly following Kant by continual insistence on the transcendent reach of moral reason,[6] Royce called upon philosophic thought to take up its responsibility of moral educator by cultivating a "deeper sense of companionship with the world."[7] In his most telling admonition, Royce brought together the thrust of his philosophic outlook: "Arise then freeman, stand forth in thy world. It is God's world. It is also thine."[8]

What I propose to do, in this brief compass, is to direct attention to three Roycean theses – intentionality, sociality, temporality – which need further phenomenological development but which attest to Royce's continuing fidelity to both his originating phenomenological orientation and his abiding, if dissenting, pragmatic allegiance. The integration of his phenomenological questioning and his pragmatism conspired to produce a speculative idealism which saw its justification in its bearing on living concerns. His culminating metaphysical vision of Pragmatic Idealism or Absolute Pragmatism saw the time and being of the world as one organized whole actively functioning in, and affected by, the temporally structured functioning of each one of us.

In many ways, Royce's prime quest was to discover the status and role of the inherent individuality of every existent in a world conceived to be a rationally coherent and organized whole. Each of these three Roycean themes, which are of prime interest to any existential phenomenology, bear on this concern. My discussion of them is primarily drawn from his central work, *The World and the Individual*, which was concerned with finding and elucidating the pervasive individuality comprising this individual world we inhabit and to which we belong.

I

Royce commenced his central work by boldly asserting the primacy of ontology for any serious systematic thinking: "you deal constantly, and decisively, with the problems of the Theory of Being whenever you utter a serious word."[9] To make any assertion about God, the world, or the human individual "implies that one knows what it is to be . . . what the so-called existential predicate itself involves."[10] In developing the meaning of the existential predicate, he sought to work out the meaning of this ontological primacy for the notions of causality, purpose, time, and what he called the Absolute.

But at the outset, in a post-Kantian age, we must immediately ask whether this ontological primacy refers to the entities we claim to be speaking about, or to attribution within the speaking thought itself. Heidegger, at least in the beginning, did *not* ask about Being-as-such, but about the 'meaning of Being' for us. Royce's insistence is that we only find meaning in our own ideas, as they are referential both to a world of things and events, and to ourselves as well; the question of the ontological predicate then immediately leads to the question of "the whole relation between Idea and Being."[11]

It is in his response to this ensuing question that Royce made one of his most innovative moves. First, he saw all ideas as acts of will; as such, ideas are essentially teleological in character: "your intelligent ideas of things never consist of mere images. . . but always involve a consciousness of how you propose to act. . ."[12] Working out the implication of this voluntaristic conception of what an idea involves, he enunciated an intentional theory of meaning: he distinguished between what he called the 'internal' or purposive intent and the 'external' or descriptive meaning of any idea. The 'external' meaning is the traditional one, the claim to some kind of correspondence between our own descriptive notion and the external entity the notion claims to describe. But, as any heir of Leibniz and Kant must recognize, any idea we enunciate is from a particular perspective and cannot rightfully claim to describe its external referent except from the speaker's own 'peculiar point of view.' That individual perspective, Royce insisted, is always forward-looking and purposive in character; its description of any external object is not teleologically neutral. To any statement made to us, we may rightfully inquire, "What is your point?," "What are you trying to say to me?," "What meaning do you want me to take from what you are now saying?," "Why do you want to tell me that?" I can only judge the aptness of a description – as, for example, a map – in terms of what I want to do with it, how it describes an area of interest in terms of my particular interest. A geological map of Pennsylvania, though fully accurate, does not meet my need if my quest for that map is to use roads to get to State College. Any particular description is always a description for a given purpose and can only be evaluated in light of its animating purpose. Insofar as the purpose must come first, external description or descriptive meaning is but the expression of its teleological intent and must be judged by how well it fulfills that intent; "the external meaning is [thus] genuinely continuous with the internal meaning, and is inwardly involved in" it.[13] The inner meaning of an idea, then, is a purpose "which is in the consciousness of the moment wherein the idea takes place."[14]

Royce's new doctrine of meaning, then, is one of teleological intentionality and is to be tested by teleological adequacy. Any meaningful idea must refer to something beyond itself, must claim to describe its referent – which is distinct from itself – for a purposive reason; the truth-claim of that description is that it meets the criteria set forth in the purposive act, the internal meaning of its initiating idea. Any meaningful idea, then, has two sides: the purpose of going beyond itself and the successful fulfillment of that initiating purpose.

Description of nature, when systematic, is what we call science; description of the world of Being or Becoming, when it claims systematic comprehension, is what we call philosophy. Neither science nor philosophy, Heidegger has argued, can be presuppositionless: both can only offer descriptive statements that apply "pre-judgments" or "presuppositions" to their referential objects.[15] Royce's insistence is that all such descriptive presuppositions or prejudgments are embedded in internal meanings, are essentially purposive in character, and provide the parameters for evaluation of the evidence for the claim embedded in the referential description.

If meaning is essentially teleological, the meaning of the verb 'to be' must ultimately be understood in terms of teleological categories. And intentional meaning, understood teleologically, will, in the end, serve as Royce's explanation of how our ideas refer to external objects, and also enlighten our conceptual understanding of individuality, causality, freedom, temporality – and, as the systematic culmination of the speculative reach, of his conception of the Absolute as well.

This consideration immediately ties into Royce's own kind of pragmatism. For, as he has urged,

> Every finite idea is to be judged by its own specific purpose. Ideas are like tools. They are there for an end. They are true as the tools are good, precisely by reason of their adjustment to this end. To ask me which of two ideas is the more nearly true, is like asking me which of two tools is the better tool. The question is a sensible one if the purpose in mind is specific, but not otherwise.[16]

If thinking itself is an activity, if purposive thinking relates to some activity in the external world, and if meaning is to be seen in the coalescence of what Royce called the 'internal' and 'external' meanings of any specific idea, then Royce is surely voicing the pragmatic tradition, and perhaps providing it with a more fundamental grounding than just announcing a maxim for thought. For Royce's worked-out conception of meaning posits what John E. Smith has pointed out as the pragmatic thesis: "the necessary connection between a concept, a belief, and an action."[17]

These considerations already entail an ensuing speculative metaphysic that, when systematically worked out, issues in some kind of idealism. Royce has been candid about this from the outset. But, at the beginning of *The World and the Individual*, he makes it clear that this is not to be a restatement of that consuming monism which the received Absolute Idealism seems to have announced. He seeks, even in the concept of the Absolute, not one "which devours individuals. . . but a whole that is just to the finite aspect of every flying moment, and of every transient or permanent form of finite selfhood. . . ."[18] Explicitly rejecting both Schelling and Hegel as "having been as far astray as a larger minded modern philosophical doctrine can be,"[19] Royce

eschews any notion of a hierarchical structure of being, instead
effectively advocates a pragmatic contextualism that reaches beyond its own confines, and speculatively proposes an idealism that
respects the finite individual as both an integral and an autonomous part of a coherent world order which "invites man to be at
home in his universe" without taking himself to be the sole
"finite end that nature seeks."[20]

Having laid out the foundations for an idealism that incorporates an originating phenomenology with a pragmatic concept of
conceptualization, Royce devotes most of his first volume to a
critical appraisal of what he terms the three traditional ontological conceptions of western thought: mysticism, realism, and
what we would today call (Marburg) neo-Kantianism. Having demo-
lished each of these in turn, at least to his own satisfaction
(largely by applying his concepts of internal and external
meaning), he turns at the end of that volume to unfolding his own
doctrine of Being. Significantly, he never really labeled it
except to call it his own "Fourth Conception."[21] It is to the
spelling out of his own "Fourth Conception" that his second volume
is dedicated. And in this spelling out, two themes, central to all
existential phenomenology, cut through and undergird Royce's presentation of his own speculative view: the essential sociality and
the essential temporality of all our thinking and doing. Let me
turn, briefly, to each of these two in turn.

II

Cognizance of the individual's self-consciousness, the assertion of the 'I,' is, Royce insists, not primary. The Cartesian
'cogito ergo sum' is a derivative assertion that can only arise in
a sophisticated social setting. As Heidegger insisted, we are
essentially beings-within-a-world, a world of other people and of
things; our world is a "with-world," Mitwelt. 'To-be-in' is to-be-
with-others.[22] Although Heidegger has developed this insight in a
more ontologically primordial way, he has done so from the vantage
point of the individual's intent on discovering the nature of his
own self. Heidegger was in many ways too beholden to the very
Cartesianism he was seeking to overturn; from the outset, he
focused on the individual's encounter with physical nature, only
at the end alluding to sociality and to the historical dimensions
of our temporality. But what is wholly lacking in Heidegger's
existential analysis of Being-with or Mitwelt is any explicit
recognition of the fact that we each function as members of organized societies, that we each function as members of overlapping

communities - and that the categories of that functioning always involve evaluative judgments.

In contrast, what we can take as Royce's existential analysis starts from elemental sociality. Our being-in-the-world, or to-be-with-others - our *Mitwelt* – he would have said, is first and foremost a social world. We are individuals only *in* social relations with others, with physical nature, even with ourselves. The social is so primordial that even our conceptions of nature, as well as of the individual self, are not initiatory but socially grounded.

> The distinction between Self and non-Self has a predominantly *Social Origin*, and that implies a more or less obviously present contrast between what we at any moment view as the life of another person. . . [and] the life of the present Ego. . . . our empirical self-consciousness, from moment to moment, depends upon a series of contrast-effects, whose psychological origin lies in our literal social life, and whose continuance in our present conscious life, whenever we are alone, is due to habit, to our memory of literal social relations, and to an imaginative idealization of these relations. . . . In origin, then, the empirical Ego is secondary to our social experience.[23]

Only as our social involvements become developed and increasingly sophisticated does self-consciousness grow. For we truly exist "only in human relations," and our aims and purposes are always "more or less social."[24] Had we no social relations, we would be able to form no conception of "the reality of any finite non-Ego."[25] Indeed, self-consciousness is a social product, something which our social experience teaches us to develop. The statement of self-consciousness, 'I exist', finds "its origin for me in social intercourse. . . [and] is secondary, for instance, to language, to which all my thinking is so deeply indebted" and which, of course, is a parameter, medium, and requisite of those social relations within which I begin to find myself; just "who I am, I have first learned from others before I can observe it for myself."[26] This social rooting of individuality is, indeed, similar in outcome if not in derivation to Heidegger's 'existential' category of authenticity which develops by differentiation of the self from those others amongst whom he first finds himself.

If we apply this general thesis to some contemporary discussion, we find that the 'problem of other minds' is then a pseudo-problem; for what Royce and Heidegger have each effectively asserted is that without an awareness of other minds I could have no consciousness of my own. Thus "it is not the analogy with ourselves which is our principle guide to our belief in our fellows. . . a vague belief in the existence of our fellows seem to antedate. . . the definite formation of any consciousness" of the self.[27]

This thought, we must note, is not entirely new; for both Royce and Heidegger, heirs of German Idealism, seem to have worked from the distinction Fichte had already drawn out of his reading of Kant - that the awareness of the Ego first depends upon its distinguishing itself from the non-Ego with which it is, from the outset, involved. In contrast to Fichte, both Royce and Heidegger developed this insight phenomenologically.

But Royce, in contrast to Heidegger, regards this originating sociality as completely primordial. Heidegger begins by pointing to our discovery of our being among things in our problematic situations of involvement with aspects of the physical world. Physical nature would thus seem, in its bits and artifacts, to have been the first discovery. Royce, on the contrary, insists, "Our belief in Man. . . is logically prior to our interpretation of Nature,"[28] just because what we mean by nature is what "we conceive *as known or as knowable to various men.*"[29] The material world, which we all take for granted and presuppose as prior to our own being, is yet discovered by us, and understood by us, as an outcome of social experience. For what we experientially mean by the physical is that "collection of actual and possible experiences"[30] which we can share with each other; the physical is, then, that about which individual experiences are indeed *public.*, and the initial differentiation of the physical from the mental is precisely the act of distinguishing those experiences which are immediately shared or shareable from those which are not. It is by comparing my fellow's response with my own that I first discover that physical reality which is common to us both. To use Royce's example, I first learn that my fellow responds to the shining sun much as I do; I soon learn that other men share this experience even when I do not, that it is reported as having been experienced before I was born, and in lands I have never visited. The sun's shining appears 'apart from the experience of any particular man, while [it]. . . is still something which every man can verify.'[31] The "order of discovery" of the world of being is first my fellow, then myself, and finally Nature as what is shared between us.[32]

Royce's statement, then, of what Heidegger later dubbed the *Mit-sein*, reads: "the general principle, 'Whatever is, is somehow linked to others,' so far amounts to the assertion that *whatever is, is in the world with others.*"[33] From this principle, as from virtually every other, Royce immediately presses the ethical implication which Heidegger just as consistently avoids – in this case: "The ethical problem [then] is not: Shall I aim to preserve social relations? but: What social relations shall I aim to preserve?"[34]

Working from this primordiality of the social in our experience of Nature as well as ourselves, Royce turns to developing its broader ramifications. Picking up from what he terms Peirce's "admirable paper," namely, "The Doctrine of Necessity,"[35] he brings into question the "so-called axiom"[36] of unvarying laws of nature and the modern attempt to make efficacious causality a fundamental ontological concept. Noting that all physical and mental activities share the predicate of time-ordering, he sees that they both exhibit irreversibility of time-order as ontological predicates; on the ground of this common essential characteristic of any-thing-that-is, he seeks to break the traditional hard distinction between matter and mind. Urging that the mathematical constructs of modern science are but interpretive instruments which cannot claim to be descriptively true of an independently existent Reality, he argues, in a remarkable parallel to Heidegger, that science itself is but "a sort of theoretical extension of our industrial art,"[37] which derives from a social practice that is teleologically oriented to specific problematic questions, and is therefore to be understood in terms of its initiating internal meanings. Science is to be respected, Royce insists, always as "an essentially social affair. The 'cosmical' fact is a fact which others are conceived to be capable of verifying besides the observer who now describes."[38] Science, as both Peirce and Dewey insist, is always public.

> For nature we know, as a fact, only through our social consciousness, and the social consciousness is ethical before it is physical, appreciates more deeply than it describes, recognizes nature for reasons which are, in the last analysis, themselves ideal, and is conscious of novelty, of progress, of significance, in general of the human, in ways which, in the last analysis, make the whole cosmical process a mere appearance of one aspect of the moral world. . . . The 'cosmos,' in the sense of empirical science, is a conceptual product of the human mind.[39]

And therefore it must be understood from the vantage point of the voluntaristic nature of human thinking, which always functions by means of internal meanings, of purposes to be fulfilled, ends to be achieved, questions to be answered, concerns to be met and shared with others.

Nature, then, is then to be conceived as a system of common being, with which we are able to establish certain communicative relationships. The natural phenomena that our daily experiences and our theoretical sciences bring to our attention are understood by us in purposive terms and convey answers to the questions we ask in the meanings we discern in our varied relationships with it. But the whole of nature is more than present physical reality. We ourselves participate, often by conscious acts, in the system of nature; and we can understand nature only as more than is immediately present to the cognitive intellect. Physical nature points us to an appreciation that "there exists, in the universe, a vast realm of fact *other than* what human minds consciously find present within their own circles of individual or private apprehension." Nature is a social system in which we participate, but which points beyond itself to a larger encompassing whole reaching into the past as into the future – both of which are integral to the experiential present. Nature then must be understood by us as "a part of Reality," and the social bases of our understanding of Nature "do indeed prove that this is true."[40]

III

Our temporally structured experience of Reality, of Nature, of our social involvements, of our own selves – all join to insist that we are, on every level, involved in "a universal time-order."[41] Time emerges, after many discussions, as the form of the will, of the expression of all meaning, of all ideas we have, of all practical activity, of the self itself. As crucial to all meaning, as the form of acting being in the world, it is ingredient to nature as to ourselves, to our understanding of Reality as such.

Royce's own treatment of time seems to have begun from James's notion of the 'specious present.' But an immediately perceived present, at most of a few seconds, can give us no consciousness of change, of irreversible succession, of time as the continuity of past with future or the presence of past and future in any living present. Beyond perception in any present moment, Royce insisted that we must have available a conception of time and it is only that conception, which points beyond the immediacy of the moment, that enables us to derive any meaning at all from what is immediately perceived. For any perceptual moment only has meaning *as* it is conceived to *tie* what is not literally present – past and future – together: any experiential present then includes ties beyond itself and is, we might note, like any idea in that it points beyond itself to its Other for its meaning.

Time, as the form of all activity, must then be not only perceptual; it must be conceptual as well. Royce's essay on time in *The World and the Individual* makes this point. Later, in *The Problem of Christianity*, he amends this to include both perception and conception as our living mode of interpretational activity. But the essay in *The World and the Individual* is revealing of Royce's general philosophic method.

For Royce here, typically, first asks about *how* we do experience the experiencing which is ours, and only then proceeds to its speculative reach. Thus, with regard to the temporality of human experiencing, we are first shown how our pervasively temporal experiential dimensions are to be understood, conceptually as well as perceptually; this essentially phenomenological description is then projected onto the connectedness of all time that is conceptually presupposed in any attempt to understand the experiential present, and thence to the speculative reach, to the encompassing 'Absolute' of all being.

Two points might be well noted. First, our consciousness of any given present includes its integral unity with both past and future; no moment of temporal experience stands alone. For consciousness exemplifies awareness of change, and change represents at least the continuity of the past into the present. But if all understanding is teleologically conditioned – as any voluntaristic doctrine must insist then the meaning of the present is always to be seen in what it portends for the future, for what is not yet but yet can-be. If any idea is pragmatically understood as a plan of action, then its presupposed conception of time is directional, and it understands the meaning of the present activity in terms of what it is yet intended to yield, in terms of what is not-yet but conceived as yet-can be. The activity of experiencing is always as an extended present – the present of consciousness *and* of the experienced world – but the understanding of that experiencing derives its meaning only by means of anticipations and expectations. Present experiencing, then, takes up the past into its forward-looking stance as expectancy and aim. In one sense, Royce comes very close to Heidegger's emphasis on futurity; important as both past and future are to the comprehension of the present, time as the form of will is always directed to what is not-yet. We each live by a continual "adjustment. . . to the reality of the future."[42] And this futural orientation appears to be the basis of the temporal outlook which builds experience:

Thought aims at constructing a notion of a future. . . . What is meant by future is not an immediately given phenomenon but only a conception of a phenomenon and yet this

conception is immediately known to be indubitable. Meaning
and justification fall together. To say what a future means
is to anticipate a future. . . . Anticipation of experience
will then be the same as the act of constructing the notion
of experience.[43]

This is phenomenologically demonstrated:

> [Each individual] inner life. . . is conscious, but
> normally very unequally self-conscious - possesses contents,
> but cannot precisely define to itself what they are; seeks
> not to hold the present but to fly to the next; scorns the
> immediate, the presented, and looks endlessly for the on-
> coming, the sought, the wished-for, the absent, so that the
> inner eye gazes on the flowing stream of events, but beholds
> rather what they hint at than what they present.[44]

Only by means of this voluntaristic integration of the three faces
('ecstases') of experiential time - present and past and future -
then, does "time, whether in our inner experience, or in the
conceived world order as a whole, [have] any meaning."[45] Internal
meanings seek "in successive stages, their union with their own
External Meaning."[46] The meaning of what Heidegger had called the
"three ['faces' or] ecstases of temporality" then depends upon
their own interpretive integration, and Royce, in the later *The
Problem of Christianity* will insist that this interpretive integration is what binds perceptual and conceptual time together.[47]
    What should concern us here is that Royce, without working
out the details of this integration or the futural priority which
his own voluntarism suggests, has suggested all the rudiments of
the constitutional structure of 'the present' which Heidegger's
own existential analyses would yet present in a more rigorous form
and with a decided priority of futurity both in constituting the
present and retrieving the germane past. This more developed
temporal doctrine would seem to be implied by Royce's fundamental
voluntarism -- even if Royce, when directly facing the three modes
of time, almost always treats them even-handedly. As Royce states:
"the future depends for its meaning upon the past, and the past in
turn has its meaning as a process expectant of the future."[48]
    But time points us to eternity, Royce maintains, continuing
in his speculative reach; and, "as a fact, in defining time we
have already, and inevitably, defined eternity."[49] For the all-
inclusive perception of the encompassing Absolute is one in which
all times "are equally present. . . as a *totum simul.* . . [which]

contains all sequences within it. . .[50] As such, "just so far as time is the final form of consciousness [what is termed the Absolute, as supreme inclusive consciousness], must have the same type of unity" that our present consciousness, "within its little span, surveys."[51] And, indeed, if we recognize "one time process as holding for all the world,"[52] then the differences between different levels of existents may be *not so much of kind* as of "processes whose time-rate is slower or faster than those which our consciousness is adapted to read or to appreciate."[53] For us any conscious present is a dynamic time-span in which what is literally past is presently held in the same view as the immediate present and the developing future. The divine perspective is then but an expansion of the kind we enjoy. For "if God is God, he views the future and the past as we do the present,"[54] as itself a dynamic stretch of process.

Our temporal experience, then, is not illusory but is rooted in the fount of all Reality. Our temporal experience is real. The knowledge of the Absolute "possess[es] a perfect knowledge at one glance of the whole of the temporal order, present, past, and future."[55] Whether God and the Absolute are interchangeable terms for Royce is a question which he implicitly - but never explicitly - leaves open.[56] But, however this may be, let us note that Royce's 'eternity' conveys no sense of timelessness but rather the all-inclusive temporality of the entire temporal order.

However this speculative theology may be, Royce sets out to assure us that temporal experiencing is an experiencing of the real world in all of its ramifications - even unto its ultimate fount in God or the Absolute itself. Again, this is a remarkable foreshadowing of Heidegger's own early speculative reach; for Heidegger, after having drawn out the dimensions of the human temporal stance always under the aegis of futurity, draws the requisite conclusion, in an often-ignored footnote: "If God's eternity can be 'construed' philosophically, then it may be understood only as a more primordial temporality which is 'unending' ['*unendliche*'].[57]

But however we regard this speculative theology - when we recall Royce's opening meditation that suggested the prime question posed out of Kant to be that of the relation of each experiential moment to every other, we can see that his developed speculative metaphysic is to see time not only as the form of all consciousness, but as the form of the Real as well. He had achieved this viewpoint by a somewhat phenomenological questioning of the structure of human experience, has seen that the temporal is not only the form of all cognition, as Kant had established, but that it is the form of all consciousness, of its volitional impetus – and of the Reality with which all consciousness deals. As Heidegger summarizes what is a prime Roycean point, Time is not only "'more Objective' than any possible Object. . . [but is] also 'more subjective' than any possible subject. . . ."[58] By either account, the universality of the temporal modes provides our assurance that our temporal form of experiencing is our experiencing of a real world, a world which stretches beyond our possible perceptions, but which sustains them in its encompassing embrace.

IV

On the basis of phenomenological themes such as these, Royce turned from what he considered to be a merely relativistic pragmatism to what he called the thesis of that "Absolute Pragmatism, of that Voluntarism, which recognizes all truth as the essentially eternal creation of the Will."[59] As he repeatedly came to argue, there must be a distinction between the criterion of truth and the nature of truth. Pragmatism's quest to find satisfaction of needs in practical activity does indeed bring to our attention specific truths about the nature of the world in which we function; but as he once said, such "truth itself must be true." What we will in seeking answers to our problematic questions are answers that accord with the nature of the whole: they work just because they instantiate or exemplify in the particular situation the whole truth of the world. What is true of the whole must be true of the part, and the part must somehow instantiate in its particularity the variegated unity of the whole.

Taking time and history seriously, taking the individual as a unique member of the larger community, Royce expands his ethics of loyalty to one of atonement, an ethic in which the individual takes upon himself in his particular problematic situation the task of reconciling and redeeming the heritage of the past for the sake of the future. The dyadic conjunction of perception and conception is developed into the essentially triadic conception of imaginative interpretation as the nature of all human knowledge. And the primordial sociality of the individual is developed into the metaphysical understanding of the nature of the life of the community – a metaphysical exposition of the sustaining meaning of 'being-with' (*Mitsein*) never before, I believe, taken with so much metaphysical seriousness.

Although some of his language suggests Hegelian-like formulations, he himself continually cites Kant to the end. And I would suggest that Royce's speculative idealism – he invariably talks about 'his conception,' not about any 'true conception' – is an attempt to build a coherent view of reality, and of our place in it, on the basis of what can be developed from Kant's own thesis that it is practical reason – morality and freedom – that leads us beyond experiential phenomena to noumenal reality itself. Time is the form of thinking, of cognition, of consciousness, of action, of will. It is the form of free individuality as well. Toward the end, Royce clearly said that his own appropriation of "idealistic theses . . . [was meant] to repudiate the frequent and groundless assertion that [his] own form of idealism regards time as 'unreal,' or the absolute as 'timeless,' or the universe as a 'block.'"[60]

Effectively anticipating Heidegger's existential analyses in many ways, he did not pursue many of these themes with as much rigor or existential depth; but he did not seek to place the same themes into a coherent outlook which never abandoned the philosophic responsibility to place critical concern for the human will within the encompassing form of what Kant had called that practical reason which is always moral reason and which takes freedom as primordial. Royce's phenomenological road to a pragmatic idealism sought no 'death of God' or estrangement from Being, but rather to call each individual to recognize his free moral responsibility to take up his own uniquely significant place in a coherent world order.

In many ways, some of which have been suggested, Royce succeeded in setting out some essential phenomenological themes. In several of these, such as the priority of sociality and the nature of community, of the moral obligations incumbent in community membership and social origin, I think that he has seen further than Heidegger has done. I think he has, in many ways, seen deeper into the ramifications of the human condition in every existential meaning of that term. Yet he was a pioneer – as Gabriel Marcel's book about Royce suggested – a pioneer who saw beyond his own vision and yet succeeded in subjecting what was given to him into a refashioned outlook while pointing it ahead to what was yet to be done.

But in one fundamental way, I think Marcel's reading was inverted; Marcel argued that Royce was "a kind of transition between absolute idealism and existentialist thought."[61] I would suggest, rather, that Royce saw that what we now term systematic phenomenological questioning provides not only categorial ways in which to comprehend existential situations – which Heidegger developed in many ways beyond what Royce had done; he also has shown that an at-least speculative metaphysics cannot be dispensed with - that serious questioning rather requires and leads to a metaphysic which, though it must remain speculative instead of dogmatically cognitive, is yet requisite to sustaining and undergirding the pluralistic community of the whole of being in which we participate.[62]

In some ways, as I have suggested, he has seen beyond what has yet been accomplished: an ontology of social being that is not only formative but also prospectively normative. But it remains as a positive comment on Heidegger's own accomplishment that what I have tried to suggest is a retrieval of the work of one prime figure out of our own philosophic past. I believe Royce and his co-workers have seen beyond their conscious limits. But *they* have seen.

What *we* are now beginning to see in the pragmatic vision has only been made possible for us by a different, though familial, vision, For - and this is urged as a somewhat Heideggerian lesson in the appropriation of philosophic history - when we approach earlier thinkers with the questions of later ones, we come to see philosophic possibilities which they had already implicitly uncovered but did not realize and somehow failed to make us see. In this case, what we have now come to see in our own philosophic past has only been made possible by a new development of thought, wrought by Bergson, Husserl, Marcel, and Heidegger. What I have tried to wrest out of Royce are precisely, as Heidegger would have suggested, those philosophic possibilities which he presented to us - but which we did not, without aid from abroad, have the ability to recover, recapitulate, and finally make our own.

But when we try to think through that new phenomenological vision, it soon becomes apparent that it cannot stand alone. Heidegger proclaimed, once again, the 'end of all metaphysics' - an interesting cry of every landmark philosopher who seems to have implicitly claimed an insight into a final vision. But re-reading Heidegger and other existential phenomenologists in the light of pragmatism suggests that like pragmatism, phenomenology itself *cannot* be self-grounding; it requires a metaphysical speculative thrust for its own deepest insights as its own primordial justification. For our *practical* functioning within-the-world tells us something about the nature of the world in which we function. Only as we are able to interpret the world in terms of our own ways of reading it can we find justification for living out our practical concerns as our phenomenological queries suggest. As Royce might have urged, our purposive ideas concerning the world in which we find ourselves suggest something about the nature of the world that we should take as a presupposition for deciding how to act in the world of which we are a part and to which we belong.

NOTES

1. Cited in J. Lowenberg, "Editor's Introduction" to Josiah Royce, *Fugitive Essays* (Cambridge: Harvard University Press, 1925), p. 31.

2. *Ibid.*, pp. 33-34.

3. *Ibid.*, p. 31.

4. *Ibid.*, p. 33.

5. Henry D. Aiken, in "Introduction" to Part One, "Pragmatism and America's Philosophical Coming of Age," in *Philosophy in the Twentieth Century* (New York: Random House, 1962), I, p. 52.

6. See, for example, Josiah Royce, *The World and the Individual* (2 vols., New York: The Macmillan Company, 1904), I, p. 417.

7. Royce, *The World and the Individual*, I, p. 418.

8. *Ibid.*, p. 470.

9. *Ibid.*, p. 14.

10. *Ibid.*, p. 12.

11. *Ibid.*, p. 27.

12. *Ibid.*, p. 22; cf. pp. 22-24.

13. *Ibid.*, p. 33.

14. *Ibid.*, p. 24.

15. See Martin Heidegger, *What is a Thing?*, trans. by W. B. Barton, Jr. and Vera Deutsch (Chicago: Henry Regnery, 1967), p. 180 and *Being and Time*, trans. by John Macquarrie and Edward Robinson (New York: Harper and Row, 1962), p. 358 (310). N.B. The latter introduces II.3.63, which discusses the 'Hermeneutical Situation for Interpreting the Meaning of Care.'

16. Royce, *The World and the Individual*, I, p. 308.

17. John E. Smith, *The Spirit of American Philosophy* (New York: Oxford University Press, 1963), p. 10.

18. Royce, *The World and the Individual*, I, p. 42.

19. *Ibid.*, p. 414.

20. *Ibid.*, p. 416.

21. In view of his explicit repudiation of Hegel – cf. n. 62 below – it would be a gross error to follow most textbooks and identify this "Fourth Conception" with Hegel's Absolute Idealism.

22. Heidegger, *Being and Time*, p. 118 (155).

23. Royce, *The World and the Individual*, II, pp. 260–64.

24. Josiah Royce, *Studies of Good and Evil* (New York: D. Appleton and Company, 1902), p. 203.

25. *Ibid.*, p. 205.

26. *Ibid.*, p. 94.

27. Royce, *The World and the Individual*, II, p. 170.

28. *Ibid.*, p. 168.

29. *Ibid.*, p. 166.

30. *Ibid.*, p. 167.

31. *Ibid.*, p. 178.

32. Cf. *ibid.*, p. 177.

33. *Ibid.*, p. 188 (Italics mine.)

34. Royce, *Studies of Good and Evil*, p. 203.

35. Royce, *The World and the Individual* II, p. 195n.

36. *Ibid.*, p. 195.

37. *Ibid.*, p. 198; cf. Heidegger, *Being and Time*, sec. 69b.

38. Royce, *Studies of Good and Evil*, p. 129.

39. *Ibid.*, p. 127.

40. Royce, *The World and the Individual*, II, p. 197.

41. *Ibid.*, I, p. 409.

42. Josiah Royce, *William James and Other Essays on the Philosophy of Life* (New York: The Macmillan Company, 1911), p. 267. (Hereafter abbreviated as *William James*).

43. Royce, *Fugitive Essays*, p. 251.

44. Royce, *Studies of Good and Evil*, p. 210.

45. Royce, *The World and the Individual*, II, pp. 132–33.

46. *Ibid.*, p. 133.

47. One might note that Royce's developed notion of interpretation as over-arching perceptual and conceptual activity comes close to Heidegger's own interpretation of Kant's 'transcendental imagination' as "the common root" of sensibility and understanding, and of practical reason as well. Cf. my *Heidegger, Kant and Time* (Bloomington: Indiana University Press, 1971), esp. chap. VI.

48. Royce, *The World and the Individual*, II, p. 132.

49. *Ibid.*, p. 133.

50. *Ibid.*, p. 141.

51. *Ibid.*, I, p. 425.

52. Royce, *William James*, p. 283.

53. Royce, *The World and the Individual*, II, p. 240.

54. Royce, *William James*, p. 263.

55. Royce, *The World and the Individual*, II, p. 374.

56. See, e.g., *ibid.*: for "God does not temporally foreknow anything, excepting in so far as it is expressed in us finite beings." Thus the total encompassing vision of all time is "ill-called foreknowledge. It is eternal knowledge."

57. Heidegger, *Being and Time*, II, V, n. xiii, p. 499.

58. *Ibid.*, pp. 471-72.

59. Royce, *William James*, p. 254.

60. *Ibid.*, p. viii.

61. Gabriel Marcel, *Royce's Metaphysics*, trans. by V. and G. Ringer (Chicago: Henry Regnery Company, 1956), p. xii.

62. Rather than being a restatement of Hegel's Absolute Idealism, Royce seems to have taken inspiration for this from Leibniz, whom Royce credits, despite some severe criticism, for having seen that "the assumed and pre-established harmony. . . [tends] to lapse into a view for which the ideal relations of the Monads, their significant unity as members of the one City of God, becomes the innermost truth of the universe." (*The World and the Individual*, II, 238.)

CHAPTER VII

EXPERIENCE GROWS BY ITS EDGES:[1]
A PHENOMENOLOGY OF RELATIONS
IN AN AMERICAN PHILOSOPHICAL VEIN

John J. McDermott (Texas A & M University)

> All my knowledge of the world, even my scientific knowledge is gained from my own particular point of view, or from some experience of the world without which the symbols of science would be meaningless.[2]

Maurice Merleau-Ponty

It is to take a precarious and even treacherous path to begin an essay on philosophy with an acknowledgement of one's "own particular view." Foundationalism, in either its Cartesian or contemporary analytic formulation, forbids such an allegedly subjective point of departure. Yet it is precisely here that phenomenology and classical American philosophy share both assumptions and endeavor. And both traditions can resonate to the description of phenomenology by Merleau-Ponty:

> The opinion of the responsible philosopher must be that *phenomenology can be practiced and identified as a manner or style of thinking, that it existed as a movement before arriving at complete awareness of itself as a philosophy.*[3]

Both American pragmatism and phenomenology have been called methods rather than philosophies. So be it. Practitioners of both know the differences which exist between pragmatism and phenomenology. Despite these acknowledged differences, some have made efforts to close the gap or at least to stress similarities.[4]

Robert S. Corrington, Carl Hausman, & Thomas M. Seebohm, eds., *Pragmatism Considers Phenomenology,* Washington, D. C.: Center for Advanced Research in Phenomenology & University Press of America, 1987.

My own predilection on this issue, if I can be forgiven a violation of the ostensible objectivity now required in philosophical discussion, comes to this. Phenomenology has taught me to take things, attitudes, ambience, and relations straight up, with no excuses. I pay little attention to the famous Husserlian bracket, which seeks for the pure essence of things, for I regard such efforts in his work and those of his followers as a form of epistemological self-deception, a result of the rigid science it deplores in a fruitless search for true objectivity. To the contrary, nothing, nothing, is ever totally bracketed, for leaks are everywhere.[5]

Yet the effort of phenomenology is salutary. Pay attention, says the phenomenologist. I listen to that warning. Intentionally, pay attention, says the phenomenologist. I listen more intently. This attending to the flow of experience is multisensorial, for it involves not only hearing but feeling, touching, seeking, smelling and tasting as well. What, then, is it for a human being to be in the world?

I

Taken straight out, and day by night, to be in the world is not to be inert, a thing among things, a bump on a log. However surprising for the tradition of Aristotelian natural place and Newtonian mechanics, quantum physics merely confirms the multiple processing which is endemic to the activity of the human organism. Merleau-Ponty writes:

> Our own body is in the world as the heart is in the organism: it keeps the visible spectacle constantly alive, it breathes life into it and sustains it inwardly, and with it forms a system.[6]

We do not fit into the world as a Lego or a Lincoln log. In fact, I believe that we have no *special* place in the organic constituency of nature. Our consciousness, so different, so extraordinary, so bizzare, especially in its dream state, is a marvelous and pockmarked perturbation of the eonic history of DNA. Following Dewey, we are in, of, and about nature. We are nature's creature, its consciousness, its conscience, however aberrant and quixotic; its organizer, namer, definer, and defiler; a transient in search of an implacable, probably unrealizable, final consummation. The human organism is surrounded, permeated, and contexted by both the natural and social environment. In speaking of William James's doctrine of the self as a relational manifold,

John E. Smith writes: "Radical empiricism is a radically new account of how the self penetrates and is penetrated by the world."[7]

The way in which the human self abides in the world is an extraordinarily complex affair. The self projects itself into the world. The self constructs a personal world, a habitation. The self, when threatened, retreats, even attempts to eject from the world, a form of dropping out. The rhythm of these transactions is often lost in the macroscopic setting of getting through the day. The algorithmic subtleties of our movements, shifts in attitude, and construction, deconstruction, setting, shifting, and bypassing of barriers are often buried in the frequently graceless syntax of duties, obligations, and habituations. So typical are our routines that the virtually infinite number of plans, plots, and variations in the rhythm of our bodily movements are lost to our attention. Recent investigations in biochemistry, especially in the human liver and in cell surface and molecular biology, reveal an utterly extraordinary network. The electron microscope has revealed a dazzling array of complexity in an endless chain of relationships. The human skin is a battleground of bacteria colonies, symbiotic, voracious, and with long memories, as found in the unerring recurrence of dermatitis, repeatedly appearing on an isolated finger or toe, over and again.[8]

The phenomenological approach to the "lived body" has been an auspicious point of departure for philosophical speculation. The arrival of phenomenological and existentialist literature after the Second World War was a bracing antidote to the positivism and logical empiricism of the emigres from the Vienna Circle. As early as 1958, Rollo May and others introduced us to the empiricism of phenomenological psychiatry and existential analysis.[9] Following the path set by Ludwig Binswanger, Kurt Goldstein, and indirectly by Aron Gurwitsch, Richard Zaner correctly sees the medical model as the most propitious for understanding the activity of the human body, since it exaggerates medical case histories, which cast light on the hidden drama of simply being in the world as a body, as an organism, and as a conscious person.

For most of us, most of the time, being in the world has an obviousness to it. We move about, little aware of our gait, presence, and interruptive activities. From time to time an event, a startle, a happening, will jog us to immediate consciousness. A snake in the yard, a tarantula in the bathtub, or the rolling red neon lights of a police cruiser at our front door is required if we are to shake off our studied state of mesmerism, of ontological lethargy.

From 1916 until 1927, a pandemic swept the European continent. Technically called *Encephalitis lethargica*, it is known to us as sleeping sickness. Its victims numbered in the millions and very few avoided death. Those who did slumbered on, kinaesthetically anonymous, until the advent of the drug L-dopa, prescribed in the later 1960's. The subsequent 'awakenings' have been described in a brilliant book by the neurologist Oliver Sacks.[10] In contrast to the way most of us are in the world, moving about in our unreflective, programmed way, I offer you, courtesy of Sacks, the movements of Lillian T., who, when she awoke, found her bodily movements, in an understatement, to be a chore. Burdened by violent "head movements" as a result of the pharmacological therapy, she was never in control of her body by instinct, only by detailed plotting. Sacks details her attempt to simply move from one place to another.

One such patient had managed to maintain an independent life outside institutions for years, in face of almost incredible difficulties – difficulties which would instantly have broken a less determined or resourceful person. This patient – Lillian T. – had long since found that she could scarcely start, or stop, or change her direction of motion; that once she had been set in motion, she had no control. It was therefore necessary for her to plan all her motions in advance, with great precision. Thus, moving from her armchair to her divan-bed (a few feet to one side) could never be done *directly* - Miss. T. would immediately be 'frozen' in transit, and perhaps stay frozen for half an hour or more. She therefore had to embark on one of two courses of action: in either case, she would rise to her feet, arrange her angle of direction exactly, and shout "Now!", whereupon she would break into an incontinent run, which could be neither stopped nor changed in direction. If the double doors between her living-room and the kitchen were open, she would rush through them, across the kitchen, round the back of the stove, across the other side of the kitchen, through the double doors – in a great figure-of-eight – until she hit her destination, her bed. If, however, the double doors were closed and secured, she would calculate her angle like a billiard-player, and then launch herself with great force against the doors, rebounding at the right angle to hit her bed. Miss T.'s apartment (and, to some extent, her mind) resembled the control room for the Apollo launchings, at Houston, Texas: all paths and trajectories pre-computed and compared, contingency plans and "fail-safes" prepared in advance. A good deal of Miss T.'s life, in short, was dependent on conscious taking-care and elaborate calculation - but this was the only way she could maintain her existence.[11]

Sacks also details the baleful motile effects of Parkinson's disease. The person afflicted with festination is subject to "forced hurrying of walking, talking, speech or thought" and takes steps which "tend to become smaller and smaller, until finally the patient is 'frozen' - stepping internally, but with no space to step in."[12]

A case history of a different kind is also illuminating. Reported by A. R. Luria, the distinguished Russian psychologist, it details the recovery efforts of a young soldier who was wounded with a bullet to the brain. He suffered "impairment of vision, loss of memory and the ability to speak, read and write."[13] This man, Zasetsky, made a heroic effort to retrieve his faculties. Over a twenty-five year period, he wrote of his journey to possible recovery. The result is a 3,000 word document, or no more than 120 words per year, for twenty-five years. By contrast, the present essay is 6,000 words and was written in four weeks, without either the human or clinical significance of that by Mr. Zasetsky. The space-time-place-object relationships that you and I take for granted were for our brain-wounded colleague a nightmare. Zasetsky reports on some disasters in doing the obvious:

> When the doctor learned what my first name was, he'd always address me that way and try to shake hands when he came over. But I couldn't manage to clasp his hand. He'd try it a second time, but as luck would have it, I'd forget I had a right hand since I couldn't see it. Suddenly I'd remember and try to shake hands again but would only manage to touch his fingers. He'd let go of my hand and try once more. But I still wasn't able to do it, so he'd take my hand and show me how.
>
> Ever since I was wounded I've had trouble sometimes sitting down in a chair or on a couch. I first look to see where the chair is, but when I try to sit down I suddenly make a grab for the chair since I'm afraid I'll land on the floor. Sometimes that happens because the chair turns out to be further to one side than I thought.

Luria comments:

> These "spatial peculiarities" were particularly distressing when he was sitting at a table. He'd try to write

and be unable to control a pencil, not knowing how to hold
it. He encountered similar problems in the hospital workshops
where he went for occupational therapy, hoping he'd be given
some work to do and thus convince himself he could be useful,
fit for some kind of job. There, too, he was up against
precisely the same difficulties.

Zasetsky continues:

> The instructor gave me a needle, spool of thread, some
> material with a pattern on it, and asked me to try to stitch
> the pattern. Then he went off to attend to other patients –
> people who'd had their arms or legs amputated after being
> wounded, of half their bodies paralyzed. Meanwhile, I just
> sat there with the needle, thread, and material in my hands
> wondering why I'd been given these; I sat for a long time and
> did nothing. Suddenly the instructor came over and asked:
> "Why are you just sitting there? Go ahead and thread the
> needle!" I took the thread in one hand, the needle in the
> other, but couldn't understand what to do with them. How was
> I to thread the needle? I twisted it back and forth but
> hadn't the slightest idea what to do with any of these
> things.
> When I first looked at those objects, but hadn't yet
> picked them   up, they seemed perfectly familiar – there was
> no reason to think about them. But as soon as I had them in
> my hands, I was at a loss to figure out what they were for.
> I'd lapse into a kind of stupor and wouldn't be able to
> associate these two objects in my mind – it was as though I'd
> forgotten why they existed. I twisted the needle and thread
> in my hands but couldn't understand how to connect the two –
> how to fit the thread in the needle.
> And then another annoying thing happened. By then I'd
> already   learned what a needle, thread, thimble, and
> material were for and had some vague notion of how to use
> them. But I couldn't for the life of   me think of the names
> for these or other objects people had pointed out to me. I'd
> sit there stitching the material with the needle, completely
> unable to remember what the very things I was using were
> called.
> The first time I entered the shop and saw people working
> there,   I noticed various things – a workbench, a slab of
> wood, a plane – and   I thought I recognized these objects
> and knew what they were called. But when I was actually given
> a plane and a slab of wood, I fiddled with them for quite a

while before some of the other patients showed me how to use these and other tools. I started to sand some wood but never learned to do it right, never did it get sanded. Each time I'd try, the surface would come out lopsided and crooked or had pits and bumps in it. And what's more, I got tired very quickly. While I was sanding the wood or looking at some of the other tools in the carpentry shop (a block of wood or a workbench) it was the same old story - I couldn't remember what any of these was used for.

When I went to a workshop to learn shoemaking, the instructor explained everything to me in great detail, since he was convinced I was very muddled and thick-headed and didn't know the first thing about making shoes. He showed me how to hold a hammer, drive nails in and pull them out, but all I learned to do was drive wooden nails into a board and pull them out again. And even then that was hard, because I couldn't see where the nails were supposed to go but kept missing the spot and banging my fingers until they bled. And I was very, very slow at it. So the only thing they let me do was bang nails into a board. [14]

Cases such as Lillian T. and Mr. Zasetsky abound in the literature and, tragically, in the everyday - our neighbors, friends and family. They are a witness to the indolent response we have to our everyday movements, perfunctory and blind to the gift that a healthy DNA double helix awards to us, idiosyncratically. These extreme versions of what it takes to be in the world, versions which are extremely intensified by anyone who has had experience with the handicapped, are intensive role models for our untapped capacities and sensibilities. The richness of the every-day, had we the will to savor our possibilities, would far exceed our fantasies. Indeed, our penchant for the fantastic is but an indictment of how casual and unreflective has become our daily posture in a world which screeches at us, though we hear not.

Classical American philosophy, represented by James and Dewey, offers us some insight in the way in which we are in the world. James stresses human energy, human proclivity, and human daring. His self is Promethean: making, constructing, reconstruc-ting and bold in its effort to transcend the accepted conceptual frames of human experience, which often tie us down, and are often chary of suspension of disbelief. James invokes the "will to believe" as an antidote to our premature resignation to limits in the variety, reach, or implication of our experiences. Acceptance of the routine, the humdrum and the obvious results in a flaccid, inert, and dull personal presence. James writes:

Some men and women, indeed, there are who can live on smiles and the word "yes" forever. But for others (indeed for most), this is too tepid and relaxed a moral climate. Passive happiness is slack and insipid, and soon grows mawkish and intolerable. Some austerity and wintry negativity, some roughness, danger, stringency, and effort, some "no! no!" must be mixed in, to produce the sense of an existence with character and texture and power.[15]

As described by James, especially in his *Principles of Psychology*, the human self is Promethean and picaresque: a venturesome, risk-oriented, and experimental prober into the widest and furthest reaches of the flow of experience. John Dewey accepts this profile as an ideal. Dewey, for example, believes "If it is better to travel than arrive, it is because traveling is a constant arriving, while arrival that precludes further traveling is most easily attained by going to sleep or dying."[16] Yet Dewey, a proletarian, in contrast to James, a New England Brahmin, realizes that the traveling is not done by an isolated self. To the contrary, Dewey's sense of a person being in the world is conflicted by the vagaries of natural forces and above all, by the bottom line admission that we are social selves, contexted, conditioned, herded, institutionalized, and tradition-laden. Despite the attraction of James's Promethean self, the cautions of Dewey with regard to the trappings that work on us as we confront the human condition must be taken with seriousness. One may lament the absence of an aboriginal approach to being in the world; but lamentation does not obviate the hard, irrepressible facticity of natural and social conditioning, a context provided throughout the work of John Dewey and George Herbert Mead.

One can posit still a third version of our being in the world, although the American intellectual scene pays little attention to it: that of the cosmological. In truth, James is right. We must seek to be prepossessive and creative in our dealings with the world in which we find ourselves. Yet Dewey is also correct in his stressing of the natural and social ambience which restricts our doings, limits our travelings, and short-circuits our desires. Still, not by the planet Earth alone do we live. In our time, increasingly, the stellar has become accessible to us and the vaunted mystery of the moon, now an extended neighborhood. Contemporary astral physics has enhanced our reach a millionfold. Although our new and approximate knowledge of the age and extent of the universe has been dwarfing in the ultimate sense, nonetheless, paradoxically, the human odyssey takes on the hue of a remarkably novel and originally self-conscious presence in an otherwise vast, unfeeling, unknowing, and uncaring panoply of sheerly natural events. Extraterrestrial consciousness is a possibility, but we have no evidence. Until such appears, the universe is not aware of itself except for the activity of human life. Merleau-Ponty tells us that "because we are in the world, we are *condemned to meaning*, and we cannot do or say anything without its acquiring a name in history."[17]

The task of building a liberating human future, as I foresee it, assumes the Promethean self of James, the social sophistication of Dewey, Mead, the Marxists and cultural anthropology, all rendered within a burgeoning social cosmology. That task, of course, remains to be done. For now, let us start at the beginning and discuss the lineaments of the potentially Promethean self and the dangers therein. The key to such a consideration is the under-standing of relations, as first proposed by William James in his doctrine of radical empiricism.[18]

II

For James, and subsequently for Dewey, the human self is urged to build a personal world, although not as *ab ovo*. Rather this personal world is to be built in response to the "push and press of the cosmos," as James would have it, or, as Dewey suggested as a response to the irreducible and ineluctable problematic which resides at the very point of transaction of the human organism with nature. Rather than there being one world, which we acknowledge from an alleged separately distant place, we have a series of worlds as constructs, as mock-ups. In the words of the neo-pragmatist Nelson Goodman, there are "ways of worldmaking," which he calls "versions and visions."[19] Anticipating modern quantum physics, James sees the world as a relational webbing with objects as results of our conceptual intrusion, rather than as fixed givens in an already structured setting. Referring to essences as "*teleological weapons of the mind*"[20] and affirming that "*there is no property ABSOLUTELY essential to any one thing*,"[21] James inverts the classical assumption that the world comes as given and need but be defined, denoted, and arranged. To the contrary, what we take to be objects in common parlance are bundles of relations, gathered first conceptually and then, by habit, perceptually. Speaking of the names of things -- in this case, a painting - Michel Foucault criticizes the supposed one-to-one correspondence between our language and the object.

And the proper name, in this context, is merely an artifice: it gives us a finger to point with, in other words, to pass surrepti tiously from the space where one speaks to the space where one looks; in other words, to fold one over the other as if they were equi valents.[22]

In modern art, the names of the paintings are often but place-holders, vestibules for entry into a world of relations that prevent any denomination or definition. If we could break the lock had on us by our inherited syntactical conceptual scheme, we could come to see, hear, feel, smell, and taste bundles of relations, rather than objects, hardly more alive than the nouns used to name them. I believe that James is right. Aboriginally, the world is not made up of objects but rather is a continuum of concatenated relations. Scandalous though it may be to those for whom logic tells the only truth, if we were to focus on a single object and detail its relations, we would have access to a perceptual entail- ment which would involve us in everything that exists. Unfortunately, we do not even attempt this, for as James notes, "We actually ignore most of the things before us."[23] Far less do we follow the relational leads which spring from these linguistically ordained things. When alert, we do better. James describes our active sense life in the following way:

Out of what is in itself an undistinguishable, swarming *continuum*, devoid of distinction or emphasis, our senses make for us, by at tending to this motion and ignoring that, a world full of contrasts, of sharp accents, of abrupt changes, of picturesque light and shade.[24]

The way in which an object is denoted on the macroscopic scale is due to one or more functional characteristics, for example, shape, size, texture, color, odor, place in space, or mobility. Once having been designated, except for occasional aesthetic considerations, the object falls into a class of conceptually identical companions: chair, glass, book. Thus we repress or ignore the relational run in every object, as in *this* book, with *that* kind of paper, smell, size, and as found on *this* table in *that* room in *this* house on *that* street in *this* neighborhood, county, state, region, country, hemisphere, planet, solar system, galaxy, and pluriverse. There is no doubt that we cut off the relations. The important question has to do with both *what* relations are cut and *how* we cut them. Who was the first human being to eat a lobster? Surely a more foreboding and less appetizing creature has not appeared to the culinary search. Yet, as with sheep brains, pigs' feet, and squid, the human being, here and there, follows a different relational trail. In those cases, relational plurality leads to delight and leaves the definition of pleasing as simply not sufficient for the longer reach.

If we were to follow each thing and event to its full perceptual implication, we would explode from experiential overload. James gives us a taste of this when he writes:

> Only in some pitiful dreamer, some philosopher, poet, or romancer, or when the common practical man becomes a lover, does the hard externality give way, and a gleam of insight into the ejective world, as Clifford called it, the vast world of inner life beyond us, so different from that of outer seeming, illuminate our mind. Then the whole scheme of our customary values gets confounded, then our self is riven and its narrow interests fly to pieces, then a new centre and a new perspective must be found.[25]

Cutting off relations is therefore necessary for personal survival. But how do we cut? Do we snip and leave a small wound which heals in time? Do we hack and leave a gaping wound which festers and, when closed, leaves an unsightly scar? Do we fold over the rejected relation, biding time until we can recover and savor it? Do we let the relational lead or inference dangle, awaiting a propitious moment to reconnoiter and relive its possibility? Do we send the relation on a journey, hoping for a return? Or do we give it a one-way ticket? Finally, do we bury the relation, hoping for its continued interment, although worried about periodic reappearance through the cracks in our vulnerable psyche?

The world we build is exactly akin to the way we cut relations, indulge relations, and celebrate relations. More, our world takes off as novel and as distinctively ours precisely in response to how we make new relations of the relations already at work in the environ in which we find ourselves. It is clear, although not for the present setting, that the way we best understand this activity of making relations is to pursue the life of the young child. Genetic epistemology has much to teach us, for children naturally make their own relations until we teach them that the world has already been named and properly codified. Against their aboriginal bent, they are told to march in step, name by name, definition by definition, until they too see the world as an extension of local grammar and hidebound conceptual designations. The social and moral result of this aberrant pedagogy is deleterious, as stressed, for example, by Merleau-

Ponty in his discussion of the presence of "psychological rigidi-
ty" as a lamentable but typical characteristic of young
children.[26] Yet for both young children and adults who are or who
wish to become alive to possibilities heretofore undreamt, the
making of relations is the way to build a distinctively personal
world. I turn now to detail some of the obstacles to a salutary
making of relations.

III

Being in the world is not a cakewalk. Our surroundings,
personal, natural and social, are fraught with potential
deception, actual invasion, and an omnipresent indifference. To
make a world as distinctively ours, by the making of relations, is
too often a rarity. The other-directedness made famous by David
Riesman and his colleagues in *The Lonely Crowd*[27] can be raised to
the status of an ontological category. In ideal terms, a person
comes to consciousness and begins to work out one's place, one's
version, and one's taste for this or that. Yet we now know that
the burgeoning self is fraught with personal freight: genetic,
familial, linguistic, bodily, climatic, ethnic, gender, racial,
and even the subtleties of gait, weight, and smile. As I see it,
the fundamental challenge is to convert the personal weaknesses
into strengths and to drive our strengths into the teeth of a
personally neutral but relatively pregnant world. The ancient
philosophers, especially the Stoics and the Epicureans, offered
sage advice on how to be in the world without getting maced. Taken
overall, their warnings focused on the dangers of excess,
indolence, and self-aggrandizement.[28] This was and is wise
counsel. The intervening 2,000 years, however, have bequeathed a
far more sophisticated environment as a setting for the
constructing of a personal world. The dangers, the traps, and the
obstacles are more subtle, more extensive, and more seductive than
they were in antiquity.

The scriptural rhetorical question, Lord, what must I do to
be saved? can be reinvoked by our children as follows: What shall
I do to make a world which is personally mine, although it
inheres, coheres, borrows and lends to others who are making a
world personally their own? Couched more indirectly, this is the
question that our children and our students ask us. The initial
response is obvious. Make relations! Build, relate, and then
reflect. Reflect, relate and then build. Seek novelty, leave no
stone unturned. Fasten on colors, shapes, textures, sounds, odors,
sights. Above all, never close down until the fat person sings.
The only acceptable denouement is death. Until then all signs are

go, that is, make relations until the maker is unmade. Still, in the making of relations, dangers lurk. We detail them as follows:

1. *Relation Starvation*

Stinginess is omnipresent in the human condition, as anyone who has lived on "tips" will attest. The novel experience carries for some of us a warning signal. We are often suspicious of the new, an unfamiliar face, a turn in the road, a break in the routine. We tend to huddle with the familiar. Even the more flamboyant of us have our schedule, our pigeon-hole for person and event. Novelty is unsettling. We prefer the familiar, the recognizable, the repetitive, for that awards personal control. In time, everything is forced to resemble something else, something prior, something already experienced. Have not I seen you before? Have not I heard you before? Repetition becomes so comforting that genuine novelty is reduced to prior experience. The width of our vision shrinks. We become more defensive about what we already know. We become less open to what we do not know.

Relation starvation is the incarnation of the *a priori.* All that happens has happened, for us, before. At least we think so. And that is because we focus only on familiarity, sameness. The novel is repressed, transformed into the familiar. We tend to chatter, over and over, about our experiences, warding off the novelty brought to us by others. We become monologic rather than open to dialogue and to those potentially liberating, yet frightening and unfamiliar experiences out of our ken. We become shrill, repetitive, and overindulgent of the significance of our own past. Others' histories hold no interest for us, for they become indices of our deprivation rather than as communal undergoings to share, however vicariously. The more committed we become to the significance of our own experiences, the less capacity we have to participate in the experiences of others. In time, the ultimate bane of human health emerges, jealousy. We soon become trapped in our own world, one which is shrinking, increasingly lonely and overesteemed. Relation-starved, we are less and less able to make relations, to break out, and build a world in which our personal style takes on meaning not by insularity but by contrast.

2. Relation Amputation

In making relations, we run the risk of being strung out. Granted that shutting out relational possibilities leads to relation starvation and an encapsulated self, yet in our counter effort to reach out, we often fail to read the map of possibilities. Knowing when to desist, to withdraw, and to close down is very difficult. How much testing is enough testing? How much experimentation is enough experimentation? The explosive world of pharmacological nostrums is constantly blind-sided by late-appearing side effects. Pesticides, thalidomide, birth control pills, L-dopa and countless other substances bequeath later "hits," events which are severely damaging to human life and which on retrospect call for earlier amputation.

On the one hand, risk is often avoided at the expense of possibility and breakthrough. The human odyssey is replete with stories of those courageous persons who defied the present data in favor of that which might emerge if one were to take the next step. One must never be cavalier. Nonetheless, surprise often awaits us as we forge a relationship heretofore banned or simply unthought. The burden is that we must learn to read the signs of implicitness. An early amputation of a lead will throw us back into the obvious. Persistence in following a relational possibility beyond its capacity to ameliorate and sustain the worth of the risk of the endeavor is foolhardy. We should not hang back and endorse the accepted slavishly. Premature amputation denies the long-standing historical message that taking a chance is usually fortuitous. Cut when necessary, but not out of fright or habit.

3. Relation Saturation

There are those of us who get the message that the making of relations is liberating. For some, this awareness turns into a frenetic activity of multiple involvement, as though the quantity of experience was sure to insure a significant life. We face here an overindulgence in the having of experiences, as though one need not bring to bear a reflective self in these transactions. Most often, those persons whose lives have been constricted by mores, repressions and systemic habituation, upon the opportunity to break it open, respond with alacrity. New experiences are collected like hash-marks. We become impervious to their significance, their dangers, their relationships to our past, our person, and our future. Unreflective in anticipation, undergoing and retrospection, these experiences follow one after the other into an unknowing bin, marked only - accomplishment. The relations, the potential implications, tumble about shy of significance and of no import to either our person or our prospects.

Relation saturation describes the fate of the person who eats without tasting. It is a relation-saturated person whose sexual activity is more characterized by a desire to do it again than to experience the doing of it in the first place. The depth of a single relation, the mastery of a technique or an instrument, as in the cello of Pablo Casals, is lost to the saturator. Endless variation replaces the nectar of a rich, single experience. The relation-saturator writes his or her autobiography at a tender age, failing to realize that it is subsequent personal history which casts genuine light on the relative importance of events once undergone without reflection. Sheer quantity of experience is misleading in its import. Following John Dewey, "Everything depends on the *quality* of the experience which is had."[29]

4. Relation Seduction

William James was fond of urging us to live on the fringe, beyond the ken of normal, everyday experience. To that end, he experienced with hallucinogens and spent considerable time in pursuing investigation of the claims made on behalf of extrasensory perception. James was also fascinated by persons who claimed to attain extraordinary insight by virtue of religious, aesthetic, or even dietary experiences. He found saints, yogis, and clairvoyants of equal fascination. For James, the present reach of the normal consciousness was puerile when compared with what he regarded as possibilities as yet unseen except by a few unusually bold and gifted persons.

Actually, James points to a double fringe. The first we have discussed, for it refers to the implicitness hidden in every object, event, and situation. That fringe is the ongoing relational leads which we too often prematurely cut in the name of obviousness and definition. The second fringe is more fascinating and more dangerous. Some persons are driven by the temptation to transcend the boundaries of common experience and belief. Through rhetoric and intense, single-minded commitment, they fasten on a vision of reality not given to the rest of us. Rooted in political or religious belief, this commitment can be liberating for others, but it can also be a snare of major self-deception. For every Abraham, Jesus, Mohammed, Marx, and Nietzsche, there are hundreds of self-benighted souls who become so enamored of their personal goal that they find themselves cut off from the stark claim of reality.

Still more dangerous is the fringe which is accessible by means of pharmacology. Mind-altering drugs are now a fact of public and familial life.[30] Yet the leap over the relational to experiences which are literally *de novo* and beyond normal capacity tends to freeze in a world of experience that has no connection with our body, our things, and our space-time relations normally undergone. I do not deny that the trip to the fringe is exhilarating. The question is whether one can ever return without experiencing severe depression in response to the comparative tawdriness of the everyday. The trouble with relation seduction, be it local fanaticism on behalf of a visionary goal or be it pharmacologically induced, is that it is addictive and therefore more manacling than liberating.

5. Relation Repression

Often we have experiences which are potentially threatening to our well-being, at least as we conceive it to be so. Instead of allowing these experiences to play out their hand, we repress them. The relational implications of the experience cannot be severed once and for all. Rather they are shoved down into the labyrinth of our unconscious but nonetheless active self. We act as if we were in a World War I pillbox complete with flamethrowers, burning out the ground around us. Bunkered down, we seem to feel on top of things. And that is precisely the problem. The repressed experiences take on a life of their own, sifting their way up and into the nooks and crannies of our conscious life, designated here as our stomach, nervous system, dreams, tics and temperament.

In the terminology of classical psychoanalysis, relation repression is often discussed under the rubric of trauma. Franz Kafka traces his comparative creative and interpersonal impotence to such an event. In a letter to his father, typically and fittingly not sent, Kafka tells of an event which set the stage for his life-long sense of alienation. As a very young child, Franz annoyed his father by constantly demanding attention while a guest was in the apartment. After repeated warnings, his father seized him and placed him outside on the *pavlatche*, the outside ledge, closing the doors on Franz in his pajamas. Locked out, cut off, and bewildered, Kafka concluded that "I was a mere nothing for him." This event, repressed and never worked out, did him "inner harm."[31] Even the final revealing of the event was posthumous and to an audience who knew neither Kafka nor his father. Such relation repression, repeated over and over in our own lives, is baleful and insidious.

IV

Being in the world is not a position of stasis. It is active, energizing, and potentially creative. Of course, it can also be enervating, treacherous and self-deceiving. For those of us who wish to become persons, the world does not come ready-made. The doctrine of natural place was a provincial fallout from the enclosed geography and cosmology of the Greek world of Aristotle, a point made in detail by Heidegger.[32] Our world is infinitely more expansive, more complex, more furtive, more demanding, and, if we have the will, more rewarding. The lattice-work of nature is intriguing. Still more intriguing is the set of relations which we ourselves fashion, knead, and impose.

Most of us have barely scratched the surface in our efforts to build a truly personal world. And few of us bequeath the ability to make relations to our children, choosing rather to pass on a shopworn box of maxims, shorn of relational excitement. On behalf of our possibilities, I tell you the story of a Polish mathematician. Our colleague, something of a dissident within the last decade, was arrested and placed in solitary confinement. He was left to himself with only a slop pail for company, having been refused his request for a pencil and paper. Seeking to keep personally alive, he did mathematical formulae in his head. Shorn of physical replication, he soon began to repeat the same mathematical relations, over and over, until they became frayed from repetition and lack of novelty. When released several years later, he said that he was about to eat his brain, for he had run out of relations and had no new formulae to revivify the inherited and so stalk out new ground. Surely, surrounded by the richest of novel possibilities, we can do as well. Or can we, oh we of little faith in the prevalence of surprise?

NOTES

This essay also appears in John J. McDermott, *Streams of Experience: Reflections on the Philosophy and History of Culture* (University of Massachussets Press, 1986).

1. The full passage from which title of this chapter is taken can be found in William James, *Essays in Radical Empiricism* (Cambridge: Harvard University Press, 1976), p. 42.

2. Maurice Merleau-Ponty, *Phenomenology of Perception*, trans. Colin Smith (New York: The Humanities Press, 1962), p. viii.

3. *Ibid.*, p. viii. (Emphasis in the original.)

4. Cf. Sandra B. Rosenthal and Patrick L. Bourgeois, *Pragmatism and Phenomenology: A Philosophic Encounter* (Amsterdam: B. R. Grüner Publishing Co., 1980). Pioneer efforts in this direction were provided by the work of James M. Edie. See, his "Introduction" to Pierre Thevenaz, *What is Phenomenology? and Other Essays* (Chicago: Quadrangle Books, 1962), pp. 13-36; "Notes on the Philosophical Anthropology of William James," in *An Invitation to Phenomenology*, ed. James M. Edie (Chicago: Quadrangle Books, 1965), pp. 110-132; and Bruce Wilshire, *William James and Phenomenology* (Bloomington: Indiana University Press, 1968).

5. Cf. John Dewey, "Having an Experience," in *The Philosophy of John Dewey*, ed. John J. McDermott, Vol. 2 (Chicago: The University of Chicago Press, 1981), p. 555. Dewey writes here of the inchoate, of the "distractions," "dispersions," "extraneous interruption" and "inner lethargy" which dog all of our attendings.

6. Merleau-Ponty, *Phenomenology of Perception*, p. 203.

7. John E. Smith, "The Course of American Philosophy," in *Themes in American Philosophy: Purpose, Experience and Community* (New York: Harper Torchbooks, 1970), p. 135.

8. Cf. Arthur Bentley, "The Human Skin: Philosophy's Last Line of Defense," in *Inquiry into Inquiries* (Boston: Beacon Press, 1954), pp. 195-211.

9. Cf. Rollo May *et al.*, *Existence* (New York: Basic Books, 1958), especially "The Case of Ellen West," pp. 237-364. Subsequent steps in a phenomenology of the body have been taken in *The Philosophy of the Body*, ed. Stuart Spicker (Chicago: Quadrangle Books, 1970), and in Richard M. Zaner, *The Context of Self: A Phenomenological Inquiry Using Medicine as a Clue* (Athens: Ohio University Press, 1981).

10. Oliver Sacks, *Awakenings* (New York: E. P. Dutton, 1983).

11. *Ibid.*, p. 316.

12. *Ibid.*, p. 328.

13. Cf. A. R. Luria, *The Man with a Shattered World* (New York: Basic Books, 1972).

14. *Ibid.*, pp. 46-49.

15. William James, *The Varieties of Religious Experience* (New York: Longmans, Green and Co., 1902), pp. 298-299.

16. John Dewey, *Human Nature and Conduct*, vol. 14 (1983) of *The Middle Works* (Carbondale: Southern Illinois University Press, 1976-1983), p. 195.

17. Merleau-Ponty, *Phenomenology of Perception*, p. xix (italics in the original).

18. For a discussion of James's radical empiricism, cf. Smith, *Themes*, pp. 26-41; and John J. McDermott, "Introduction" to James, *Essays in Radical Empiricism*, pp. xi-xlviii.

19. Cf. Nelson Goodman, *Ways of Worldmaking* (Indianapolis: Hackett Publishing Company, 1978). Acknowledging the influence of James, Goodman writes: "Our universe, so to speak, consists of these ways rather than of a world or of worlds." (p. 3); "universes of worlds as well as worlds themselves may be built in many ways." (p. 5)

20. William James, *The Principles of Psychology*, vol. 2 (Cambridge: Harvard University Press, 1981), p. 961 (italics in the original).

21. *Ibid.*, p. 959 (italics and emphasis in the original).

22. Michel Foucault, *The Order of Things* (New York: Pantheon Books, 1970), p. 9. Cf. the ironically perceptive critique of the deception of words in Michel Foucault, *This Is Not A Pipe*, (Berkeley: University of California Press, 1982).

23. James, *Principles*, vol. 1, p. 273. See also William James, "The Stream of Thought," in *The Writings of William James*, ed. John J. McDermott (Chicago: University of Chicago Press, 1977), p. 70.

24. James, *Principles*, vol. I, p. 274. See also James, *Writings of William James*, p. 70.

25. William James, *Talks to Teachers on Psychology* (Cambridge: Harvard University Press, 1983), p. 138. See also, "On a Certain Blindness in Human Beings," in James, *Writings of William James*, p. 634.

26. Maurice Merleau-Ponty, *The Primacy of Perception*, ed. James M. Edie (Evanston: Northwestern University Press, 1964), pp. 100-108.

27. David Riesman *et al.*, *The Lonely Crowd* (New Haven: Yale University Press, 1950).

28. For an exquisite instance of a symbiotic relationship, witness that the jellyfish and the nudibranch in the Bay of Naples, as described by Lewis Thomas, *The Medusa and the Snail* (New York: Bantam Books, 1980), pp. 3-4:

> Sometimes there is such a mix-up about selfness that two creatures, each attracted by the molecular configuration of the other, incorporate the two selves to make a single organism. The best story I've ever heard about this is the tale told of the nudibranch and medusa living in the Bay of Naples. When first observed, the nudibranch, a common sea slug, was found to have a tiny vestigial parasite, in the form of a jellyfish, permanently affixed to the ventral surface near the mouth. In curiosity to learn how the medusa got there, some marine biologists began searching the local waters for earlier developmental forms, and discovered something amazing. The attached parasite, although apparently so specialized as to have given up living for itself, can still produce offspring, for they are found in abundance at certain seasons of the year. They drift through the upper waters,

grow up nicely and astonishingly, and finally become full-grown, handsome, normal jellyfish. Meanwhile, the snail produces snail larvae, and these too begin to grow normally, but not for long. While still extremely small, they become entrapped in the tentacles of the medusa and then engulfed within the umbrella-shaped body. At first glance, you'd believe the medusae are now the predators, paying back for earlier humiliations, and the snails the prey. But no. Soon the snails, undigested and insatiable, begin to eat, browsing away first at the radial canals, then the borders of the rim, finally the tentacles, until the jellyfish becomes reduced in substance by being eaten while the snail grows correspondingly in size. At the end, the arrangement is back to the first scene, with a full-grown nudibranch basking, and nothing left of the jellyfish except the round, successfully edited parasite, safely affixed to the skin near the mouth.

29. John Dewey, "The Need of a Theory of Experience," *The Philosophy of John Dewey*, Vol. 2, 508. (Italics in the original.)

30. Cf. R. E. L. Masters and Jean Houston, *The Varieties of Psyche-delic Experience* (New York: Dell Publishing Co., 1966).

31. Franz Kafka, *Letter to His Father* (New York: Shocken Books, 1953), p. 17.

32. Cf. Martin Heidegger, *What is a Thing?*, trans. W. B. Barton, Jr. and Vera Deutsch (South Bend: Gateway Editions, 1967), pp. 82-85.

CHAPTER   V I I I

HODGSON'S   INFLUENCE

ON   JAMES'S

ORGANIZATION   OF   EXPERIENCE

Charlene Haddock Seigfried (Purdue University)

Shadworth H. Hodgson, founder of the British Aristotelian Society and a voluminous writer, unfortunately now fallen into oblivion, was one of the earliest and continued life-long influences on William James.[1] A measure of the debt James felt he owed him can be gathered from his letter to Hodgson, January 1, 1910, in which he said that, in answer to a Belgium student asking him to name the sources of inspiration for his doctrine of pragmatism, he could recognize only two: Peirce and Hodgson, "with his method of attacking problems by asking what their terms are 'known as.'"[2]

In his privately bound collection of Hodgson's essays James singled out (and underlined part of) this sentence from "Common-Sense Philosophies": "We are brought back once again to the *same practical common-sense* of our starting point, the pre-philosophic attitude with which we originally confront the visible world."[3] Both Hodgson's striking re-working of the question of 'being' in terms of what being is 'known as' and the centrality of his re-working of common sense to his philosophic system seem to have greatly impressed James, if one may judge from James's own testimony, from his familiarity with many of Hodgson's writings, from the passages in Hodgson's works which he singled out, and from a careful comparison of their texts.

As usual, James's sources are filtered through his own preconceptions, which keep him from grasping them in their original integrity and work such a transformation on them that their originators frequently eschew their paternity. The passage about common sense, for instance, is given in the context of the infinite universe. Hodgson was saying: "In this infinite universe,

Robert S. Corrington, Carl Hausman, & Thomas M. Seebohm, eds. *Pragmatism Considers Phenomenology,* Washington, D. C.: Center for Advanced Research in Phenomenology & University Press of America, 1987.

the known or conceivable parts are everywhere surrounded and limited by an Unknown, out of which they arise, into which they pass, and to which they must be referred in respect both of their efficient and their final causation."[4]

James, strangely enough, does not seem to have equated Hodgson's "unknown" with Spencer's or with Royce's Infinite. He seems, instead, to have assimilated it to his own notion of a vague sense of "more," and it was only later that he realized that Hodgson was talking about an Absolute infinite.[5] Typically, James's originality, despite his voracious reading habits and frequent citations from the works of others, largely consists in his idiosyncratic appropriation of the material. As faithful expositor of the thoughts of others, he was a complete epigonic failure, but as revealing his own position, his misreadings are accurate renditions.

One of James's most challenging and puzzling innovations, the substitution in the *Principles of Psychology* of the passing thought for the ego, soul, principle of identity or center of action, can be better understood in relation to the Hodgson sources he is drawing on.[6] Hodgson is referred to, for instance, in the passage where James is seeking to explain how thought can appropriate its object, thought being the agent "vehicle of choice as well as of cognition." Such thought, being experiential "in a perfectly verifiable and phenomenal way," accomplishes from "the psychological or naturalistic point of view" what other philosophers try to explain from an associationist, transcendental or spiritual point of view (PP, I, p. 360, p. 401). Since thought can never be an object to itself, the only self it knows is past, and "thought may conceivably have no immediate knowledge of itself. . . . The present moment of consciousness is thus, as Mr. Hodgson says, the darkest in the whole series" (*ibid.*, p. 341). What it feels as its own immediate existence is the bodily part of its present Object of Thought. The bodily movements and feelings are the experiential 'kernel' into which the represented Self of personal identity is accreted. The 'I' and the 'me' are words of emphasis, useful in delineating aspects of thought, just as 'here' and 'now' are "distinctions possible in an exclusively *objective* field of knowledge" (*ibid.*). The influence of Hodgson is also acknowledged in the sections on "The Consciousness of Self," where these structures of thought, superimposed on the flux of thinking, are apparently taken to be retrospective and classificatory (*ibid.*, p. 347).

For James consciousness is always thought going on, and he rejects as scholastic subterfuge any appeal to a non-phenomenal world (PP, I, 359). James distinguishes between the 'me' as "an empirical aggregate of things objectively known" which is "always the bodily existence felt to be present at the time" and "a *Thought*, at each moment different from that of the last moment, but *appropriative* of the latter" (*ibid.*, pp. 400-401). Although obviously based on the Kantian distinction between the empirical and transcendental ego, James explains *both* phenomenologically, as experiential.

The passing thought can be experienced in that it is directly verifiable; one can prove that thought is going on. In any case, James points out that no one has denied that the passing thought is a directly verifiable existent, but various schools have disagreed about the relationship of the ego to that thought. James rejects the transcendental ego, for example, on the grounds that such a postulate is needed only if one denies any direct knowledge of the thought as such. But since we do experience thinking as such and, furthermore, can prove it, then there is no need for a metaphysical solution to a phenomenal problem. By 'proof' James means that "all the experiential facts find their place in this description" of each passing thought appropriating the immediately preceding thought, "unencumbered with any hypothesis save that of the existence of passing thoughts or states of mind" (PP, I, 401).

It seems that for James the passing thought that involves a consciousness of self is a valid scientific hypothesis because it makes sense of all the experiential data at hand, while the transcendental hypothesis fails because it explains away, rather than incorporates, experiential facts. He particularly repudiated the primary role of the transcendental ego – that of unifying otherwise chaotic impressions – because experience is always already organized in perception. Indeed, this is a founding fact in its appeal both to the chaotic multiplicity of impressions always available and the selective interest which carves out human worlds. There are many problems with this critique, as enunciated in the *Principles*, not the least of which is James's holding, simultaneously, that selective interest carves out personal worlds from an otherwise chaotic sea of impressions and that experience is always of an already ordered world of perceivable relations.[7] Another difficulty arises as soon as one tries to identify the subject of attribution of the practical and aesthetic interests which organize experience, since James says that the passing thought is organized according to these interests. Such attention picks out from the excess of possible impressions just those which will become objectified. But it makes more sense to attribute attention and interests to someone holistically rather than to a passing thought. The transcendental ego, once denuded of an explicit rationality and of subsumption to an all-inclusive ego, could perhaps still function as an historically justifiable term for such organization. By substituting the term "passing thought" for it, James intends an empirical reduction of the transcendental ego, but he is curiously blind to the very organizing function that his own explanation demands. If the denial of the transcendental ego is meant to attack the explanation that two things must be brought together by a third in order for 'a world' to exist, i.e., that an ego somehow 'within' the person must take impressions and organize them into objects by subsuming them under categories, then such a critique can be supported. But the fact that we find ourselves in an already organized world does not obviate the necessity of explaining how it comes to be organized. The appeal to the passing thought as an organizing principle is thus unsatisfactory.

It is difficult to make sense of James's appeal to the efficacy of causal agency while denying the substantial identity of the agent ego or self without examining the positions in Hodgson that he is drawing on. Why, for instance, does he insist that relations are found in experience, thereby rejecting both Kant's argument that relations must be organized by the transcendental ego and Hume's claim that experience originally consists of disconnected sense data, and nonetheless argue that attention, guided by aesthetic and practical interests, picks out from the big bloom-ing buzzing confusion just those aspects it wants to objectify? The appeal to conscious agency both in practical, i.e., moral, matters and in organizing a human perceptual world is pervasive and constitutive of his philosophical position. But what is the nature of this ongoing subject that is not itself organized?

Hodgson correctly argues, in "The Metaphysical Method in Philosophy," that the "assumption of a chaos in sensations, out of which experience results, involves the assumption of causal agency in the Subject."[8] Although it is true that sensations are ordered into the various perceptual objects we recognize as such, Hodgson counters that they already have duration and succession apart from such ordering. It was the assumption of an original chaos of sensations that led Kant to account for the genesis of experience by taking over the substantial subject of the Scholastics as the noumenal subject as a constituting agency of the objective world. But the assumption of the causal agent outside experience was taken as equivalent to a knowledge of what causal agency consisted in, thus turning a general term into an actual or real thing. Hume was on firmer ground in pointing out that we do not have any knowledge of what constitutes causal agency (M, pp. 54-55). Calling for a radical change in philosophy, Hodgson wants to replace the method of proposing hypotheses to account for the genesis of experience, which, by definition, must be prior to or transcend the objects they are proposed to account for, by the more defensible method of having "recourse in the first instance to experience itself, and see what its content is, apart from any hypothesis of its cause or mode of production" (*ibid*, p. 55). The proper philosophic method involves examining experience without bringing in any presuppositions. This "method of getting experience pure" requires a determined effort to maintain an indifference, receptivity, and freedom from bias (*ibid.*, p. 56).

Hodgson distinguishes between what things are *known as*, i.e., their nature, and their genesis or history, how they came to be what they are known as (M, p. 57). But "the subjective analysis of the stream of consciousness, *without assumptions*, is the whole business and function of philosophy" (*ibid.*, pp. 61–62). We can't, therefore, entertain a theory both of how we can have experience and attend to what it is. Experience must simply be taken as it is given, as an ultimate datum. We must prescind from considering the agent of consciousness, whether soul, mind, ego, or subject, because all these involve inferences and none are a matter of immediate inspection, pure and simple. Such agency is not denied, but held in abeyance, until the descriptive marks of such agency are gathered from experience, rather than being merely speculatively assumed (*ibid.*, p. 63).

By refusing to speculate about the genesis of experience Hodgson does not have to decide whether the external world is orderly or chaotic or whether sensations are one or the other. Instead he turns to a pure analysis of what is found in experience. In this way he avoids making the illicit assumption that both Hume and Kant made in calling original sensations chaotic. Hume assumed that disorder and isolation are primordial facts and that order and nexus must be accounted for as derivative facts. Kant pushes this to an extreme and accounts for the genesis of order and nexus by assuming causal agency in the subject. But *finding* order and nexus in sensations, as inseparable and primordial facts of experience, is very different from *assuming* them, and, therefore, they do not have to be accounted for nor their genesis sought. Philosophers have only to trace the development of one kind or mode of order and nexus out of another kind; i.e., the order and nexus in the external world and the order of logical ideas, out of the primordial order and nexus in the stream of consciousness (M, p. 65).

I will briefly summarize these original positions of Hodgson which had such a powerful formative influence on James's philosophy. Hodgson rejects a primordial chaos of impressions for an experiential quasi-chaos, partially ordered already and further objectified by us. A "pure description" of experience is substituted for the transcendental method. This method of "immediate inspection" is to be free from all bias or presuppositions. We cannot ask the question of the genesis of experience since this would be to speculate about what is not, in fact, experienced. The question of agency, therefore, must be deferred while the philosopher instead gathers experiential evidence of the marks of such agency in experience. Order in both the external world and in the logical and theoretical domains can be traced from the fundamental order and nexus in the stream of consciousness. Since such order is found and not merely assumed, a firmer foundation for philosophy can be established.

But James, like Nietzsche, makes sense of the physical world, consciousness, and formal systems, including science, art, ethics and religions, by reference to individual agents willing a world which answers to their needs. His fundamental theoretical problem becomes how to develop a philosophic position grounded on personal efficacy which answers the objection raised to such a position by Hume, Comte, and Hodgson, while at the same time heeding their empiricist critiques of the causal agency advocated not only by Kant and Hegel, but by the post-Kantian romantics of both the Emersonian and Fichtean variety. Despite his infatuation with Hodgson, for instance, he confronts him in an early letter (1879) with the admission that, despite Hodgson's reservations, the relations of the individual consciousness to universal thought are so obscure that he still wants to ascribe causality "to individual volitions and reactions of attention." [9] While adhering for the most part to the Hodgson philosophy summarized above, James subtly shifts the terms of the discourse to accomodate causal agency. That he was not able at first to thoroughly reconstruct his borrowings is evidenced by some of the incompatible assertions and unresolved dilemmas that remain, especially in the *Principles of Psychology.*

One transformation that James effects is to redraw the boundaries of psychology and philosophy. Hodgson objected to the traditional division based on the genesis of experience. Psychology was defined by its attribution of the genesis to individual conscious agents in the presence of the external world, while philosophy was defined by its attribution of the genesis to some transcendent, immanent, and/or absolute source. He instead wants to categorize psychology as a positive science and therefore its subject matter is the genesis of experience, with philosophy defined as its subjective counterpart, limited to analysis only (M, pp. 63-64). What Hodgson attributes to philosophy – staying within the stream of consciousness, refusing to consider the genesis of experience, and not dealing with the causal efficacy of the subject -- James sees as the properly positivistic definition of psychology. He tried to stay within these strictures in the *Principles of Psychology*, but he did not always succeed. He turned to philosophy in order to legitimately take up the questions proper to philosophy, which are the reverse of Hodgson's distinctions, namely the genesis of experience, the relations of the stream of consciousness to external reality, and the subject as a conscious agent.

Already in the *Principles of Psychology* James takes up Hodgson's admonition to look for evidence of agency, without attributing such activity to some separate entity behind the scene. His use of the "passing thought," for instance, avoids the attribution to an unseen agent while allowing him to talk about the actual organizing taking place within the stream of consciousness. He sets up the chapter by stating that every psychic state can be studied by way of analysis, asking what it consists in, and by way of history, i.e., "its conditions of production, and its connection with other facts" (PP, II, 913). True to the Hodgson model, he quickly disposes of the way of analysis and gets on to the proper psychological discussion of the genesis of beliefs. But he also subverts this model because the genesis is an internal one, and he leaves the question of the relationship of our subjective beliefs about reality to the actual being of reality as one of the unsolved puzzles of both psychology and philosophy, but totally beyond the scope of psychology to answer (cf. *ibid*, pp. 1230 ff.).

The "various orders of reality" are introduced as clarifying the second, and more accessible, historical question, that of the genesis of beliefs: " *Under what circumstances do we think things real?* " The startling answer is that anything is thought to be real which is uncontradicted by anything else of which we think (PP, II, pp. 917-18). This real existence for the mind cannot be contrasted with *extra mentem* existence, since the latter is only available to contradict erroneous belief insofar as it is itself believed. And this belief in the real objects of my world remains as such by the same criterion as the erroneous belief itself, i.e., in its not having been contradicted by other beliefs. To conceive a proposition is to believe in it, unless it clashes with other propositions believed at the same time. "The whole distinction of real and unreal, the whole psychology of belief, disbelief, and doubt" are said by James to be grounded on two mental facts – that we can think differently of the same and that "we can choose which way of thinking to adhere to and which to disregard" (*ibid.*, p. 920). Cognition of the real is thus subordinated to choice. (This puts James solidly in the post-Kantian romantic tradition of Fichte and Schopenhauer.)

This is not to be taken in the crude sense that we choose, despite evidence to the contrary, to believe anything we wish. By no means - our choices are constrained by what we habitually pay attention to. For the most part we distinguish between what exists and what does not, but this division does not exhaust our classification system, since non-existent objects are further discriminated according to their inner relations, recognizing them " *as* objects of fancy, *as* errors, *as* occupants of dreamland, etc." The question remains as to how the categorizations get formed in the first place. This is done by each thinker's "dominant habits of attention," which "practically elect from among the various worlds some one to be. . . the world of ultimate realities" (PP, II, 923). For most people the world of ultimate realities from which we don't appeal is that of the "things of sense." The prerogative reality is given only to this nucleus of the absolute real world.

But since in the strict sense of the word 'existence,' everything exists as some sort of object, whether as mythical object or as an object of science fiction or as a delusion, to believe in only one set of objects as truly existing is to demonstrate the irreducible part choice plays in our human nature. What we therefore call real is whatever appears to us to exist. But in order to do so, the objects must have some relation to us. This practical reality, as opposed to metaphysical reality, (i.e., reality in itself or for an infinite intelligence) is achieved insofar as objects appear both *interesting* and *important*. These practical and aesthetic interests disclose reality and not the other way around. The mere existence of sensible objects does not constrain us to privilege them as the only or even preeminent reality. Therefore, reality means primordially "relation to our emotional and active life" (PP, II, 924).

The appeal to some relation to our practical and emotional life, rather than to the thinking subject or causal or moral agent, is made to keep within Hodgson's strictures that only the evidence of agency which operates within experience can serve as a legitimate, non-speculative grounding. James participates in the empiricist deconstruction of the substantial ego, but not in order to get rid of its function. On the contrary, he also goes to great lengths to replace it with a defensible substitute. He insists that something remains, even after the empiricists successfully criticize the practice of turning functions into entities. Personal identity doesn't altogether vanish for Locke, but consists in pragmatically definable particulars. Likewise, for Hume, nothing is left of the substantial soul but "verifiable cohesians in our inner life."[10] But such remnants, modest though they be, can become part of the experiential basis for larger claims. So do our aesthetic and moral needs. We need "a permanent warrant for our more ideal interests," chief among which is the "need of an eternal moral order."[11] James thought that Kant's transcendental deduction of the moral order was vulnerable to criticism and tried to develop an experiential and experimental deduction instead.

The fundamental issue is whether human actions have any significance. To acquiesce in the nihilistic denial of such significance, to regard the world as not only indifferent to, but untouched by, moral consequences, is to inhabit a meaningless world. This would be a world completely foreign to humans, "reptilian," so "*unheimlich*" that there would be no reason for living.[12] In such a context talk of the nature of the causal agent is vacuous, as is the philosophical discussion of free will versus determinism. What we want to know, and need to be assured about, is whether our actions can bring about real arrangements in the world, whether real evils can be overcome. The center of gravity of philosophy must alter from authoritarian pronouncements to the "really vital question" of what the world is going to be. The question is not the self-centered one of who I am, but what I can do to better the world.[13] As he says in a letter to Hodgson, he is not interested in agency as such, in the sense of assigning ownership to actions, but in establishing experientially that moral reactions are efficacious.[14] This differs from the emphasis in traditional morality on the autonomous agent as supplying the ground for assigning praise or blame. His method of showing that changes are brought about in situations helps explain his otherwise curious indifference to assigning moral or causal agency when describing organizing situations, whether of objectifying sensory experiences or of imposing new moral standards.

The pragmatic principle or "principle of practicalism," as he first calls it in 1898, is developed to dissolve metaphysical problems by displacing merely dialectic disputes analyzing abstract differences of meaning by asking what is practically meant by the metaphysical terms or issue in question.[15] To ask what something means practically is not to ask about the mere usefulness of any means to ends but is an existential referent to the development of the individual person's sense of self as a moral agent, which always involves responsible rearrangements of the world of experience. Thus, to ask what any metaphysical issue means practically, e.g., to say that the universe is a unified system, is to ask such questions as: "In what ways does the oneness come home to your own personal life? By what difference does it express itself in your experience? How can you act differently towards a universe which is one?"[16]

In the last expressions of his mature philosophy he again returns to an examination of agency. He replaces the notion of agency as a substantial metaphysical principle with that of "personal activity-situations."[17] He re-defines free will, for instance, not as the assertion of a metaphysical principle of activity, but as the "character of novelty in fresh activity situations. It is a manifestation of the phenomenon of the field of consciousness as being not just repetitious, but the succession of novel events."[18]

Although James's most original contributions to philosophy arise from his concentrating on the 'eaches,' i.e., careful descriptions of the unique configurations of particular living moments of experience, rather than the 'alls,' i.e., a systematic comprehensive theory of such experiences, he clearly wanted his individual percipient taken in interaction with the environing social and physical world, and though his tolerance for competing frames of reference was high, he passionately wanted to understand how these multiverses made a universe, after all. The search for a comprehensive explanation which would preserve, or even enhance, the varieties of human experience was a dominating motive which simultaneously drove him toward panpsychism and kept him from it as long as it seemed to submerge differences.

His own developing methodology, however, strictly enjoined importing into a problematic situation a ready-made theoretical scheme not derived therefrom. Since he also clearly recognized that scientists do not gather facts at random, but only insofar as they contribute to a pre-existing theoretical framework, he must have something else in mind besides the observation versus theory dichotomy in his frequent critique of merely theoretical explanations overcome by his factual reporting. It should be recognized that he has shifted the terms of discourse without his being fully aware tht he has done so. He is obviously more interested in describing the pre-theoretical, lived world on which science and all consciously explanatory schemes are parasitic than in carrying out the experiments he thinks constitutive of a respectable science of psychology. His many laments over his inability to write something strictly philosophical are an exact analogue, since he was fascinated with the lived world out of which philosophers worked rather than with the philosophic systems themselves.

This world of ordinary experience is pivotal in two distinctive, but related ways.[19] On the one hand it provides the context out of which more specialized organizational schemes, whether scientific, moral, or esthetic, emerge. Furthermore, these specialized worlds bear ineradicable traces of their origin, and James spends a great deal of time showing how some development, aberration, tendency, or privation in a particular sphere is due to the continuance on another level of the attitudes, limitations, and structures of the ever present, though often ignored, context of ordinary experience. By making these connections explicit James demystifies important aspects of science, technology, ethics, and esthetics.

On the other hand, the acceptability of the final outcome or overall movement or overriding tendency of any coherent theory, system, project, way of life, or style within the sub-worlds is best determined from the point of view of the world of ordinary experience. The justification for the right to veto systems which in complexity may be beyond the competency or comprehension of anyone working out of the level of ordinary experience, is that such systems, as products of persons, bear an inescapably personal signature. Thus, although ordinary experience shares the status of one sub-world among others, depending on the context of discourse, it also enjoys a privileged status within Jamesian philosophy.

The system as a whole will instantiate tendencies identifiable in human terms. One cannot obliterate the human dimension of experience. Even the attempt to do so, to make a system approximate as nearly as possible to a self-starting, self-regulating machine, reveals the cravings and refusals of a certain type of temperament. In fact any self-consciously objective system, which puts itself on a level of operation seemingly impregnable to charges of temperamental bias, whether by claiming to be an instantiation of pure rational thought, or divine fore-ordination, or scientific realism, or necessary logical relations, will be recognizable by someone not of the temperament to make such claims, as revealing obvious biases.

Because systems, no matter how abstruse, are the creations of persons, something distinctively personal not only will remain embedded in them, but will characterize them as a totality. This personal element James calls temperament. Only out of the clash of temperaments will some mutuality evolve. Mechanisms of mediation can and should be developed and recommended, but the last word belongs to the spontaneous acceptance or rejection of the individual person, which is the result of their accumulated life experiences. As always, James's expression is most felicitous:

> What the system pretends to be is a picture of the great universe of God. What it is - and oh so flagrantly - is the

revelation of how intensely odd the personal flavor of some fellow creature is. Once reduced to these terms. . . our commerce with the systems reverts to the informal, to the instinctive human reaction of satisfaction or dislike. . . . The finally victorious way of looking at things will be the most completely *impressive* way to the normal run of minds.[20]

The retrospective glance, accordingly, just because it is imported into the present moment cannot reveal reality as it is and necessarily falsifies. James nowhere draws this startling conclusion, but assumes it in his criticisms of other positions. They are considered false because they import into their explanations of present experience structures that can be at most merely regulative and then substantialize such classificatory schemes as part of the original experience. James, it seems, imagines he is doing otherwise. Although he recognized the importance, the efficacity, of such non-experiential, created structures in everything from scientific theories to artistic creations and moral ideals, and even grounds human dignity on such 'spontaneous' creations of genius, he just as firmly believes that the test of such structures is their successful congruence with immediate experiencing.

As his later writings and notebooks make clear, James wanted to be methodologically 'pure' in deriving all his categories from immediate experience. An unremarked accomplishment of James is his skill in showing how many philosophical constructs, howsoever sophisticated, are disguised elaborations of common sense categories and share the drawbacks of their unreflective origins. The irony is that James's own method, as he was himself aware on one level, necessarily reflects back on immediate experience. Although he sometimes thinks, as do many contemporary phenomenologists, that he can do so without importing any categories not derived therefrom, at other times he clearly understands that the present moment is the multidimensional 'specious present,' which Miller has so well elucidated, in which retrospection is legitimate because the immediate present includes both the past and the emergent future.[21] In introducing a long passage by Hodgson on the duration of even the smallest unit of consciousness James says: "These lingerings of old objects, these incomings of new, are the germs of memory and expectation, the retrospective and the prospective of time" (PP, I, 606). He is paraphrasing Hodgson's statement that "the rudiments of memory" and "a former and a latter are included in the minimum of consciousness" (*ibid.*, p. 607).

The retrospection inherent in the specious present is of the living moment just passing away. This experience is self-contained and "leans on nothing," i.e., no extrinsic categories need be imported or invoked. But our attention in the present moment is always partial according to our interests. How is this related to retrospection as a methodological principle? "Just as in the original sensible experience our attention focalized itself upon a few of the impressions of the scene before us, so here in the reproduction of those impressions an equal partiality is shown, and some items are emphasized above the rest" (PP, I, 572). That the past is recalled and conceptualized according to our interests is axiomatic for James. It is noteworthy that he related interests to the vitality of the aesthetic sense: Hodgson's 'law of redintegration,' (i.e., that every object, which has occured in a variety of combinations, has a tendency to redintegrate, or call back into consciousness, all of them), "will be least obeyed by those minds which have the smallest variety and intensity of interests – those who, by the general flatness and poverty of their aesthetic nature, are kept for ever rotating among the literal sequences of their local and personal history" (*ibid.*). [22]

As to which interests predominate, where Hodgson insists that habit is the sole determinant, James adds three more determinants: (a) recency in experience, (b) vividness in an original experience, and (c) "*congruency in emotional tone* between the reproduced idea and our mood" (PP, I, 574-577). Habit would produce mere repetition, and James is much more interested in rearrangements and the logic of discovery. He consistently values the creative over the repetitive and recognizes its pervasiveness where others do not see beyond the sameness of social constructs. Thus, while ostensively explaining how we observe present objects and record the past, he actually shows how present experience is selective and the past reconstructed.

James's borrowings from Hodgson are extensive and especially important because they help set up the boundaries within which he operates. Some themes are clearer in the original and a better understanding of, for instance, the way perceptual experience is already ordered and yet we carve recognizable objects out of this pre-existing but rudimentary order could direct us to a more promising reading overriding James's own waffling on the subject. The "pure description" of Hodgson can likewise help illuminate the puzzling "pure experience" of James. Even where James diverges deliberately from his mentor, as in insisting on the causal efficacy of human agency and resisting the temptation of the premature closure characteristic of rational systems, Hodgson still sets the terms of the debate. As with most cases of influence between two original thinkers, James never simply repeats nor totally frees himself from Hodgson, and tracing the subtleties of their give and take can add significantly to understanding and going beyond both positions.

NOTES

This paper replaces the one given at the conference, which was already accepted for publication in Michael H. DeArmey & Stephen Skousgard, eds., *The Philosophical Psychology of William James*, Washington, D.C.: Center for Advanced Research in Phenomenology & University Press of America, 1986.

1. Cf. Andrew J. Reck, "Hodgson's Metaphysics of Experience," in *Philosophy and Archaic Experience*, ed. John Sallis, (Pittsburgh: Duquesne University Press, 1982), pp. 29–47.

2. Ralph Barton Perry, *The Thought and Character of William James*, I, (Boston: Little, Brown, 1935), p. 653.

3. Shadworth H. Hodgson, "Common-Sense Philosophies," *Proceedings of the Aristotelian Society*, I, no. 2 (1888), 25. (Houghton Library, Harvard University, no. WJ 539.19, p. 21.)

4. Hodgson, "Common-Sense Philosophies," p. 25.

5. In a letter to Hodgson, dated December 30, 1885, James complains that for the first time he understands the foundation of Hodgson's philosophy and he rejects it. Apparently, James has not been paying much attention to Hodgson's appeals to the absolute Infinite. For James the Absolute means total intelligibility, and he finds this notion, and the philosophic tradition it represents, more mystifying than enlightening. He says to Hodgson, "For what is your famous 'two aspects' principle more than the postulate that the world is thoroughly *intelligible* in nature?" Perry, *Thought and Character*, p. 631.

6. William James, *The Principles of Psychology* (3 vols.; Cambridge: Harvard University Press, 1981). All page references to this work, abbreviated as PP. are incorporated into the text of my essay.

7. This problem is treated at length in my *Chaos and Context: A Study of William James* (Athens, Ohio: Ohio University Press, 1978).

8. Shadworth H. Hodgson, "The Metaphysical Method in Philosophy," *Mind*, IX (1884), 52. Page references, abbreviated as M. are in the text.

9. Perry, *Thought and Character*, p. 616.

10. William James, *Pragmatism* (Cambridge: Harvard University Press, 1975), p. 48.

11. James, *Pragmatism*, p. 55.

12. William James's letter to Hodgson, Sept. 12, 1886, in Perry, *Thought and Character*, pp. 637-639.

13. James, *Pragmatism*, pp. 55 ff.

14. James letter, 1886, in Perry, *Thought and Character*, pp. 637-639.

15. William James, *Collected Essays in Review*, ed. Ralph Barton Perry, (New York: Longmans, Green, 1920), p. 431.

16. James, *Essays*, p. 135.

17. William James, *Some Problems of Philosophy* (Cambridge: Harvard University Press, 1979), p. 106.

18. William James, *Essays in Radical Empiricism* (Cambridge: Harvard University Press, 1970), p. 93 n.9.

19. See my "James's Reconstruction of Ordinary Experience," *The Southern Journal of Philosophy* XIX (Winter, 1981), 499-515, and "The Philosopher's 'License': William James and Common Sense," *Transactions of the Charles S. Peirce Society* XIX (Summer, 1983), 273-290.

20. James, *Pragmatism*, pp. 24-25.

21. David L. Miller, "William James and the Specious Present," in *The Philosophy of William James*, ed. Walter Corti, (Hamburg: Felix Meiner, 1976), pp. 51-79.

22. Shadworth H. Hodgson, *Time and Space* (London: Longmans, Green, 1865), p. 267.

CHAPTER IX

TOWARD A HERMENEUTICAL REALISM

Thomas Olshewsky (University of Kentucky)

In an earlier paper on semiotics and hermeneutics,[1] I made some comparisons between Peirce's and Gadamer's work, with some brief suggestions about hermeneutical realism. I want here to retrace those steps briefly (for those not familiar with the earlier paper), but spend most of my attention on extending the notion of a hermeneutical realism.

Gadamer's Problematic

In his *Truth and Method*, Gadamer gives us an account of the history of hermeneutics that shows at once a synchronic dialectic between the formulation of the hermeneutical problem and the understanding of interpretation in vogue at the time, and a diachronic dialectic of the shifting epistemological perspectives through time. The Classical view was a simple realism, in which the text as object was taken to be the problem for interpretation, moving from lack of understanding to understanding of the text presented. Schleiermacher's post-Kantian Romantic View saw any encounter with an object as already interpretive, so the task was to move from misunderstanding to understanding with a problem shift from text to author, and the problematic became how to transcend one's own historical bounds to represent the context of the author. With Dilthey's Empiricist-historic View, hermeneutics shifted from interpretation of texts to a *Geisteswissenschaft*, a science of human existence, and the problematic became a tension between a base in the relativity of experiential immediacy and the goal of comprehensive accountings for the human situation. Gadamer sees at the roots of these dialectics a reflective alienation based upon subject/object tensions of the epistemological formulations of the problems which are out of touch with the lived experience that requires integration. The traditional treatments of hermeneutics all contain epistemological

Robert S. Corrington, Carl Hausman, & Thomas M. Seebohm, eds., *Pragmatism Considers Phenomenology,* Washington, D. C.: Center for Advanced Research in Phenomenology & University Press of America, 1987.

prejudices that separate off the subject (interpreter) from his object (the text). The problem seems to be how to transcend the prejudices that underlie the alienated consciousness. The answer does not lie in substituting one epistemological frame for another, but in a shift from conditions for human knowledge to conditions for human being-in-the-world, in a shift from epistemology to ontology. Also, the problem is not quite one of transcending prejudices either. So cast, this would put us back into the dialectics of the earlier treatments of hermeneutics. Our prejudices are not defects to overcome. They are conditions upon our openness to the world. "It is not so much our judgments as it is our prejudices that constitute our being."[2]

The hermeneutical problem, then, must be recast: How can we accept our prejudicial condition as integral to our being, and yet critically rise above particular prejudices? This formulation accomplishes the move from epistemology to ontology, and with it the rejection of the Cartesian frame that generates the dialectical tensions between subjectivity and objectivity. The acceptance of prejudicial conditions as conditions for being human shifts the focus of the problematic of interpretation from objectivity to critique. Gadamer would find a base for that critique in a dialogue of question and answer between the interpreter and his text. Not only does the interpreter ask questions of the text, but the text also questions the interpreter. As a genuine dialogue, not only must the text respond to questions raised by the prejudiced-motivated interpreter, but the text also calls into question some of those very prejudices in the answers it offers.

Gadamer's interpretation of this dialogue of inquiry can be characterized by what I call the "thesis of linguisticality." Language is not a mere tool of communication of our understanding of the world as some prelinguistic given. "Learning to speak does not mean learning to use a preexistent tool for designating a world already somehow familiar to us; it means acquiring a familiarity and acquaintance with the world itself and how it confronts us."[3] Our understanding is always linguistically informed. Language is the medium of human understanding. "Being that can be understood is language."[4] So questioning takes place in a language, and interpreting a text is often analogous to learning a foreign language. When we have learned effectively to ask questions in that new language, we have in effect learned to respond to questions posed to us by that text. "Thus, the dialectic of question and answer always precedes the dialectic of interpretation. It is what determines understanding as an event."[5] "understanding is language-bound."[6]

This resolution to the reformulated hermeneutical problem is not without its critics. Habermas, for instance, finds in Gadamer's thesis of linguisticality (which he calls an "idealism of linguisticality") a latent Hegelian strain that provides only for hermeneutical appropriation and cultural transmission, and thus fails to meet the task of critical reflection.[7] Gadamer's retort that Habermas's own proposals regarding critique of ideology themselves presuppose a language-bound orientation is little more than a *tu quoque*, and does not itself give a response to the critique.[8] Indeed, as I shall shortly note, Habermas is himself involved with a modified thesis of linguisticality. The question remains for both programs of how to acknowledge the language-bound character of understanding on the one hand, and not lapse into a cultural relativism on the other. The temptation to construe the thesis of linguisticality as a collapse of thought into language, as a nominalistic hermeneutics, exacerbates the problem rather than alleviates it. Besides, in Gadamer's critique of Wittgenstein, it seems to be a move that he himself explicitly rejects.[9] How then can the hermeneutical problem be resolved, and the understandings of human communities be put into critical contact with the constraints of reality, without lapsing back into the epistemological bifurcations which gave the problematic its birth? What are the prospects for a hermeneutical realism? For this, I think the pragmatic realism of C. S. Peirce can be a help.

Peirce's Pragmatic Realism

The Peirce offered a realistic pragmaticism (distinct from James's more nominalistic strain of pragmatism, for instance) is a point widely acknowledged, but that he offered a pragmatic realism, as I have often stressed,[10] is a point equally worthy of note. It is in an orientation simple in conception, but rich in implication. I will risk laboring the familiar only because popular construals distort and truncate the implications by taking inadequate account of the base. This lies, I think, in failure to take account of the interdependencies of his phenomenology with his semiotics and his pragmatic maxim. Some understanding of these will provide a basis for some comparison and contrast with Gadamer's program, and point the way to a hermeneutical realism.

Peirce's ontological categories admit of a myriad of manifestations depending on the context of concern, but are most fundamentally articulated in terms of logical relations. Firstness is a monadic relation, a one-place predicate requiring relation to nothing else for its being. Secondness is a two-place predicate, requiring interaction between two for its being, and thirdness is a triadic relation in which there is mediation between two predicates by a third. On these three relations, Peirce maintained, the whole of a logic of relations can be built, and on these three three categories, all of being can be understood. Phenomenologically, they are immediacy, reaction and reflexion; ontologically, "they are the being of positive qualitative possibility, the being of actual fact, and the being of law that will govern facts in the future":[11] temporally, they are present, past and future; psychologically, they are feeling, acting and willing; modally, they are possibility, actuality and potentiality.

Phenomenologically, nothing exists in the immediate present. The present of firstness is pure possibility. For that possibility to be actualized, it must interact with a second. It thus enters into an event, and becomes part of the existent past. No truth second is intelligible without a third to interpret it. An interpreted event presupposes continuity and generality, and thus has implications for the future. By virtue of this implicative character, any meaningful event (interpreted existent) is a sign (a text) to an observer (interpreter).

Peirce's semiotics begins with the conception of all signs as thirds. "A sign stands *for* someting *to* the idea which it produces, or modifies."[12] In this context, thirdness is mediation. The sign, as a conveyer of meaning, mediates between the object and the interpretant; the interpretant mediates between the sign and the object to interpret the meaning; the object mediates between the sign and the interpretant to ground the meaning. Without this three-fold triadic relation of mediation, there can be no semiosis. All understanding requires this thirdness, and so all understanding is semiotic. Firstness and secondness are known derivatively as the logical presuppositions of thirdness. I cannot *conceive* the pure firstness of unbounded quality nor the pure secondness of dyadic interaction, however closely I may approximate them in my phenomenological bracketing. My most immediate awareness of feeling and quality, of action and interaction, is already mediated by semiotic processes.

Failure to understand this triadic character of the semiotic processes is failure to understand Peirce's pragmaticism. Meaning is not rooted simply in the relation of signs to users ("ask not for the meaning, but for the use") nor in the relation of the signs to their objects (meaning-as-reference). Rather, it requires the interaction of actuality on the one hand and the interpretation of conceptualization on the other. Thus it is not our conception of the conceivable practical effects of the object is the whole of our conception of the object.[13] The meaning is our conception which serves as the interpretant, but the possibilities of the range of that meaning are constrained by the actualities of the object. The actuality is always a second, and so is manifest in effect.

If meaning thus requires thirdness, it follows that conceptions can only be thirds. They cannot exist in themselves; they can only exist in relation to an object that they are about on the one hand, and to a sign that they interpret on the other. This triadic relation is thus a three-way street of interdependency. Just as thought is required to bridge language and object, so object is required to bridge thought and language; indeed, signs of some sort (whether linguistic or not) are required to bridge thought and object. The concepts can then be thought of as signs themselves, standing for the relation between language and object, and themselves requiring interpretation in that relation by some prior interpretant. The resulting conception of conception is that there is no first thought (with all of the conceptual difficulties that conclusion brings), and that a concept can only be understood in its relation to sign and referent through the interpretation of other concepts.

The resultant picture of thought is as "a thread of melody running through the succession of our sensations."[14] Thought differs from raw sensations in that it cannot be immediate. It is mediated by time as well as by signs and by other conceptions. Concepts provide us with ways of thinking about something, and the aim of thinking about something is always the production of a habit of action. The concept is a tool of the act of thinking that results in belief. The result of this process is made successful by the absence of doubt, and doubt arises from the failure of our habits of action to correlate with the habits of the object we act upon, and that correlation can only be known on the basis of sensation. "Our idea of anything is our idea of its sensible effect."[15]

Concepts are required in a triadic relation with sign and referent as interpretants of meaning. They are themselves semiotic by virtue of their correlations in the conceptual scheme, they are tools of thought, which is always an activity to establish habits of action, and they are correlated through action and sensation with the effects of their referents. That "our conception of these effects is the whole of our conception of the object" derives simply from the fact that our relation to the objects is just through such actions and sensations. If our conceptions of the object's effects are inadequate to our habits of action in relation to it, then our actions will relate us to those effects in such a way that they produce in us unanticipated sensations producing the perturbations of doubt. The sole object of inquiry is to avoid such surprise.

The limits of inquiry are that we can never guarantee that we will not be so surprised. However comprehensive our conception of an object, we can have no infallible guarantee that the implications of the concept would ever comprehend the effects of the object. "The total meaning of the predication of an intellectual concept is contained in an affirmation that, under all conceivable circumstances of a given kind. . . the subject of the predication would behave in a certain general way - that is, it would be true under given experiential circumstances. . . ."[16] Here we get a glimmer of a theory of meaning, just enough to distinguish it from the maxim for clarity. Our conception of the effects is the whole of *our* conception of the object, but this may not approach what is conceivable. Further, even though we might ascertain all conceivable effects relative to a certain predication, that would give us the total meaning of the predication, but not of the conception of which it is predicated. The meaning of an assertion may thus in principle be determined in terms of pragmatic conditions - though in practice even this seems unlikely. The meaning of a concept may not be so determined, but develops and interacts with the development of inquiry as it seeks convergence upon that ultimate consensus of competent inquirers.

Some Convergencies and Divergencies

The possibility of a hermeneutical realism based upon Peirce's ontology is masked in part by Gadamer's own contrasts of his approach to hermeneutical reflection with the semiotics of Charles Morris. He rightly notes a psychologizing of semantics in Morris's hands, but this is quite contrastive with Peirce's phenomenological base. Indeed, in what little has been said here of Peirce's treatment, we can already see many points of convergence with Gadamer's approach to hermeneutics. Because each sign is subject to interpretation by other signs, there is no first truth, no absolute beginning to the process of interpretation. Peirce's way of putting this matter is that there is no cognition not determined by a previous cognition; that there are no intuitions in the Cartesian sense.[17] Gadamer's formulation is that "there is no first word."[18] Because semiotic processes are ways of coming to terms with being, and the only ways that we can come to terms with being, it does not make sense to talk about being in mysterious, inaccessible terms. Peirce's way of putting this matter is that "we have no conception of the absolutely incognizable";[19] Gadamer says, "We can express everything in words and can try to come to

agreement about everything."[20] Because our understanding of the
world is always semiotic, always a matter of thirdness, always a
relation mediated by signs, it is an interpretation subject to
reinterpretation. This leads Peirce to his fallibilism, that "we
cannot in any way reach perfect certitude nor exactitude;"[21]
Gadamer's way of putting the matter is that "the standpoint that
is beyond any standpoint. . . is a pure illusion."[22]

Even their differences in starting point prove superficial on
examination. Peirce's accent on scientific inquiry needs to be
seen in the light of his ordering of human inquiries (where issues
of logic are based in ethics, and then aesthetics, and then ultimately in phenomenology). Gadamer's start in aesthetics is not for
him a necessary start, and he must in the end incorporate scientific inquiry into his universal hermeneutics.

These commonalities and compatibilities should not blind us
to points of divergence. Everywhere that Peirce speaks of conception and signs, Gadamer speaks of language and words. While Peirce
maintains that there is no thinking without signs,[23] this does not
imply that there is no thinking without language, much less that
we think linguistically. Gadamer's contention for no thinking
without language puts him in terms of Wittgenstein's tendency
toward "Augustine's nominalistic theory of language," and cites
Wittgenstein's own self-critique: "'If language is to be a means
of communication there must be agreement not only in definitions
but also (queer as it may sound) in judgments.'"[24] This latter
suggestion (queer as it may sound) points us in the direction of
something like Peirce's treatment of semiotically informed
thought. It is not a direction in which Gadamer chooses to go. His
thesis of linguisticality, that the field of language is "itself
an actual whole of interpretation," by attempting to avoid these
horns of the Wittgensteinian dilemma, places him squarely in a
Neo-Hegelian orientation, where the framework offers no base for a
critique. To treat the encounter of dialogue between interpreter
and text as a confrontation with a foreign language invites us to
confront once again the dilemma of a nominalistic reduction of
thought to language or an appeal to a non-linguistic dimension to
thought.

This is the point, as already noted, where Habermas takes
issue with Gadamer's hermeneutical program. Habermas's own solution is to break out of the hermeneutical circle in two directions. On the one hand, he supposes that the relation of observer
to observed in observation is an immediate relation of experience
to reality, unmediated by the interpretive role of understanding.
It is this that grounds understandable meaning in reality. On the
other hand, understood motives and intentionally devised actions

enable us to break out of established prejudices to form new orientations for understanding. Between the base of experience and the critique of action, the hermeneutical enterprise operates on the basis of a thesis of linguisticality. It is just not as ubiquitous as the one that Gadamer proposes.

One might suppose that this account by Habermas is an echo of Peirce's treatment of the roles of perception and action, but such is simply not the case. For Peirce, even the most rudimentary perceptual consciousness is semiotically informed, and significance has to do with the effects of the referent, not just the purposes of the interpreter (here, dimensions of reference and implication are just as important to the notion of intention as purpose). It is because the significance of signs exceeds the purposes of the interpreter in their implication, and conditions for experience are not given in the sensory intake of observation, that inquiry can lead us into surprise and to the need for interpretive reorientation. He thus avoids both the myth of the given and the intentional fallacy (that the sum of the significance of the text lies in the purposes of the author) while maintaining a basis for critique. He thus avoids the difficulty of both hermeneutical orientations (Habermas's and Gadamer's) by displacing the thesis of linguisticality with a broader semotic base.

The pragmatic realism also integrates epistemological and ontological concerns with interpretation instead of bifurcating them. The object as a reality to be accounted for in inquiry is a *dynamical* object, not an actual object of consciousness. The object as ground is a determinate referent for an interpreted sign in the semiotic process. Considered in itself, as immediate and present, the object is pure abstracted possibility, and uncognizable. Ontologically, the object requires secondness to give it determinate existence and thirdness to give it continuity and connectedness with other events in reality. Epistemologically, the object must be a second to relate it in some respect or quality to consciousness, and it must be a third for interpretation of its significance. For there to be truth and meaning and all, there must be a reality of the generality of thirdness, and all objects of knowledge must be generals as well. The object of knowledge (the dynamical object that we inquire into) is distance from the ground of knowledge. The ground is present to our consciousness, and "everything which is present to us is a phenomenal manifestation of ourselves. This does not prevent its being a phenomenon of something without us, just as the rainbow is at once a manifestation both of the sun and of the rain."[25]

This gives us a dialogical relation between our world as semiotically informed and reality as confronted in perception and action, mediated by reflective interpretation. Peirce's dialogue with the object of inquiry may seem as Kantian as Gadamer's dialogue with cultural history seems Hegelian. About such transcendental overtones, some qualifications need to be made. For Peirce, concepts make sense only in terms of the practical effects of their referents. This means that the constitution of the world can be understood only at the end of inquiry, not at the beginning. There is something in Peirce's notion of the convergence of competent observers on the truth comparable to Heidegger's notion of being on the way to language. Nor does Peirce's ontological realism allow for anything like Kant's unintelligible *Ding-an-sich.* Human inquiry cannot make sense if the reality accounted for does not have order and continuity. The re-presenting of that reality in human formulation does not require some copy-theory for such con-formity. "That to which the representation should conform, is itself something in the nature of a representation, or sign – something noumenal, intelligible, conceivable, and utterly unlike a thing–in–itself." [26]

Toward a Hermeneutic Realism

It remains to be explored where this grounding in Peirce's realism can take us in our understanding of hermeneutics. If there is anything that Gadamer's critique of the history of the hermeneutical traditions has to teach us, it is at least the importance of the formulation of the hermeneutical problem. It makes a difference how you say things in your questions as well as your answers, and the primacy of question and answer is no more antecedent to the hermeneutical conditions of human understanding than is the primacy of perception or action. Gadamer is also right in pointing out that we do speak *in* a language, not *with* a language. Human understanding (habits of action, belief networks, schemata, etc.) is not always (indeed, not often) with conscious intention, and is seldom of conscious construction. Against such a background, not only does the significance of the dialogue of question and answer take on new light, but the history of the dialectics of the hermeneutical problematics does as well. To what extent is a new formulation of *the* hermeneutical problem a *re*formulation of what hermeneutics is all about?

Basic to the whole of the hermeneutical traditions is the discrimination of the world as we understand it and reality as we confront it. This requires that we not treat the world as we understand it as coincident with reality as we confront it (fallibilism), and yet that we take our understanding to be in some sense an accounting for that reality (realism). This is not the kind of solipsistic realism in which *my* world and *the* world are coincident either (cf. Wittgenstein's *Tractatus*).[27] The very notion of hermeneutics seems to presuppose not only a confronted reality for which we must give account, but a community of interpretive inquiry in which that accounting is given. This is why the theatre model of individual spectator perceiving detached reality does not work. It posits an alienated subject detached from reality and community in ways that make unintelligible human conditions for interpretation.

The problematic for a hermeneutical realism might then be: How are we to account for world/reality discriminations and interactions without lapsing into the alienations of the subject/object dichotomy that characterized earlier hermeneutical traditions?

Beginnings for an answer, as I have been suggesting, are already implicit in Peirce's philosophy, informed by his semiotics, and undergirded by the categories of his phenomenology. Essences (firsts) do not exist, but they determine the limits of possibility, and as such are conditions on existence. Activities (seconds) exist, but are indeterminate except as opposition to further action, and thus set limits on interpretation. Interpretations (thirds) are determinate, but never absolute, and can be evaluated as adequate to the extent that their generality gives articulation to the continuities of reality for which they are intended to take account. Interpretations inform human activity in interaction with the realities that stand as potential opposition to that activity. Reinterpretation is required when the semiotic forms of concepts, beliefs, and other habits of action fail to fulfill the projected purposes of action because the realities of opposition are not adequately accounted for. This is what Peirce describes as doubt forced upon the inquirer; it is what Gadamer describes as the text questioning the interpreter. It is meaningful interaction between an inquirer and his environment, a dialogue between an interpreter and his text, an engagement of a person through his commitments with the realities that confront his action.

Ontologically, reality is thus conditioned by modalities of the categories. These are logical conditions in the sense that the actuality of existence presupposes the possibility of quality and implies the regularity of law. These are conditions for reality to even be thinkable. These are phenomenological conditions in the sense that for an object to appear to consciousness, it must already be a third, but implicit in thirdness is already secondness of encounter and firstness of presentness. These conditions are conditions upon reality, but only upon reality as we come to terms with it. Conceptions of reality independent of its appearance to us and our reflections upon it simply do not make sense (What would an object look like if no perceiver were around to look at it?). Any reality with which we have to do must be so conditioned, and reality otherwise we are not even capable of considering.

Our encounters with reality are through perception and action mediated by thought. Such encounters are not between a transcendental subject and a phenomenological object, but between an organism and its environment. Coming to terms with reality through reflection and action is the human condition for being in the world. I regard *my* world as *the* world insofar as that constitution is compatible with the limits of reality. I become aware of those limits only when encountered as impediments to perception and action. Epistemologically, I know reality as distinct from the world I live in only negatively, as an opposition to be taken account of. I regard the accounting as adequate if it provides sufficient coherence and completeness and applicability to facilitate my action. To that extent, I may be said to have incorporated the opposition into my world by taking account of it, and the tension between the organism and its environment has been reconciled through thought and action.

This picture of reality is complicated by the realization that seldom do we confront the brute shock of uninterpreted opposition, and then usually as a momentary disruption (running into a glass door, for instance). Oppositions (social and psychological as well as physical) admit of degrees of resistance and unintelligibility. Surd opposition, that which defies intelligibility (as in Sartre's phenomenon of being) is not possible, but stands as a non-existent limit, as a vanishing point off the canvas that gives perspective to the structures of the world.

This orientation also requires the context of a community of interpretation as a condition for consciousness. This is a semiotic community, not just a linguistic one, in which we acquire cooperation of action and attention of perception in indexical and iconic fashion as a base for object permanence before linguistic symbols ever take on hermeneutical significance. Such a conception of communities of cooperation and communication, along with the conception of reality as opposition, obviously need further exploration. I have only been concerned to put us on the path toward such a hermeneutical realism.

NOTES

1. "Hermeneutics and Semiotics," *The University of Dayton Review*, Vol. 17, No.1 (Summer 1984).

2. Hans-Georg Gadamer, "Universality of the Hermeneutical Problem," in *Philosophical Hermeneutics* (Berkeley: University of California Press, 1976). p. 9.

3. Hans-Georg Gadamer, "Man and Language," *Philosophical Hermeneutics*, p. 63.

4. Hans-Georg Gadamer, *Truth and Method* (New York: Seabury, 1975), p. 450.

5. Gadamer, *Truth and Method*, p. 429.

6. Gadamer, "Universality of the Hermeneutical Problem," p. 15.

7. Jürgen Habermas, *Knowledge and Human Interests* (Boston: M.I.T. Press, 1972).

8. Hans-Georg Gadamer, "Scope and Function of Hermeneutical Reflection," in *Philosophical Hermeneutics*, pp. 29 ff.

9. Hans-Georg Gadamer, "The Phenomenological Movement," in *Philosophical Hermeneutics*, p. 176 ff.

10. See my "Realism and Semiosis," "Peirce's Pragmatic Maxim," "Hermeneutics and Semiotics," etc.

11. Charles S. Peirce, *The Collected Papers of Charles Sanders Peirce*, Vols. I-VI, ed. Charles Hartshorne and Paul Weiss (Cambridge: Harvard University Press, 1931-1935), Vols. VII-VIII, ed. Arthur Burks (Cambridge: Harvard University Press, 1958), 1.23. All references to this work follow the standard form of volume number followed by a period and paragraph number.

12. *Ibid.*, 1.388.

13. Cf. *ibid.*, 5.402.

14. *Ibid.*, 5.395.

15. *Ibid.*,   5.401.

16. *Ibid.*,   5.467.

17. *Ibid.*,   5.259 ff.

18. Gadamer, *Truth and Method*, p. 492.

19. Peirce, *Collected Papers*, 5.265.

20. Gadamer, *Truth and Method*, p. 493.

21. Peirce, *Collected Papers*, 1.147.

22. Gadamer, *Truth and Method*, p. 339.

23. Peirce, *Collected Papers*, 5.250, 5.283.

24. Gadamer, "The Phenomenological Movement," p. 177.

25. Peirce, *Collected Papers*, 5.283.

26. *Ibid.*,   5.553.

27. Ludwig Wittgenstein, *Tractatus Logico-Philosophicus*, trans. D. F. Pears and B. F. McGinness (London and Henley: Routledge & Kegan Paul, 1961).

AFTERWORD

CONSIDERATIONS OF AN HUSSERLIAN

Thomas M. Seebohm (Universität Mainz)

In his reflections on the papers in this volume Robert Corrington concludes that pragmatism in general has more in common with Merleau-Ponty, Heidegger, and Schutz than with Husserl.[1] This is doubtless correct to the extent that the criticisms against Husserl mentioned in the papers are very similar to those raised by Heidegger, Merleau-Ponty and other members of the so-called Phenomenological Movement. The main criticisms attack: (1) the insufficiency of Husserl's theory of perception and memory,[2] (2) his failure to recognize the significance of the social character of experience and his concomitantly solipsistic phenomenology,[3] (3) his method of "bracketing," i.e., the strict restriction to the phenomenologically given,[4] (4) his metaphysical subjectivism,[5] and finally (5) his foundationalism, his Cartesianism, the futile proposal of a presuppositionless philosophy.[6]

I will deal with these criticisms later. Before doing so I want to note that there are at least some characteristics of Husserl's phenomenology which it has in common with the pragmatist's descriptive approach to experience.

Beth J. Singer shows how close Alfred Schutz's investigations are to par inquiries by pragmatists.[7] Schutz was earlier mentioned in the company of Heidegger and Merleau-Ponty, but a simple comparison of literary styles clearly shows how little Schutz's descriptions have in common with either the characteristic techniques hermeneutic phenomenology employs to treat language or with the typical abundance of narrative elements and poetical metaphors to be found in the writings of Merleau-Ponty. On the contrary, Schutz (like Husserl generally) describes certain general structures of the experience of social life with a precisely determined terminology. His descriptions have the character of "eidetic universality" in Husserl's sense. It the

Robert S. Corrington, Carl Hausman, & Thomas M. Seebohm, eds. *Pragmatism Considers Phenomenology,* Washington, D. C.: Center for Advanced Research in Phenomenology & University Press of America, 1987.

in Husserl's sense. If the term "eidetic" is not acceptable, it can — also in Husserl — be replaced by "typological," i.e. by a referring to universal types.[8]

The links between Husserl and James are well known. Charlene Haddock Seigfried shows the connection between James's approach and the methodical principles proposed by Hodgson.[9] However, what Hodgson says can also be regarded as an outline of the essentials of a pure description in Husserl's sense and as practiced by Schutz. There is a common root to both – descriptive psychology – which for Husserl is represented by Stumpf and has behind it the descriptive tradition of English empiricism.

Charles Sherover has convincingly shown that in the realm of a properly understood "metaphysics" Royce can be regarded as a forerunner of Heidegger's existential phenomenology. Richard J. Bernstein also correctly illuminates (so it seems to me) the opposition between the treatment of *praxis* and *phronesis* in Heidegger and pragmatism, especially with respect to Heidegger's downgrading of calculative and manipulative thinking. What is involved here is the function of science and scientific method for philosophy in Heidegger, pragmatism and Husserl. According to Heidegger scientific thinking is (a) at the greatest possible distance from Being, (b) inseparably connected with technology and in this connection a threat of eschatological dimensions, and finally (c) not of significance for philosophical thought but on the contrary the opposite of philosophical thinking.[10] Needless to say, such a position is incompatible with pragmatism and especially with Peirce. The turn against Cartesianism is in Heidegger also a turn against every position for which science has a positive function for philosophy. It seems to me that the turn against Descartes in Peirce's pragmaticism is a rejection of what Descartes says about science, but not of the positive function of science for philosophy and the corresponding predominant interest in the methodology of science.

In answering the pragmatists's above-mentioned (3) critique of Husserl I will deal with the differences in their respective treatments of this issue. Nevertheless, it is clear at the outset that for Husserl science is the highest achievement of the human mind, despite the shortcomings of the *degeneration* of the idea of science into technology. He also holds that a radical philosophy is possible only as a correlate of the development of science and that one of the main tasks of phenomenology is the clarification of scientific objectivations, beginning with the analysis of scientific method. Already in the Prolegomena to the *Logical Investigations* he starts with the methodology of logic and mathematics. Thus, the character of the descriptive techniques used as well as the evaluation and function of science for philosophy are two aspects in which Husserl is closer to pragmatism than are Merleau-Ponty or Heidegger.

I will now turn to the criticisms. The first two, concerning Husserl's theory of perception and his insufficient appreciation of the social character of experience, are strongly connected because of the close relation between his theory of intersubjectivity and his "transcendental aesthetics." Criticisms of a similar type have been raised against Husserl by phenomenologists, originally, and most adequately and subtly, by Aron Gurwitsch. I have dealt with them in detail elsewhere and will therefore restrict myself here to some historical remarks about why such in part unjustifiable criticisms have been raised again and again.

Having read the *Logical Investigations*, the *Ideas Pertaining to a Pure Phenomenology and to a Phenomenological Philosophy*, the *Formal and Transcendental Logic*, and the *Cartesian Meditations* (setting aside the Fifth Meditation), i.e., having read the material known in the first half of the twentieth century, a reader is easily prompted to raise the first two criticisms. Even after a careful reading that gives great weight to the *Phenomenology of Inner Time Consciousness*, the Fifth Meditation and *Experience and Judgment*, one may still come to the conclusion that Husserl in some places hinted at topics that he did not successfully integrate into the "solipsistic metaphysical idealism" which is predominant in his philosophy. However, it should be noted that when Husserl in 1918 responded to the suggestion that the structure of experience has a socio-emotional character with the ambiguous answer, "perhaps you have something," [11] Edith Stein had already finished the second redaction of *Ideen II*.[12] The material collected therein clearly indicates how the social character of experience – which is rooted in the last instance in animalic and emotional experience at the deepest levels of association and passive synthesis – is essential for Husserlian phenomenology. This has become clearer with the publication in 1966 of the *Analysen zur Passiven Synthesis* (Hua XI) – a work without which in my opinion the Fifth Meditation cannot be understood. Furthermore, such phenomenological research is not restricted to the late Husserl. From at least 1900 it was a main topic of his interest. As he himself in part recognized, the results of such descriptions have certain consequences not only for the evaluation of the "Cartesian path" to the transcendental-phenomenological reduction but also for a really appropriate presentation of phenomenology. But such a presentation requires that certain misunderstandings with which I will deal below are avoided. Furthermore, in these texts Husserl deals extensively with perception, memory and expectation. Thus, it is an open question what would result from a comparison of pragmatism and transcendental phenomenology concerning either (a) the deeper levels of perception, memory, association, affection, emotion, and the like or (b) the social intersubjective character of experience. It is possible and perhaps advisable to restrict such comparisons to purely descriptive contents, bracketing so to speak everything brought in by criticisms (4) and (5), but one would have to keep in mind what will be said with respect to criticism (3).

Let us then take up this criticism. Husserl's concept of "bracketing" and the phenomenological reduction can be understood in a two-fold way. Following the *Ideas I* and the *Cartesian Meditations* the reduction can be linked immediately with the transcendental turn and *epoche* as an *epoche* from everything which is not given through the subject. In this case criticism (3) will receive most of its force through the viewpoints mentioned in criticisms (4) and (5). However, the "bracketing" can be understood in a much more elementary manner. It is a reduction to what can be grasped descriptively. Thus, it excludes all theoretical explanations -- be they scientific, theological, metaphysical, or "transcendental arguments" of any style - that refer to conditions that are entities only *ex definitione* but not given for a descriptive approach. It holds as well that causal explanations, even if they refer to descriptively explicable conditions, do not properly belong to the realm of phenomenological analysis. Further explication could show that already this bracketing reduction implies an inhibition of the interest in the actual existence of objects.

It seems that the analyses of lived experience given in pragmatism do not concern themselves explicitly[13] or implicitly[14] with such methodical "fixations." At the outset - as in phenomenology - the concern is always to give a purely descriptive analysis of experience and of scientific experience as well. But then facts and explanations given by the sciences are introduced at a very basic level in order to analyze experience. Subsequently a variety of explanations having a speculative-metaphysical character are brought in. Thus we have Royce's idealistic pragmatism and Buchler's naturalistic pragmatism. In any event, "The pragmatist is led ultimately to an explanatory hypothesis."[15] It should be mentioned that such a step beyond pure description is by no means parallel to the step which leads Heidegger beyond phenomenology. Pragmatism's step is mediated by science, and just for that reason it exemplifies the type of metaphysics that Heidegger tries to overcome.

But here our concern is with phenomenology of the Husserlian type. From its viewpoint (a) the pragmatist in most cases tends to fall back on the sciences long before it is really necessary, i.e., for Husserl pure description can stand on its own feet much longer. Furthermore, (b) though it might be in general desirable to formulate some philosophical cosmology once again, such attempts must nevertheless be considered as uncritical and adventurous. In short: despite the interest of pragmatism in lived experience and its use of certain descriptive methods, the method of pragmatism cannot be called phenomenological – not even in the most elementary sense just mentioned.

With respect to criticism (4) it has to be admitted at the outset that Husserl himself – by talking about the "absolute being" of the ego and the only "relative being" of the world – has provoked interpretations of transcendental phenomenology as metaphysical idealism or as an idealism in the style of Fichte. Despite inconsistencies that occur in Husserl's claims to criticize all traditional types of metaphysics and idealism – Kant's included – I would not dare deny that he himself at least sometimes understood himself in this way. In these passages the "absolute being" of the transcendental would have to be interpreted as a necessary being in the sense required by the ontological argument or in Fichte's speculation about the absolute I. This interpretation leaves transcendental phenomenology wide open to criticisms of all sorts, including the ones originally raised by Heidegger. I have elsewhere argued that this interpretation has to be abandoned.[16] Transcendental phenomenology speaks of "givenness": it is throughout an epistemic theory and has no ontological (understood in the old ordinary sense) implications. So interpreted, transcendental phenomenology is not a "metaphysical idealism." Nor is it a Kantian transcendentalism with a hypothetically presupposed subject. Rather, it is a "methodological idealism." That is, it contends that in every critically grounding reflection the givenness of the subject to itself has priority over the givenness of any other object and even over the givenness of the sum total of objects, i.e., the world.

This leads us to criticism (5). It can be said that Husserl is a foundationalist even if one restricts oneself to a purely epistemic understanding of his transcendental phenomenology. He wants to create philosophy as rigorous science. According to the *Cartesian Meditations* the idea of science requires that philosophy be absolutely grounded. Moreover, since it is meaningless to search for presuppositions of an absolute ground, philosophy has a presuppositionless beginning. This idea of science is for Husserl at the outset an anticipatory or "precursory"[17] presumption. He also says that Descartes and all post-Cartesian attempts to realize this presumption ended in seductive aberrations and so failed.[18] Thus, Husserl's foundationalism is first of all a critique of all preceding types of foundationalism. A fair criticism of transcendental phenomenology as a type of foundationalism should take this into account.

Before returning to Husserl I want to make some general remarks concerning different types of foundationalism, i.e., attempts to give *Letztbegründung*. It is sometimes argued that because nobody can start without presuppositions, no presuppositionless philosophy is possible. This argument rests on an equivocation and is thus an informal fallacy. To search for and find a *relative* ground, e.g., some necessary conditions of a certain event, implies not only the knowledge of the event but also the foreknowledge of all the circumstances in which the relatively necessary condition is somewhere hidden. Hence, this foreknowledge is the relative presupposition of searching for and finding a relative ground. The search for an absolute ground likewise has a relative – albeit a more extensive – presupposition in the foreknowledge of what it grounds, namely, everything. However, to admit that this search has a relative presupposition is not to admit that the absolute ground itself has a presupposition; such an admission would be self-contradictory. Therefore, to say that the idea of science requires a presuppositionless beginning is only another way of saying that it requires an absolute ground. It does not imply the meaningless requirement that it should search for such a ground without any foreknowledge. At least what is to be grounded must be known.

Moreover, the statement, "Absolute grounding is impossible," is in general – as Fichte pointed out – stronger than the statement, "Absolute grounding is possible." Granted that the idea of science is not yet fulfilled and that the next attempt to point out an absolute ground will most likely have its flaws (as borne out by the experience of thinking since Descartes), the statement that the idea of science is impossible presupposes more than the statement that the idea of science will *possibly* be realized at some time in the future.

Furthermore, it has to be kept in mind that there are different types of foundationalism, so it might be very difficult to find one single argument to defeat them all. One way to classify the types of foundationalism is through the character of the founding or grounding relation, i.e., the relation between ground and grounded. Another way is the method of deriving the grounded from the ground or in general the method of connecting them. With respect to the second way one could point, e.g., to derivations *more geometrico*, transcendental arguments, various types of dialectic. For the general problem of foundationalism the first way is the most important. In the original Cartesian type an absolute ground is first found, and then everything else is deduced logically from it via proofs. Another type of foundationalism, e.g., Kant's, is much weaker. He claims to identify the transcendental unity of apperception and the manifoldness of sensibility as absolute grounds in the sense of "conditions of the possibility of experience." Fichte's criticism of Kant makes the difference between the two types of foundationalism sufficiently clear. He complains that Kant has only shown that the ego conditions (*bedingt*) the object but should have shown how the ego determines (*bestimmt*) the object.[19]

There is another version of foundationalism that has the biconditional as its logical counterpart. Since the deduction goes both ways, the system is a "circle." The universe of differentiated objects is deduced from the Absolute, and the Absolute in turn can be reached and is itself determined by the shapes (*Gestalten*) in which it differentiates itself. This strongest version of foundationalism is represented – at least according to many interpreters – by the system of Hegel. Finally, there is a version of foundationalism that defends the self-givenness of the subject. Ironically enough, the pragmatist Royce defended this variety of foundationalism against the idealist Bradley, who in defending a weaker version of foundationalism wrote:

> The actual subject is never, in any state of mind, brought before itself as an object. . . , [it] never feels that it is all out there in its object, that there is nothing more left within, and that the difference has disappeared.[20]

As I will discuss below, such a statement could be a conclusion drawn from Husserl's phenomenology of inner time consciousness, which is the keystone of the final grounding in his "critique of the critique."

As mentioned, according to Husserl all pre-Husserlian types of foundationalism ended as "abberations." They all – and not only Descartes – failed to ask the prior phenomenological question of *how*, i.e., through what kind of "evidence," an absolute ground can be given. Husserl answers that this "evidence" must itself be absolute. He claims that what is required is a phenomenological critique and analysis of what "absolute evidence" and its counterpart, "relative evidence," can mean. He maintains that such an analysis will show that these terms can have quite different meanings. Hence, in order to specify what Husserl has to say about "absolute ground" it is first necessary to distinguish these meanings rather carefully.

For the sake of brevity I skip the essential difference between "predicative" and "prepredicative" evidence.[21] It is tacitly assumed that this difference with all of its implications (including the truth and falsity of judgments) is involved in the four types of absolute and relative evidence that will be considered. It is, in addition, useful to keep in mind, that the Husserlian term "evidence" is not a possible predicate of objects. It is only a possible predicated of modes of experience of objects.

(a) Absolute evidence can be understood as original evidence.[22] What is originally evident is the given as bodily present in perception. By contrast, relative evidence can be understood as only signitive evidence, which is either signitive evidence proper – in which the object is present only via a sign representing it – signitive evidence in an improper sense – in which the object is present not bodily but only via imagination, e.g., through expectation or memory.

(b) Absolute evidence can also be understood as adequate evidence,[23] while relative evidence can be correlatively understood as inadequate evidence. Inadequacy can here mean incompleteness, indistinctness or one-sidedness. Complete adequacy can be reached only in a process that is open. Thus, it follows that adequate evidence cannot be original evidence. It can be called "original" only in an improper sense, namely, to the extent that all of its contents – which are otherwise only given as remembered and/or expected – can be brought to original evidence again.

(c) A third type of absolute evidence is apodictic evidence.[24] Apodictic evidence in general is "necessary evidence" or "indubitable evidence." Such an indubitability is given with respect to objects of consciousness, i.e., in "direct intention," only with respect to certain objects of eidetic intuition. It is given if something cannot be thought and/or represented "otherwise." Apodicticity of this sort does not imply adequacy or original givenness. Even in a mathematical proof nobody can have all of the steps together in original evidence; the premises, lemmas and rules of derivation are not always known adequately. This holds also for simple cases, like the "law of non-contradiction." Although it is a good candidate for this sort of apodicticity, it is nevertheless true that concepts involved in its formulation (and there are several formulations!), like "truth" and "falsity," are not adequately known, and complex philosophical reflections concerning them do not have their objects as originally given as a whole in some present phase of consciousness.

The disadvantage of apodictic evidence in "direct intention" is that it is not given originally and so is subject to unlimited possible questioning. Though I cannot think it otherwise, there remains the open and very often empty possibility that a further penetration of the subject-matter may change it considerably. Thus, such an apodicticity is still open to relativistic objections. This would not be the case with (d) a second sort of apodictic evidence, which is both an original evidence and fulfills the requirement that it be reenacted in every act which reflects upon it, i.e., it only occurs in "oblique intention." If this is the case, then it is obvious that "indubitability" has here the specific meaning that the very act of doubting reenacts in itself that which it doubts, e.g., in the case of doubting the evidence in which consciousness is given to itself.[25]

What has to be shown is that such apodictic evidence can be found with respect to the self-givenness of the subject, but not with respect to the givenness of the world (the precise meaning that this statement has cannot be explicated here). We have in phenomenological reflection an *epistemic* and *not* an ontological priority of the subject.[26] All "relative" evidence is investigated in the relation it has to this absolute evidence, which is "apodictic" in the second sense just mentioned.

Some further restrictive remarks are necessary. (a) The apodictic self-givenness is an original evidence, but that does not exclude that the subject is also given to itself in an evidence that is only "signitive" and that even points to spheres that cannot be given originally in principle. Thus, to every original self-givenness in the present there belongs the past, which is only given in an evidence that is not original. But that this is the case is given in an apodictic and original evidence. (b) It follows from what has been said in (a) that apodicticity of self-givenness does not imply adequacy, either with respect to existence or with respect to "essence." (c) Phenomenology is interested not so much in the self-givenness of the subject as regards its existence as in the general structures of givenness in general, in eidetically given structures. The mere fact that such structures are given on the basis of an apodictically given existence does not imply that they are themselves apodictically given. As a "critique of the critique" can point out, only some very general structures concerning intentionality, temporality, and the genesis of consciousness are themselves given apodictically, i.e., occur in every phase of conscious life and hence also in those in which they are themselves investigated. But these apodictic evidences about the general structures of consciousness are sufficient to prescribe, to "ground," a general methodical framework for further phenomenological investigations concerning contents which are by no means "apodictically" given. As pointed out in (a), it can even be the case that it follows from the apodictically given temporal structures of consciousness that some contents cannot in principle be brought to original givenness. They are – in different degrees and in different forms – only given in signitive evidence in the broadest sense. But to repeat: that this is the case is itself known in apodictic evidence.

What has been said is far from being a sufficient explication of the "foundations" of transcendental phenomenology. It is, hopefully, sufficient to justify two comments. (a) The Husserlian is not very impressed by criticisms (3) – (5). They are not specific enough; they in part presuppose interpretations of transcendental phenomenology that transform it into an intellectual monstrosity, and they overlook that Husserl's so-called foundationalism is itself a critique of foundationalism in that it is itself "grounded" in a critique of "absolute evidence." (b) If phenomenological methods are applied, it is not necessary to provide a phenomenological justification of their application. They might simply be applied. One might also attempt a justification via transcendental arguments, speculative methods, and the like. However, if the thesis is that phenomenology should replace – and not merely be just another type of – traditional first philosophy, then it is phenomenology itself that has to point out phenomenologically the rights and the limits of this approach. This should be done without implying any ontological claims. In the wake of phenomenology's critique of the "idea of science," implying, as it does, the ideal of "absolute grounding," perhaps only pragmatism and pragmaticism provide a framework within which "metaphysics" and "cosmology" can be meaningfully done. In any case, because phenomenology does not imply any sort of ontologically tinged foundations or employ any results of the sciences to advance ontological statements concerning the world, it is completely neutral with respect to pragmatism as well.

NOTES

James H. Wilkinson gave highly valuable advice concerning the presentation of the material in this essay.

1. Cf. Robert S. Corrington, "Introduction and Reflection," this volume, p. 2.

2. Cf. Charles Hartshorne, "An Anglo-American Phenomenology: Method and Some Results," this volume, sec. 5.

3. *Ibid.*, secs. 2, 6.

4. See notes 13 and 14 below.

5. See Corrington, "Introduction and Reflection," pp. 22-24.

6. Hartshorne, "An Anglo-American Phenomenology," p. 59, and Corrington, "Introduction and Reflection," loc. cit.

7. Cf. Beth J. Singer, "Signs, Interpretation, and the Social World," esp. pp. 102 ff., cf. p. 93.

8. Edmund Husserl, *Cartesian Meditations*, Secs. 20 and 34 in Volume I of *Husserliana* (The Hague: Martinus Nijhoff, 1950).

9. See Charlene Haddock Seigfried, "Hodgson's Influence on James's Organization of Experience," pp. 190 f.

10. I admit that there are less radical readings of Heidegger, but it seems to me that *Der Satz vom Grund* (Pfullingen: Neske, 1957), pp. 166-170 is one of the places that allows a "radical" reading of Heidegger as diametrically opposed to Husserl's evaluation of science.

11. Cf. the final remark in the contribution of Hartshorne.

12. Edmund Husserl, *Ideen zu einer reinen Phänomenologie und phänomenologischen Philosophie II* (Hua IV, 1952 – its first publication!). The second part, "The Constitution of Animalic Nature," is of special significance; it clearly indicates that the material of the Fifth Meditation concerning the intersubjective character of experience is not something that occured to Husserl only towards the end of his life. See my "The Other in the Field of Consciousness," in Lester Embree, ed., *Essays in Memory of Aron*

Gurwitsch, Washington: Center for Advanced Research in Phenomenology and University Press of America, 1984, pp. 283-303.

13. See, e.g., the introductory remark in John J. McDermott, "Experience Grows by its Edges: A Phenomenology of Relations in an American Philosophical Vein."

14. This is at least the impression one can get from the presentations of pragmatism in the contributions of Sandra B. Rosenthal ("Classical American Pragmatism: Key Themes and Phenomenological Dimensions") and of John E. Smith ("The Reconception of Experience in Peirce, James, and Dewey").

15. Sandra B. Rosenthal, "Classical American Pragmatism," pp. 48 f. Cf. also Robert S. Corrington on Husserl and Buchler, pp. 21-25.

16. See my "Die Stellung der phänomenologischen Idee der Letztbegründung zur Seinsfrage," in K. Gloy and E. Rudolph, eds., *Einheit als Grundlage der Philosophie* (Darmstadt: Wissenschaftliche Buchgesellschaft, 1985), pp. 303-321.

17. *Cartesian Meditations,* Sec. 3. The translation of D. Cairns (The Hague: Martinus Nijhoff, 1977) has "precursory," which is one of the connotations of "*vorläufig,*" but I think that "anticipatory" better expresses the connotation Husserl had in mind here. For a more detailed account of what follows, see my chapter, "Transcendental Phenomenology," in J. N. Mohanty and W. R. McKenna, eds., *Husserl: A Textbook,* Washington: Center for Advanced Research in Phenomenology and University Press of America, forthcoming.

18. *Cartesian Meditations,* Sec. 2 (at the end of the section).

19. J. G. Fichte, *Zweite Einleitung in die Wissenschaftslehre,* in I. H. Fichte, ed., *Gesammelte Schriften* (1845-1846), Vol. I, pp. 476-477.

20. F. H. Bradley, *Appearance and Reality. A Metaphysical Essay* (2nd ed., Oxford: Oxford University Press, 1978), p. 96. Claudia Moser gave me valuable information concerning this dispute between Bradley and Royce. Cf. Claudia Moser, *Die Realitätsproblematik bei Francis Herbert Bradley und Bernard Bosanquet* (Diss., Mainz, 1986), sec. 2. 1. 8 Anmerkung.

21. *Cartesian Meditations*, Sec. 5.

22. *Ideen zu einer reinen Phänomenologie und phänomenologische Philosophie*, Vol. I, 1913, Secs. 51, 52, 139, 140. (*Hua III*, 1950)

23. *Cartesian Meditations*, Sec. 6. *Ideas I*, Sec. 138.

24. *Ideas I*, Sec. 137.

25. *Cartesian Meditations*, Sec. 6.

26. Nevertheless, it is *compatible* with the ontological statement that the subject is a "being in the world." Cf. fn. 16 above.

CONTRIBUTORS

Richard J. Bernstein (Ph.D., Yale University, 1958) is T. Wistar Brown Professor of Philosophy at Haverford College. He is a former editor of *The Review of Metaphysics* and *Praxis International*. His publications include *John Dewey (1966)*, *Perspectives on Peirce* (ed.), 1965, *Praxis and Action* (1971), *The Restructuring of Social and Political Theory* (1976), *Habermas and Modernity* (ed.) (1985), and *Philosophical Profiles* (1986).

Robert S. Corrington (Ph.D., Drew University, 1982) is Assistant Professor of Philosophy at The Pennsylvania State University. His publications include articles on Heidegger, Schleiermacher, Royce, Buchler, John William Miller, hermeneutics, and American naturalism. His book, *The Community of Interpreters* is forthcoming from Mercer University Press. He is currently working on a systematic hermeneutics emerging out of dialogue with ordinal metaphysics and Continental thought.

Charles Hartshorne (Ph.D., Harvard University, 1923) is Ashbel Smith Professor Emeritus of Philosophy at the University of Texas at Austin. During his long and distinguished career he has developed a comprehensive metaphysics of process. Among his many books are *Whitehead's Philosophy* (1972), *A Natural Theology for Our Time* (1967), *Creativity in American Philosophy* (1984), *The Divine Relativity* (1948), *The Logic of Perfection* (1962), *Insights & Oversights of Great Thinkers* (1983), *Omnipotence and Other Theological Mistakes* (1984), and *Born to Sing: An Interpretation and World Survey of Bird Song* (1973). He is also the subject of a forthcoming Schilpp Volume in the *Library of Living Philosophers* series.

John J. McDermott (Ph.D., Fordham University, 1959) is Distinguished Professor of Philosophy and Humanities (College of Liberal Arts) and Professor and Head of the Department of Humanities in Medicine (College of Medicine) at Texas A & M University. He is co-founder and advisory editor of a Critical Edition of *The Works of William James* and editor of scholarly editions of the writings of Josiah Royce (1969), John Dewey (1974, 1981), and William James (1968, 1977). He is the author of *The Culture of Experience: Philosophical Essays in the American Grain* (1976); the first volume of a two-volume *Cultural Introduction to Philosophy* (1985); and *Streams of Experience: Reflections on the Philosophy and History of Culture* (1986). He has taught and been visiting lecturer at more than one hundred universities, symposia and conferences, both in America and abroad, in Europe and China, and published more than 50 essays in scholarly journals and university press collections of essays.

Thomas Mack Olshewsky (Ph.D., Emory University, 1965) is Professor of Philosophy at the University of Kentucky and is Chairman both of the Department of Philosophy and of the Program in Linguistics there. He wrote *Foundations of Moral Decision* (1985) and *Good Reasons and Persuasive Force* (1983), and edited *Problems in the Philosophy of Language* (1969). His articles in various journals include studies on Peirce, Aristotle and Plato, and work on problems in religion, psycholinguistics, philosophical psychology and philosophical linguistics.

Sandra B. Rosenthal is Professor of Philosophy at Loyola University, New Orleans. She is past president of The Charles S. Peirce Society and The Southwestern Philosophical Society, has served on the executive committees of The Society for the Advancement of American Philosophy and The Southern Society for Philosophy and Psychology, and is a consulting editor for several journals. Her publications include a book on the pragmatic philosophy of C. I. Lewis, two co-authored books on pragmatism and phenomenology, and *Speculative Pragmatism* (1986), plus numerous articles dealing with pragmatism and the relation between pragmatism and phenomenology.

Thomas M. Seebohm (Dr. phil., Mainz, 1962; vinia legendi, Mainz, 1969) is Professor at the Johannes Gutenberberg Universität, Mainz and a Director of the Center for Advanced Research in Phenomenology, Inc. He has published *Die Bedingungen der Möglichkeit der Transzedental-philosophie* (1962), *Zur Kritik der hermeneutischen Vernunft* (1972), *Ratio und Charisma, Ansätze zur Ausbildung eines rationalen Weltverstandnisses im Russland Ivans III* (1977), *Philosophie der Logik* (1984), and articles on Kant, German idealism, phenomenology, and hermeneutics.

Charlene Haddock Seigfried (Ph.D., Loyola University of Chicago, 1973) is Associate Professor of Philosophy and member of the American Studies Committee at Purdue University, West Lafayette. She is on the Executive Committee of the Society for the Advancement of American Philosophy. Her publications include *Chaos and Context: A Study in William James*, and articles on the impact of Darwinian evolution on philosophy, Nineteenth Century American and Continental Philosophy, aesthetics, and feminist theory.

Charles M. Sherover (Ph.D., New York University, 1966) is Professor of Philosophy at Hunter College. He has been Visiting Professor at Duquesne University, SUNY-Stony Brook, and The Graduate Faculty of the New School for Social Research. His publications include *Heidegger, Kant and Time* (1971), *The Human Experience of Time* (1975), a just pbulished new and annotated translation of Rousseau's *Of the Social Contract*, and articles on political philosophy, Kant, Heidegger, and the philosophy of time.

Beth J. Singer (Ph.D., Columbia University, 1967) is Professor of Philosophy at Brooklyn College of The City University of New York. Her publications include *The Rational Society: A Critical Study of Santayana's Social Thought* (1970), *Ordinal Naturalism: An Introduction to the Philosophy of Justus Buchler* (1983), and articles on various American philosophers, including Dewey and Whitehead, as well as on the concepts of experience, communication, and community. She edited *Philosophy After Darwin: Chapters for "The Career of Philosophy," Volume III, and Other Essays* by John Herman Randall, Jr. (1977). She is currently President of the Society for the Advancement of American Philosophy.

John E. Smith (Ph.D., Columbia, 1948) is Clark Professor of Philosophy at Yale University. He is past President of the American Philosophical Association, Eastern Division, and of the Metaphysical Society, the American Theological Society, and the Hegel Society of America. His publications include *Reason and God* (1961), *The Spirit of American Philosophy* (1963), *Royce's Social Infinite* (1950), *Experience and God* (1968) *Religion and Empiricism* (1967), *Themes in American Philosophy* (1970), *The Analogy of Experience* (1978), and *Purpose and Thought: The Meaning of Pragmatism* (19##). He is a former Director of the National Humanities Institute in New Haven, and is currently the General Editor of the Yale Edition of the *Works of Joathan Edwards*.

INDEX OF NAMES

INDEX OF TOPICS